FINAL FLIGHTS

Dramatic wartime incidents
revealed by aviation archaeology

As part of our ongoing market research, we are always pleased to receive comments about our books, suggestions for new titles, or requests for catalogues. Please write to: The Editorial Director, Patrick Stephens Limited, Sparkford, Near Yeovil, Somerset, BA22 7JJ.

FINAL FLIGHTS

Dramatic wartime incidents revealed by aviation archaeology

Ian McLachlan

Foreword by Len Deighton

Patrick Stephens Limited

© Ian McLachlan 1989

Illustrations © Ian Garstka 1989

First published in 1989
Reprinted in 1994 and 1996

British Library Cataloguing in Publication
Data

McLachlan, Ian
 Final flights.
 1. World War 2. Air operations by Great
 Britain, Royal Air Force. Fighter
 aeroplanes. Pilots. Biographies. Collections
 I. Title
 940.54′4941′0922

 ISBN 1-85260-122-1

*Patrick Stephens Limited is an imprint of
Haynes Publishing, Sparkford, near Yeovil, Somerset BA22 7JJ*

Printed and bound in Great Britain by
Butler & Tanner Ltd, Frome and London

10 9 8 7 6 5 4 3

CONTENTS

AEROPLANES

The wings, some still in remarkable shape,
The bodywork supreme,
The pilots must have been so proud;
So happy, to see them gleam.

Mens favourite names adorned the shell,
With numbers beside identifying them well,
So many fought and flew so high,
It's a shame so many had to die.

Heroes, planes, bombings of the past,
Destruction and deaths by the score,
Some still bear the scars of these times,
And bear not to think of the war.

Apart from the bravery of men in those days,
When they had to take flight to the sky,
Many planes still remain,
With their beauty unshamed,
These hold more memories than you or I.

by Nicola Jervis
25/11/87.

FOREWORD

by Len Deighton

In the uncertain world of writing and publishing there are few things more pleasing than seeing a worthwhile project come to fruition. When I first encountered Ian McLachlan's it was one more reading task piled high at my bedside. It was at my bedside because I simply couldn't get through my work during daylight hours. So I was tired and weary when I first picked up Ian's typescript. It was then titled 'Wreckage recovered — courage recalled' and told me exactly what his book was about. I'm not so sure I would have read it had it had its present title 'Final Flights' which I suspect is the invention of someone working in a publishing company. However we must be delighted that a publisher saw the potential in this fascinating book.

'Wreckage recovered — courage recalled' was self-evidently about what some people are calling aviation archaeology. Sometimes I hear it deplored: I hear people saying that there is something bad about recovering wreckage, and sometimes the bodies, of fallen aviators. I don't quite follow the argument and urge no relative to feel distressed. If it was my father, my brother or my son I would not prefer that he remains forgotten in some unmarked spot.

And anyone who reads this book will see that people such as McLachlan are serious, knowledgeable and dedicated. It is an important part of the history that many of us lived through, and which many prefer to forget. Here are true stories that no fiction can match. When so long ago I pulled that typescript from the heap I stayed awake half the night reading it. I hope you will find the stories he tells as fascinating as I did.

Len Deighton.

PREFACE

In the 1950s, my brother bought me a model Spitfire and, like many lads then, and now, I spent hours gluing and painting as well as learning aviation history off box-lids. From my bedroom ceiling, the Battle of Britain was re-fought; a damaged Fortress limped home trailing cotton-wool smoke, I was hooked on aircraft.

Growing up in East Anglia, I was aware of its aviation history from tales told by adults who lived through the war. Living in Lowestoft, I learned of attacks on the town and, like other children, played happily in some of the bomb-sites. The Americans were remembered for the night German intruders trailed them home (the subject of a future book) and, of course, for their social influence.

One day, my father handed on some souvenir pieces of aircraft and triggered an inquisitiveness leading, ultimately, to, 'Final Flights'. Instead of models, why not find pieces of a real Spitfire or Flying Fortress? In 1964, standing where 21 men died on a desolate marsh, I realized it was the men who counted. This is not a book about digging up aircraft. Fragments of shattered warplane became clues to unearth the history they represented.

Few parishes in this region are without their crashed aircraft. Few people in those parishes remember and fewer still know the facts. Fine young men often died where we now enjoy the countryside, others died on sites now in back gardens. The least we can do is record the passing of these lives.

Ian McLachlan.

ACKNOWLEDGEMENTS

In this endeavour, I am indebted to many individuals and organizations whose help I acknowledge. In particular, I would like to thank author Martin Bowman for advice, guidance and encouragement, authors Chaz Bowyer and M.J.F. Bowyer, Roy Child for his recollections, historian Bob Collis, Christopher R. Elliott, Stewart P. Evans, the late John Ford, N.L.R. Franks, Roger A. Freeman, Chris Gotts, Jim Goudelock, Ian Hawkins, Dr John W. Kelly, Walker M. Mahurin, the late Jim Munro, Lord Somerleyton.

Also the following people and organizations: P. Adcock, J. Aicardi, R. Allard, P.H. Anderson, E. Aspinall, D. Aylard, Mike Bailey, Roy Baker, Mrs N. Ballinger, R. Barber, R.A. Barber, A. Barrell, M. Barnard, S. Batchelor, R. Bateson, Mrs V.E. Batten, N. Beckett, A. Bedford, C.H. Bennehoof, Mrs R. Benton, F. Berry, H. Binns, Mrs I. Bird, S.P. Birdsall, Rose Mary Bishard, C. Bishop, S. Bishop, R.G. Borst, Brig. Gen. H.W. Bowman, USAF, R. Brooks, C. Brown, D. Brown, T. Brown, R. Buxton, D. Buxton, S.G. Bryant, J. Calver, C. Cansdale, J. Carless, T. Chaplin, D. Chapple, P. Claydon, F.H.P. Clear, P. Clegg, S. Cochrane, E. Cole, F.R. Cole, K. Collinson, H.E. Comstock, K. Connolly, M. Cookman, M. Coombs, P. Cornwell, P. Cox, P. Crickmore, Helen Creegan, A. Dann, M. Davany, L.S. Davis, A.F. Dirks, A. Dowdle, A. Downing, S. Dunham, C. Durrant, A. Dykstra, E. Eastwood, J. Ellingsworth, K. Ellis, D. Engle, T. Everett, K. Everitt, F. Falkenstine, D. Field, J.P. Flanagan, P. Foolkes, M. Forrest, Mrs J. Foster, Royal D. Frey, C.E. Fuller, F. Fuller, Adolf Galland, H. Gabbott, J. Gardiner, L. Garnett, C. Garton, H.E. Gayfer, E.W. George, M.L. Gibson, Air Comm, J.H. Giles, DSO, DFC, A.G.S. Glover, R.L. Goldsmith, A. Goodrum, S. Gotts, C. Goss, Rev. G. Green, Mrs L. Greatbatch, Mrs A.Griffiths, V. Grimble, A. Hague, Charles Hall, Cliff Hall, H. Hall, K. Harbour, R. Harper, S.F. Hartman, M.D., M. Harvey, D. Heany, W. Hoagland, H. Hoehler, G. Holmes, J. Hood, M.T. Hopkin, D. Hudson, W. Ingle, R. James, Mr E. Jarvis, J. Jenkins, Miss N. Jervis, K. John, W.D. Jones, J.D. King, D.G. Knight, B. Lain, L.C. Lanigan, E.W. Lark, N. Laws, H.C. Lawrence, R.W. Leggett, F. Leyland, C.J. Liggins, Frantisek Loucky, J. Loyst, Mr & Mrs R. Loyst, D. Mallett, R. Mallett, Dr J.T. Mason, Jr, USN, P. McDonough, E.R. McDowell, E. Mingay, B. McLachlan, R. McLachlan, R. More, D. Morris, Gp. Capt. O.A. Morris, DSO, K. Mould, Mrs R. Moy, C.C. Murfitt, B. Mynn, C.H. Newlin, A. North, M. Nice, Heinz J. Nowarra, Merle C. Olmsted, M. Osborne, S.R. Palmer, J.R. Palmquist, Mr & Mrs S.J. Parr, S. Parry, M.A. Paul, M. Payne, R. Peacock, J. Pemberton, L. Pennow, J. Pettenger, Maj. W.A. Pleumer, Alfred Price F.R. Hist. S., C. Rhodes, W.G. Richmond, Miss E. Rodger, J.T. Rose, M. Ross, Ken C. Rust, A. Saunders, John F. Scott, J.J. Sloan,

P. Snowling, K.J. Sorace, C.E. Soucek, J.R. Spurgeon, E. Stern, E.E. St John, A. Stubbs, H.V. Sturgeon, F/Lt A. Swann, D. Syrett, G. Target, Mrs C. Taylor, S/Ldr G. Taylor, J. Taylor, W.J. Taylor, Mrs S. Tedford, C.A. Thrower, P. Thrower, G. Thompson, M. Thompson, M. Tipple, T. Tipler, S/Ldr E.S.T. Tout, MBE, A Tovell, P.E. Underwood, Jan J. van der Veer, J. Vasco, G. Vyse, D. Wade, F. Walls, J. Warner, J. Watling, K. Whittle, K.C. Wicks, Jack Willburn, Mrs D. Willett, S. Williams, P. Wilson, J. Winder, A.J.A. Woollard, Lt. Col. John H. Woolnough USAF, S. Woods, R.H. Youngs, Russ Zorn, Gunther Zerhusen, G.J. Zwanenburg.

Air Historical Branch, Air Mail, American Aviation Historical Society, American Battle Monuments Commission, Anglia Television Ltd., Anglian Aeronautical Preservation Society, Aviation News, Bendix Corporation, Boeing Company, Buddies of the Ninth, Cambridge American Military Cemetery and Memorial, Canadian High Commission, Commonwealth War Graves Commission, *Coventry Evening Telegraph*, *Croydon Advertiser*, *Croydon Borough News*, de Havilland Canada, *East Anglian Daily Times*, *Eastern Daily Press*, *Eastern Evening News*, *Ely Standard*, East Anglian Aircraft Research Group, East Essex Aviation Museum, Fenland Aircraft Preservation Society, *Flypast Magazine*, *Forfar Dispatch*, Friends of the Eighth, *Gateshead Post*, Hawker Siddeley Aviation Ltd., Imperial War Museum, 100 BG Museum, 390 BG Museum, Norfolk and Suffolk Aviation Museum, RAF Museum, Tank Museum, Ministry of Defence, *Manchester Evening News*, Norton AFB HQ USAF Inspection and Safety Center, *Oldham Evening Chronicle*, Pioneer Parachute Co Inc., Pratt and Whitney Aircraft, RAF (EOD), RAAF, Republic Aviation, *Toronto Star*, *Toronto Sun*, USAF Historical Division, USN Historical Center, Warplane Wreck Investigation Group.

Appreciation is expressed to Graham Truscott and other PSL staff who made my introduction to the world of publishing a pleasant experience.

Particular thanks go to my wife Julie for her support and for typing the manuscript. To Ian Garstka for his superb illustrations and his wife, Pauline, for encouraging the project.

Finally I express my thanks and appreciation to Len Deighton for helping a novice even if the publisher did change the original title.

Ian McLachlan
Norwich, April 1989

WHEN ACES MEET

The early hours of 17 November, 1940, saw much activity on the famous RAF Station of Martlesham Heath near Ipswich, Suffolk. While airmen shivered over their frozen Hurricanes, the pilots of 17 and 257 Squadrons attended briefing for a convoy protection patrol. The fury of the preceding months had subsided into mundane but vital matters intermingled with sporadic combats recalling the ferocity of high summer. Of the pilots present, one had established himself as a master of the trade but has undeservedly been accorded less fame than many of his contemporaries.

One reason for this may be that this holder of the King's Commission, Count Manfred Beckett Czernin, DSO, MC, DFC, was born on 18 January, 1913, in Berlin — now capital of Hitler's Third Reich — and was a member of the Austrian aristocracy. His mother, Lucile Katharine Beckett, daughter of Ernest William Beckett, 2nd Baron Grimthorpe, had married an Austrian nobleman, Count Otto Czernin von and Zu Chudenitz of Dimokur, and Manfred was her fourth son. In 1920 the Count divorced and Manfred came with his mother to settle in England. In 1926 she married Captain Oliver Henry Frost OBE, MC, a former pilot in the Royal Flying Corps. His step-father's stirring recollections of aerial combat so strongly influenced Manfred that, in 1935, he joined the RAF to train as a pilot. Even fighter pilots were instilled with basic procedures and the Count became one of countless airmen to pound the parade ground at RAF Uxbridge. These less glamorous aspects of service life did not suit his ebullient nature and he was to come into conflict with military disciplines and authority throughout his career. Suitably indoctrinated the fledgling airman was then sent to Number 6 Flying Training School at Netheravon, Wiltshire where, in May, he soloed in an Avro Tutor. Five months tuition later, he moved from the 240hp Lynx engine in a Tutor and converted to the Hawker Hart Trainer, a derivative of the famous bomber likewise powered with a 525hp Rolls-Royce Kestrel X. Manfred eventually satisfied his superiors that he was competent enough for his role in an operational squadron and February 1936 saw him with 57 Squadron flying Harts and, later, Hind bombers from Upper Heyford. The coveted wings on his tunic, Count Czernin's aristocratic background typified the cliché for an RAF pilot of that period: handsome, wealthy, owner of a sports car and successful with women. For two years he enjoyed this lifestyle then, ever a restless spirit, he left the RAF to embark on a business venture based on observations made during a visit to America. Impressed with the fast food system, Manfred founded a snack bar entitled, 'The Hot Dog' in the West End. However, his generosity and many friends soon created friction within the partnership and, not being an entrepreneurial spirit, Manfred became disenchanted and the enterprise folded.

The darkening political scene drew Count Czernin's attention from commerce to concern over events in Europe. His personal life was to be subordinated by the on-coming war but on the threshold of that worldwide disaster he married a very pretty English debutante, Maud Hamilton. It was November 1939, and the aristocrat was again an airman.

Bombers did not suit Manfred's highly individualistic approach and an application for fighters found him training on Hurricanes with 504 Squadron, Debden. In February, 1940, he went to 213 Squadron, Wittering and, three months later, he was posted to 85 Squadron in France where he landed only hours before the Germans launched the blitz that overwhelmed Europe. Courageously, the Allied Air Forces fought superior odds but limited numbers were soon whittled away in a desperate struggle to stave off the inevitable. Sortie followed sortie but the initiative and momentum of the opposition was inexorable and the Allies reeled in retreat. Despite all this, the Count's indomitable sense of humour prevailed and, with his background, he kidded younger pilots that he previously served in the Luftwaffe piloting the highly respected Me 109! On 19 May, that his 'service' was conclusively terminated was demonstrated by the destruction of two Heinkel III bombers! At the beginning of June, 85 Squadron was withdrawn but the Count stayed only days in England before returning to France, this time with 17 Squadron. Czernin was tired but undaunted and his personal contribution in the Battle for France was to knock five enemy aircraft to earth and fly many dangerous ground-attack sorties against advancing columns of the Wehrmacht. No amount of courage, however, could contend with insufficient resources, inadequate planning and lack of suitable preparation for the fast moving war waged expertly by the enemy. Soon German armies stood glowering across the Channel and a battered Royal Air Force prayed for time to recuperate.

To some it seemed that God granted that prayer: history relates the logistical difficulties and German High Command prevarication over a decision to invade. Whatever the reason, the RAF had a few weeks' respite before the Battle of Britain. Participants and historians have well described and adequately analysed this conflict elsewhere, here the unusual situation of a man born in Berlin fighting to defend London concerns us more. Pressure during those months was intense but Count Czernin coped

competently with the demands, often leading sections of 17 Squadron in combat. Manfred again demonstrated his talent on 25 August in a mêlée near Portland Bill by accounting for two Me 110s within moments of each other. Recognition of his skill came on 11 September 1940, when he was awarded the DFC.

Tenaciously the Luftwaffe persisted and the days blended into a hot summer of attrition of men and machines as the Germans sought air superiority, the pre-requisite for invasion. Even the exuberant Manfred wearied of the nerve-sapping situation as he experienced the stress of coming from readiness to combat, combat to calm and then the stomach-retching strain of scrambles. Faces came and went: he lost many friends but seemed himself to have a guardian angel affording protection. At the end of the Battle, Count Czer-

Me 110s from Erprobungsgruppe *210 in combat formation. Fighter protection proved necessary for the unit's aircraft* (J. Vasco).

nin had increased his tally of kills to nineteen without serious mishap but, a few weeks later, his escorting angel failed to take-off.

By November, both sides found the need to replenish aircraft and rest pilots — 17 Squadron now resided with 257 at Martlesham Heath and provided cover for the south-east of 11 Group and the coastal convoys passing within its jurisdiction. At 08.48 hours on 17 November, the Sunday morning peace broke under the powerful crackle of Merlins as 257 jostled out and took-off, followed fifteen minutes later by eleven Hurricanes of 17 Squadron, climbing for the coast. As Woodbridge slid by, the Count thought of Maud in their boat home on the Deben — she was expecting their first child and her concern would be intensified as she listened to the strain of climbing engines. Today, Manfred as Yellow One, flew an unfamiliar Hurricane I, coded YB-D, V7500. His own kite, 'Kyro' — after his

elkhound and squadron mascot, was being serviced. However, the Rolls-Royce Merlin III of this fighter pulled sweetly enough and the patrol appeared routine.

Any introspection was abruptly erased by a crackling voice from control cancelling their original mission and vectoring them on to an in-coming raid of fifty-plus bandits which had penetrated 11 Group's airspace and was roaring towards their target, the bomber base of RAF Wattisham. Immediately, the Hurricanes swung to intercept, increasing power as they did so. Converging courses brought the enemy into sight just short of their intended target, additionally protected by a layer of cloud. The German formation turned east, diving to increase speed for their secondary objective: dock installations at Harwich.

Banking to port, the Hurricanes positioned themselves to attack, but Manfred became detached from his unit in cloud and missed the initial contact at 09.15 over Ipswich. Alone in the sky, a fighter pilot is at his most vulnerable: formations were devised so that pilots act as eyes for their comrades. It is necessary for a pilot to twist and turn his head as well as manipulating his machine, constantly covering the blind spots from which an assailant might strike. Despite the danger, Manfred pressed ahead and broke cloud to find himself confronting a formation of enemy aircraft.

The Germans were in two waves of twenty aircraft each. Czernin's squadron tackled the rear element while Manfred, having been separated, faced the leading section alone, a formidable task for one fighter but Czernin drove straight at them. The enemy aircraft were twin-engined Me 110s from the specialist Luftwaffe fighter-bomber unit, *Erprobungs-gruppe* 210. This *Gruppe*, now based at Denain, had established a reputation for its activities, notably the devastating, if erroneous, attack on Croydon during the evening of 15 August. The experimental unit's operations had not been without severe losses and it was always necessary to provide adequate escort for the cumbersome fighter-bombers. Today the 110 crews were comforted by the Me 109s of *Jagdgeschwader* 26 led by *Oberstleutnant* Adolf Galland, one of Germany's top fighter aces, about whom a few words are worthwhile.

Born in Westerholt, Westphalia, Galland began flying gliders when only seventeen and entered the then clandestine Luftwaffe in 1932, his training being carried out surreptitiously in Italy the following year. During 1937/38 he flew with the Legion Condor in Spain and was operational from the moment World War 2 began, flying his plane against Poland on 1 September, 1939. For the next fourteen months his renown climbed as rapidly as his record of vic-

tories. Galland was the epitomy of the fighter pilot and not unlike the Count in character. Czernin was, perhaps, a little more the Aryan in appearance, with light hair, blue eyes , and over six feet tall, but the dark, handsome Luftwaffe pilot shared his penchant for living life to the full. Both men smoked, but Galland even went to the extreme of having a cigar tray modification in the cockpit of his fighter. Another similarity was the bearing of a personal motif on their aircraft. Czernin's usual Hurricane carried a painting of Kyro while Galland also had a caricature of a small creature, Disney's famous Mickey

Adolf Galland, one of Germany's most skillful fighter pilots and air-war strategists (M. Payne).

Mouse. It has to be said that his adaption of the well known rodent was a little less than friendly, judging from the chopper and pistol being wielded by it. The pilot's passion for a good Havana was emphasized by a fat cigar gripped in the animal's teeth. In addition to standard markings, unit crest and leader's chevrons, the rudder of his fighter bore an impressive array of victory symbols, fifty at that time, but later to reach 104! Being very outspoken, Galland clashed with his superiors, notably the rotund *Reichsmarschall* Goering, and was adamant in his view that the Luftwaffe's interpretation of the fighter-bomber at this juncture in the war was almost totally ineffective.

Luftwaffe tacticians mismanaged the Battle of Britain, rancour existed between fighter and bomber branches and Goering sided with the bomber crews' desire to have fighters closely escorting them which, while visually stimulating bomber personnel's morale, severely restricted the fighter in combat because it lost the advantages necessary for success: height, choice of approach and surprise. Nearly four years later USAAF fighter Command proved the point when they took the traces off their Mustangs — with devastating results against the Luftwaffe. In 1940, the end of massed bomber attacks during daylight found the German fighter pilots themselves lugging bombs to England and Eg210 was the test unit for these operations. Having been pronounced as a 'Zerstorer' — destroyer, or long-range fighter, the Messerschmitt 110 proved so dismal in this role that it required protection itself and even utilization of the type as a fighter-bomber escorted by 109s had only limited success. But Galland had no time to ruminate on his opinion of operational techniques as his

This caricature was painted below the cockpit of Galland's Me 109.

force drew near their target and the defending RAF fighters strained to cut them off. His unit, JG26, would fight skilfully and tenaciously to protect their charges from the RAF squadrons rising to engage.

An air battle, unlike movements of land armies, is very difficult to detail. Because of the speed and dimension in which it occurs, one rarely gets precise altitude, time and location of individual actions and, moving at 300 mph plus, many participants found themselves too busy struggling to survive let alone take notes for the benefit of historians. However, pilots did keep log books and records were maintained by both Air Forces. Information from these and careful examination of material from other sources does allow a reconstruction of the battle which scattered over Suffolk that Sunday morning.

Czernin, confronting the enemy formation, mistakenly identified his selected target as a Fiat Br20 of the Italian Corpo Aereo Italiano which, as

Galland flew this Me 109, W.Nr 5819, from August 1940 until April 1941. Czernin's Hurricane was just one of its victims (M. Payne).

far as is known, was not active in the area, nor any other part of the UK that morning. Exactly a week earlier, 17 Squadron had been one of several RAF units to intercept the Italians on their first, major assault against British defences. Mussolini's men flew machines inadequate for the occasion and suffered serious losses in a singularly one-sided fight. Czernin missed that particular scrap but returned from leave to hear numerous accounts and, since the Italians were expected to return, his identification error is understandable. He was not the only RAF pilot to report encountering Italian aircraft on 17 November, Pilot Officer Lock of 41 Squadron made a similar mistake.

Whatever their nationality, Czernin was in no doubt of their intent and certain of his duty to deter their attack despite his vulnerability without Yellow Two protecting his tail. Manfred may not have seen the escorting 109s but should surely have expected their presence and how swiftly he needed to

act to get at the more important bombers before the fighters found him. An instant appraisal of his position showed his best approach was to hit the rear of the bomber formation in a traditional attack and all 1,029hp of his Merlin were thrashed as he banked aggressively into action. In these vital moments, his trained eyes double-checked the controls before he attacked: gunsight on and set, safety ring on the control column switched to, 'fire' — the rear view mirror was empty, but for how long? Selecting a target to the rear of the formation, Count Czernin closed behind it and pressed the gun button. He was a superb marksman and the Hurricane a stable platform for the eight .303 machine guns it carried. This combination unleashed a stream of bullets — converging on the Messerschmitt, tearing away part of its twin tail unit and smashing its port Daimler-Benz engine to a halt, streaming smoke.

Unknown to Manfred, he may have avoided death by only fractions of a

Obergefreiter *Carl Stoff hesitated and may have saved Czernin's life* (J. Vasco).

and his gun jammed. The Me 110's port engine ignited and the pilot, Uffz. Werner Neumann, jettisoned their bombs and turned for the coast. The Hurricane was coming in again — where was their escort?

Flying above the bombers, Galland spotted the Hurricane moments after it broke cloud but was too far away to prevent it opening fire on one of the fighter bombers. He immediately called his wingman to follow him down to ward off a further pass by the British fighter. Then, manoeuvring to attack, Galland was dazzled by the sun and momentarily lost the RAF machine. Czernin's gamble looked like succeeding but then the German caught sight of his Hurricane as it banked away from the bombers, apparently preparing to swing in for a renewed attack. The German ace slipped neatly behind the turning Hurricane, deftly co-ordinating the 109's controls to stay tucked into Czernin's blind spot, below the tail, as he closed range. His opponent was about to pay for the courageous audacity of his single-handed attack. Unseen by Czernin, the Messerschmitt stalked to 150 ft before Galland fired a short burst from cannon and machine-guns. The effect was devastating. Bursting into flames and shedding a trail of shot-away parts amid the smoke, the Hurricane keeled sharply over on its right wing and went down. Resisting the often fatal fascination of following victims earthwards, Galland climbed away to meet more British fighters. His assistance had been too late for the 110 Czernin had hit and Galland last saw it falling away from the formation, smoke trailing from both engines.

The work of others that morning had been less dramatic and the routine of rural life continued on Red House Farm,

second because the Me110 gunner. Obergefreiter Carl Stoff hesitated in case the fighter was an escorting Me 109. Years later, Stoff recalled the combat and related that the last two Me 110s of his formation became separated, weakening their defensive firepower. Suddenly, a fighter appeared about 400 metres astern. Stoff's hesitation gave Czernin the advantage. At the very moment Stoff fired, his machine was raked by the Count's guns. Stoff was hit in the head

Ufford. Young Ron Buxton was fetching his father's horses for grooming and the usually recalcitrant animals behaved no better today, having taken nearly an hour to chase off the meadows. They were about to enter the stables when the roar of aero engines and clatter of machine guns sent them fleeing, panic-stricken, across the fields, and an equally frightened farmhand flung himself flat for cover. From the prone position, Ron looked up to see what he thought was a Dornier 17 heading towards Bromswell and the coast with a Hurricane firing in pursuit. He kept his head down. There was more gunfire, then, looking skywards again, he saw the Hurricane just above cloud, steeply banked to starboard and coming rapidly earthwards. Clouds obscured his vision but the Merlin screamed a funereal threnody, which ceased abruptly on impact. Ron could not be sure if the pilot had escaped.

Czernin hunched instinctively for the protection offered by his armour plate as cannon and machine gun bullets slammed into his fighter. The fury of that spasm stunned him. Never had he been so frightened or felt so helpless as hood and instrument panel shattered, all controls were shot away, and flames seared from ruptured fuel tanks. Miraculously he was unscathed. The horizon swung sickeningly to the vertical and over as the Hurricane lunged earthwards. Self-preservation quickly overcame shock and he fought vehemently to escape as 'g' forces pressed him against the seat which had just saved his life but now seemed as though it might trap him. Unsnapping the Sutton seat harness, he released the canopy frame, hauling it back as far as he could. Then, discarding his flying helmet, he struggled to his feet and, exerting all his strength, kicked himself clear of the cockpit and fell into the cold, November air. He had been hit at 8,000 ft and was desperately aware of lost altitude. In those terrifying, tumbling moments, Manfred, who thought himself an atheist, prayed vigorously and unashamedly as his right hand located the metal 'D' ring and tugged hard. The canvas pack burst into a stream of silk. A second later it smacked open with a breath-taking jerk: his own descent decelerated sharply while his Hurricane plummeted into clouds below. His senses regained some semblance of self-assertion and, smiling inwardly, he remembered some of the standard jokes told about parachutes during pilot training: 'If it doesn't work, bring it back' and so on. Thankfully, he had no need for complaint but his respite from fear was brief. He heard engines and watched with mounting horror as two Me 109s hurtled ominously towards him. Galland had given explicit orders that no parachuting airmen should be fired upon but there were those on both sides who ignored this code of conduct and Manfred thought it wise to play dead, head and arms dangling. A short burst was aimed at him but missed, and the fighters swept past and away as RAF fighters appeared to defend their helpless comrade.

On Red House Farm, Ron had missed this series of events. He could hear aircraft and machine-guns but large clouds hid the drama from vision until he spotted Czernin's parachute drifting earthwards. Calling his brother, Donald, the two lads set off to where they estimated the pilot would land.

The last second of his descent caught Count Czernin unawares and he crashed heavily through a hedge, badly twisting his ankle. Not wishing to be dragged along by the wind, he quickly pressed the release box and pulled off the parachute webbing. Seeing the Buxton brothers approaching, he began limping towards them but had not gone many paces when a 15 cwt Bedford truck rattled on to the scene and disgorged a gaggle of Homeguardsmen and Constabulary, armed and wary of the airman's identity. Manfred was in no mood for kidding now and soon established he was no Nazi. A car was sent from Martlesham and the Count drew thankfully on a cigarette as he awaited collection, only twenty minutes had elapsed since he took-off, yet it could have been a lifetime.

Unable to speak to the pilot there was little excitement to detain the Buxton boys so Don went home but the elder Ron was keen on aircraft and set off to find the downed Hurricane which he located in a field close to Bredfield Church. The fighter had entered the ground vertically, shedding both wings, the condition of which offered mute testimony to the accuracy of Galland's fire. Ron was not allowed near the fuselage which protruded heavenwards from a deep crater effusing exploding ammunition and puffs of smoke. A number of RAF personnel were discussing removal of the wreck and Ron heard an officer issue orders for clearing only the surface debris and that which might interfere with ploughing — the remainder would be left. Ron Buxton never forgot that eavesdropping.

The Count had survived, but what became of his victim? Stoff was stunned as Neumann struggled to keep their ailing machine airborne. If they reached the sea, their own rescue services might snatch them to safety. Neumann soon realized this was hopeless since their burning aircraft could explode at any moment and so he instructed Stoff to

jump. Still dazed, Stoff struggled to get out and his landing near Ufford was poor, injuring his left shoulder. His reception by British soldiers was also unpleasant. Ordered to raise his arms as they approached, the wounded airman painfully raised only his good, right arm, a gesture misinterpreted by his captors as a Nazi salute so his injured, left arm was struck angrily by the butt of a rifle.

Records show that, at 09.16, an enemy aircraft came down in the sea off Aldeburgh and the motor lifeboat, *Abdy Beauclerk* was launched with a doctor, Major R. Acheson, on board. Neumann got a ducking but was soon retrieved by the lifeboat whose crew later received £22 14s 6d for their catch.

However unpleasant their welcome, Stoff and Neumann were luckier than their comrades. In an analysis of events that morning the Luftwaffe achieved little for the loss of four aircraft: bombs were scattered over several East Anglian parishes and two soldiers and a civilian were killed in Felixstowe, where the departing Eg210 made a cursory attack. Three of the aircraft destroyed were Me 110s. *Uffz* Herman Strobel and gunner *Uffz* Willi Rademacher are believed to have fallen to Flight Lieutenant Alfred Bayne of 17 Squadron. Bayne damaged a 110 and was attacking Strobel's plane when driven off by more 110s. Strobel's aircraft is thought to be that reported leaving the coast near Butley on fire and losing altitude. Just off the French coast, Strobel had to ditch but both he and his gunner died, their bodies being washed ashore some time later.

Flying Officer Niemiec, Bayne's number two, also hit a 110 but had to break away when himself attacked. Pilot Officer F. Kordula, 17 Squadron, and Sergeant Cameron also attacked Me 110s. Kordula saw no results on his ini-

Like their adversaries, Lutfwaffe pilots relaxed when they could: Uffz Werner Neumann is on the extreme right, leaning forward (J. Vasco).

tial pass but split the fighter-bomber formation and then pursued a 110 out over Southwold leaving the lamed Messerschmitt with its right engine asmoke. Cameron also gave chase to three 110s and saw them off over Aldeburgh, one dragging a black plume from its port engine. *Uffz* Johannes Kowatsch (pilot) and *Uffz* Hans-Georg Bade (gunner) were both reported missing. Bade's body was washed ashore but Kowatsch was never found. It is felt they fell to Pilot Officer Kordula or Sgt Cameron. Other RAF units entered the affray and Galland is credited with the destruction of Sergeant B. Henson, 257 Squadron, who crashed into the sea near Lightship Sunk. In retaliation, 257 claimed two Me 109s while 41 Spitfire Squadron pitched in and Pilot Officer Eric Lock claimed two more 109s before being wounded and shot down on Buckenay Farm, Alderton. Despite claims totalling four Me 109s, Luftwaffe records acknowledge only the loss of one aircraft and pilot, *Oblt* Eberhard Henrici of 1/JG 26. Confusion in combat resulted in over-claiming by all air forces during World War 2.

It was a long, weary war and the soil of East Anglia enveloped many more aircraft before the skies were still again. Czernin's Hurricane was left where it had fallen and would remain undisturbed for 29 years.

Count Czernin's RAF career lasted another eighteen months during which time he commanded several squadrons and served against the Japanese in the Far East. Owing to his error in identifying the Me 110 as an Italian Br20, the Count thought he had seen action against all the major Axis powers but had not, in fact, fought directly against Italian forces. This was just as well, for Italy was a country he had become fond of during holidays spent at the family villa in Ravello. He was fluent in Italian and understood the country, two attributes that affected the next stage of his military career. Now aged thirty, he was considered too old to continue as a fighter pilot much as he still sought the excitement of active service and, in September 1943, he left the RAF to enrol as a Special Operations Executive. He was twice dropped behind enemy lines in Italy and was instrumental in unifying scattered and disorganized partisans. Fighting two vastly different forms of warfare, Count Czernin proved adept at both but he, like many others, found the adaption to post-war life difficult. Manfred gave his best to his country and this sacrifice adversely affected his health. In 1948 he was operated on for cancer and won the battle against it. Despite this and other problems, he eventually became a senior executive with the Fiat Company in Britain. On 6 October 1962, this valiant nobleman, fighter pilot and SOE operator, died peacefully in bed of a heart attack.

Adolf Galland, the Count's protagonist, became General of the Luftwaffe Fighter Arm before confrontation with Reich political and military ineptitude ensured his dismissal and return to operations, flying the Me 262 jet fighter. After the war, his organizational ability and business expertise helped reconstruct the West German economy and he remained active in aviation circles.

In 1969 the author's interest in crashed aircraft brought him into contact with Ron Buxton and discussion

Ron Buxton with pieces of the downed Hurricane.

soon turned to the Hurricane Ron recalled going down. Remembering the RAF officer's instructions, Ron felt sure the engine was still buried and ought to be worth recovering. Permission to dig was given by farmer Peter Taylor and, appropriately, it was Armistice Day, 9 November, when a small team of enthusiasts met in a field some 800 yards west of Bredfield Church. The land was between crops so we had only three weekends to find and remove the fighter before the soil would be sown again. Metal detectors were not light, simple or common in 1969 and my fruitless efforts to coerce noise from a very cheap Army surplus back-breaker caused us to discard it and rely on the memories of Ron and Mr Taylor senior. One optimist had some divining rods.

The field bore no immediately apparent trace of disturbance and, to complicate matters, had been enlarged by combining a number of small fields. Luckily Mr Taylor's familiarity with his land enabled him to step confidently to a point near the middle and push a stick in. Surprisingly, the divining rods agreed and study of ground close to his marker revealed a small piece of aluminium on the surface. This could have been carried by years of ploughing but we felt certain and began digging. The soil was compacted and grudged every inch we penetrated. At 11.00 am we paused to observe the moments of remembrance, made the more poignant by our purpose. At a depth of one foot we came across clusters of bullets mostly broken or exploded, but convincing evidence of the exact position and any lingering doubts were eliminated when we removed the remains of a tyre, wheel and brake drum. Pieces of the Warren-trussed, tubular aluminium primary fuselage structure were then revealed, crumpled but still attached to the buried forward section. Darkness forced a halt and a week of rainy weather ensued to soften soil for our next visit and good progress was made. A trail of miscellaneous debris had been left as the Hurricane augered in and we picked up pieces of perspex, cockpit frame and fragments of the shattered Rotol, three-bladed wooden propeller. At a depth of 5 ft we found a jumble of debris crushed into the back of the armour plating which had saved Czernin's life. Included amongst this were remnants of the radio-accumulators and transmitter but nothing worthy of preservation had sur-

A prized find: the control column spade from Czernin's Hurricane with the gun-button used by the ace moments before being attacked.

vived the intense fire when his oxygen bottle exploded. Corrosion had reduced much of the aluminium to crystals and doubts were expressed about the condition of the engine and other artifacts; would they be worth the effort of removal?

Below the armour plate we found the cockpit but the space normally occupied by a pilot was compressed into a layer not more than 8 in thick between the rear armour and that of the forward bulkhead. A fierce blaze had melted many fittings but the prize trophy, Czernin's control column spade, was extricated in fine condition. The tit could be squeezed but the rest was imagination. Rejuvenated by our find, we continued digging and hauled the forward bulkhead out for our first view of the Merlin. Use of a plumb line could not have positioned it more accurately on its nose and we now stood on the air uptakes mounted on the rear of the engine and fed from an external scoop mounted beneath the fighter's forward fuselage. Retrieval of the engine would be no easy task — it stood embedded in clasping clay which gripped boots and spades alike as we dug. Anxious not to cause more damage than 6,500 lb of aircraft impacting at 400mph had already done, we increased the diameter of our workings for freedom of movement and left the engine encased in a column of clay as the depth of our hole increased. The Merlin is nearly seven feet in length and, by the time we had exposed the oil pump unit, about a quarter of the way along, bad light prevented further excavation. We had only one more weekend to attain our objective.

Dawn on 23 November 1969, found diggers already at work toiling in teams of three in the cramped crater. Half way down the length of the engine we found the propeller boss, torn off on impact but carried in with the Merlin's momentum. A small monkey winch, capable of raising five tons, had been carried to the site and we soon had the cable from this looped around the propeller. For safety, those in the hole moved clear in case the hawser snapped and whip-lashed but all went well as the prop boss was winched slowly away from the engine and up the side of the crater. Three feet from the rim a problem occurred when the cable slipped off the pulley, jamming the winch. Not wishing to slacken right off and drop our catch in the hole, we eased back and fastened a rope to it before calling the complete labour force into action to drag it clear.

Then for the engine itself: digging continued until the curve of the sump became apparent. There was now a risk of the engine tilting to crush those working in the crater and we felt sufficient soil had been cleared for the winch to cope with the weight and suction. To fully utilize a monkey winch, it is necessary to anchor it to an object with enough strength to resist being dragged forwards, trees being the most obvious choice. Here there were no trees within reach so a 'dead man' was created to tether the winch by hammering in a stake. It was now mid-day and time was short: lunch boxes sat untended as we scurried about preparing to lift the engine. Morale was high as a suitable fixing point and angle of removal were determined and the winch line again flexed into life. For the first time in 29 years, the Merlin moved, almost imperceptibly at first, but a small gap opened between it and the earth on one side, confirmation that it had shifted. Then it stopped. The winchmen still levered energetically. What was wrong? Puzzled for a moment, we then realized the 'dead man' had lost his grip. Winching ceased, the stake was driven deeper into the soil and supported with armour plating before a renewed attempt but, again, disappointment as the dead man was drawn remorselessly towards the engine.

Obviously we needed greater anchorage and less weight to haul, so two further 'dead men' were duly interred and a complicated cable system devised to incorporate their additional strength. The position of the winch was altered to a more favourable line of attack and, risking it might topple, two volunteers worked anxiously beside the Merlin clearing more clay. This time the stubborn brute just had to shift. Nerves tightened along with the cable. The first 'dead man' leant ominously while the engine remained motionless. Late afternoon light faded as did our hopes in the tenebrious gloom — this great, metal tooth certainly required tough dentistry and looked as if it would have to wait another year for extraction. Then, without warning, the Merlin lurched free and sagged on to the cable. Steadily it was pulled to the surface while a band of jubilant beavers busily filled in the cavity behind it.

We were pleased with its condition and as proud as the name 'Rolls-Royce' on its casing. Cleaning away remaining clay, we found the engine specification and number plates and Merlin number *30527* took its place in the history of aeronautical archaeology.

As related in ensuing chapters, the fields and fens of Eastern England have yielded numerous aviation artifacts since the recovery of Count Czernin's Hurricane. Ron Buxton has established a

Giving up its struggle, Rolls-Royce Merlin engine number 30527 is winched to the surface.

museum to house them and it is situated, appropriately, in a former control tower on the wartime airfield at Parham, Suffolk. He restored the Merlin as an exhibit and, now the enmity has faded, it is preserved in tribute to two aerial adversaries. Air combat is a cold, sharp war but this find is enough to admire the skill and courage displayed 'when aces meet'.

IN MEMORIAM

During World War 2, Royal Air Force Bomber Command lost over 72,000 airmen, the majority of whom perished in the bitter struggle against Hitler's Reich. Books aplenty have been written about this battle and some question whether the resources committed were wisely used. I do not intend to add to this controversy and will comment only that it is easy for historians from four decades on to criticize judgements made in time of war. One undeniable fact was the courage of the airmen who took the war to Germany and faced a skilful enemy in an element itself often hostile. Today their loss is history and many young people are incognizant of the contribution a generation their own age made for the freedom they enjoy.

Imagine a queue of 72,000 men. Somewhere in there are nine men whose story would have vanished but for the recovery of their bomber 32 years after it crashed. The circumstances surrounding their loss means they have no individually identified graves, only a series of stones, each bearing the poignant epitaph, 'An Airman of the 1939-45 War'. An RAF heavy bomber usually had a crew of seven — the reasons for nine casualties will be explained later. However, six men did come from one crew and the seventh would have perished but for an accident which saved his life. The author eventually traced this survivor, former mid-upper gunner, Warrant Officer Roy Child, and this modest man only agreed to provide his recollections because they reflect the quiet heroism of his comrades.

Roy enlisted in the RAF on 24 August 1942. His aspiration was to be a pilot but the service sought air gunners, and the shorter training necessary meant action earlier, so Roy opted for the single, upswept wing and the proud abbreviation, 'AG'. After basic training, he was posted to No 4 Air Gunnery School at Morpeth where relegated Blackburn Bothas were used to teach turretry to the tyro. He accrued 15 hours 20 minutes air time during May 1943, before being posted to 11 OTU, flying the much safer Wellington out of Westcott.

At Westcott, he first crewed with a tall, slenderly built Scot named Robert Young Rodger who, at 27, had the inherent qualities most suitable for a bomber pilot. Gifted with natural leadership, Bob Rodger commanded by consent in preference to rank and this ability undoubtedly came from his father, a Science Master at Forfar Academy. Emulating his father, he was educated at the Academy and became top pupil in Science and the Arts as well as a proficient golfer, eventually playing for the Scottish Junior International team against England. Another talent was music and it is poignant to recall that one of his favourite pieces was the Warsaw Concerto written for the aptly named, wartime film, *Dangerous Moonlight*. On leaving Forfar Academy he joined the Scottish Union and National Insurance Company. His initial military service was in the Royal Corps of Sig-

2

Early days with 90 Squadron, the crew pose with X Y-Y, EF458. Back row, L-R: Bob Rodger; 'Tug' Wilson; Howell Jones; Cliff Mitchell. Front row, L-R: Ed Davany, Leslie Griffiths; Roy Child (E. Rodger).

nals but in July 1941 he transferred to the RAF as a volunteer for aircrew training and, after three months, commenced pilot training.

Superior climate and peaceful skies in the USA made it logical for the Allies to train aircrew under the aegis of Uncle Sam and an agreement was reached to teach 8,000 pilots in American flying schools during 1941/2. Bob Rodger was one of those to leave a blacked out and well-bombed Britain to train in safer skies and in January 1942 he started his American flying tuition at Turner Field, Georgia. The course was demanding and less than half met the standard sought, some failed in tragic fashion and never re-crossed the Atlantic. There were periods of leave and these he used to learn something of America, her history and culture. Washington was visited but, being based in the South, he developed an interest in the Confederacy and visited some of the battlefields of that earlier conflict. His Pilot Training Diploma was awarded on 4 October 1942 and he returned to the UK the following month for continued advance training and flying acclimatization on Oxfords with 6(P) Advanced Flying Unit at Little Rissington, and Wellingtons with 26 OTU, Wing, before joining 11 OTU where he met Roy Child.

There was no rigid procedure of crew assignment, kindred spirits were encouraged to gather on the sound principle that airmen who selected one another would bond into natural crews. The catalyst for the successful crew depended strongly on the pilot and Bob Rodger's personality engendered both loyalty and affection from those who orientated towards him as their 'Skipper'. When, on 1 July 1943, he transferred to 1651 Heavy Conversion Unit, he had the genesis of a crew to train with him on the enormous Short Stirling bomber. Their lives would be interdependent and the task for 1651 HCU was to harmonize seven airmen into a team capable of serving with maximum effect in an operational squadron.

Navigating the bomber was 27-year-old Pilot Officer Clifford Mitchell, a Lancastrian whose personal commitment to the war effort was very deep. He was a widower and the decision to leave his young son to be cared for by his sister must have been heart rending. Perhaps this was why he was introspective and spoke little of his future hopes, for his inner self may have acknowledged little hope of a future. To an extent, they all felt a hint of this but some things were best unspoken. On one occasion Bob allowed Cliff to fly the aircraft so he had some experience should the contingency arise but, when

'Skipper', Flight Lieutenant Robert Young Rodger, a natural leader who commanded by consent in preference to rank (E. Rodger).

the crisis occurred, there was nothing any man could do. By sad coincidence, another of Bob's crew, Air Bomber Sergeant Robert Wilson was also a widower, his wife having died in 1941. Their three-year-old son, Peter, was adopted by his grandparents when Bob Wilson entered the RAF.

Known as 'Tug' to his crewmates, Bob worked for Daimler in Coventry before the war and loved flying. It was his task

In a picture for his girlfriend, Leslie Griffiths models an airman's attire (Mrs D. Willett).

codes he used were vital for the crew's survival. A quiet, conscientious lad, he studied to develop his enforced career and was granted a Commission only a week before he died. On home leave he spoke little of service life preferring to stroll in the country making plans with his fiancée for the future the war so ruthlessly smashed.

Manipulating the mechanics of the bomber was the crew's eldest member, 32-year-old Sergeant Edward Francis Davany from Gateshead, County Durham. A short, narrow-featured man, he followed the crew's trend for quieter personalities and was a devout Roman Catholic. Educated at the Blessed Sacrament School, he became apprenticed to a painter and decorator and worked hard through those difficult days of unemployment. In the late 1930s, he established his own business and gained contracts for a number of major projects. He was a kind, caring person who gave much of his time and energy in church work to aid the poor and it is not surprising that his beliefs would not let him stand aside from the responsibility of fighting for a free world. In January 1941 he entered the RAF and, after initial reception, he moved into a series of technical training schools for Flight engineers. In August 1941 he had leave to get married but the days he and his bride Theresa would share were subordinated by the RAF's need for replacement aircrew.

In June 1943, he completed his course at No 4 School of Technical Training and was posted to 1651HCU at Waterbeach where he blended into Bob Rodger's crew. His station in the Stirling was reminiscent of a submarine's control deck, with its banks of gauges monitoring the bomber's complex, electrical, hydraulic, pneumatic and fuel sys-

to see that the bombs struck the designated objective. Wireless operator for the crew was 21-year-old Sergeant Leslie Mayberry Griffiths, who came from Keresley, near Coventry. His mother had been seriously injured in the infamous Coventry raid of 14/15 November 1940 when a landmine shattered the family home. 'Les' Mayberry was an accounts clerk, also in the motor industry but, after that dark winter of raids, he put balance sheets aside and enlisted in the RAF. Only a few years earlier, he had arranged passwords and transmitted signals for his childhood chums, now the tems. The four Bristol Hercules VI engines sucked fuel from seven tanks in each wing giving a normal capacity of 2,254 gallons which they consumed at over 200 gallons per hour. Ed's role was to co-ordinate consumption to optimize operational performance. He had to know his aircraft intimately and be capable of conducting emergency repairs that might keep them airborne after damage by enemy action. Their most feared adversary was the fighter and the remaining crew members were gunners. Their Stirling was equipped with three Frazer-Nash hydraulically-powered turrets: an FN15 in the nose with two .303 machine-guns; an FN50 dorsal turret with two guns and an FN20 tail turret with four guns. Only the mid-upper and rear turrets were manned regularly. Tug Wilson could operate the FN15 should it prove necessary.

Roy Child occupied the mid-upper while the most boisterous member of the crew, Australian Flight Sergeant Howell Idris Jones was their, 'Arse-end Charlie' in the FN20. This ebullient 28-year-old was of Welsh descent and came from Randwick, New South Wales. He enlisted in the RAAF on 13 September 1941 and embarked for the UK just over a year later. Short in stature, his approach to military discipline was typically Australian and his tendency to fall asleep on cross-country training flights was disconcerting but, on operations, there was none more vigilant than 'Hal' Howell.

1651 HCU was based at Waterbeach near Cambridge and was, in its way, a university dedicated to students graduating in airmanship on Stirlings. Day and night, the sound of Hercules engines reverberated across the fens as crews did circuits and bumps, beacon stooges, cross-country exercises, fighter affiliations and bombing practice missions. Bob and his crew accumulated their education in the great, black-bellied bomber without major mishap but the Stirling took some getting used to. After Wellingtons, she seemed, and was, enormous, standing 22 ft 9 in high with a deep sided fuselage 87 ft 3 in long. Shorts originally sought a wingspan of 112 ft but Specification B12/36 restricted it to under 100 ft because the Air Ministry insisted on a bomber suitable for existing runways and hangar sizes. Consequently, the first of the modern heavies was seriously handicapped by this imposition and proved unable to achieve the operating altitudes of her later wider-spanned sisters, the Halifax and Lancaster.

The Stirling's sturdy appearance engendered confidence although she had an Achilles Heel, which was again caused by concern over take-off length, which had forced Shorts to increase wing incidence by 3°, but the requirement came too late to alter production tooling so the undercarriage was lengthened to create the required slope for the aerofoil. This created a complicated retraction mechanism with inherent weaknesses which dogged the Stirling through her career and deposited many ignominiously on their bellies, particularly at the Conversion Units. Once airborne, however, the Stirling demonstrated a manoeuvrability belied by her size and, as their flying time increased, Bob's crew established a rapport with the aircraft and faith in their pilot's ability. Having accomplished 49½ hours of daylight plus 50½ hours night flying, they were one of 45 crews turned out by 1651 in July and, as with most of its neophytes, they went to 3 Group whose units were based in the Cambridge/Ely area.

One of the Group's finest squadrons was No 90 then based at Wratting Common, not more than a dozen miles from Waterbeach, on the south-eastern side of Cambridge. Earlier in the war, this unit had the distinction of introducing the American Flying Fortress to combat, but the debut was not successful and the squadron eventually disbanded to reform with Stirlings in November 1942. Initially there were two flights, 'A' and 'B', but the complement later expanded with the addition of 'C' flight, whose aircraft adopted their own fuselage code 'XY' as opposed to the standard Squadron code 'WP'.

The CO, Wing Commander J.H. Giles, DFC, allocated his new crew to 'C' flight but, before allowing them to fly an operation together, it was customary for the pilot to fly as 'Second Dicky', or number two pilot, with an experienced crew. Two days after his arrival, Bob Rodger flew his first operation when he accompanied Flight Lieutenant Peryer to the crematorium that was once Hamburg. Bomber Command and the Eighth Air Force conducted a plan of pulverizing attacks on the port and over 40,000 people died in the resultant firestorm. This awesome display of Allied air power portended the fate of Hitler's Reich, sending shudders through the nation and its leadership. Fortunately for the battered city, the weather deflected the final blows and Bob Rodger experienced the difficulties of target location. Contrary to the Met reports, they faced 10/10 cloud to the target and little better in the target area, quite apart from icing and freak electrical storms that sent St Elmo into his eerie antics. Unsure of their position, they bombed what they believed was Bremerhaven, fifteen miles east of Hamburg, and headed home dispirited by the doubtful contribution of their attack.

Bob was now a little more prepared than his crew but training still formed an important part of Squadron life and the first flight they all made with 90 Squadron was a fighter affiliation. A Spitfire was their 'attacker' and the purpose of this exercise was primarily to practise evasive action but it also accustomed gunners to respond from a manoeuvring bomber against a target, itself speeding through range and field of fire. The most successful tactic developed by bomber crews was appropriately named the 'Corkscrew', and called for superb cooperation between gunners and pilot. The intention was not to be there when the fighter fired. Judge it too late and you received a formidable blasting from cannon and machine-gun — go too soon and the fighter followed you through: nemesis bomber. Gunners had to be alert, first to spot the assailant and then time the command and direction of corkscrew. Co-ordination was essential. Either gunner calculated the fighter's direction of attack and called for Bob to 'Corkscrew Port' (or Starboard), 'Go!'. Their precision timing had to be matched by Bob's dexterity piloting 25 tons of aeroplane. On the command 'Go', Bob swung the Stirling into a near vertical bank and killed lift by prodigious application of bottom rudder. This dropped the bomber sharply out of position and shed anything up to 2,000 ft, quite apart from the crew's breakfast. Bob then hauled her into a climb ready to repeat the procedure if the fighter still threatened. Such extreme gyrations tested airmen and aircraft and numerous casualties resulted from structural failure or loss of control but, to be of value, the simulation had to be realistic, and Roy revelled in this aspect of their training.

A week after Bob's induction flight, the entire crew were briefed for their first operation. Following a general policy of breaking in new boys on softer sorties, they were ordered on what was termed a 'gardening' attack to 'plant' mines in the sea near La Rochelle. Throughout the war, Bomber Command made a significant but little credited contribution to the sea war by mining sealanes and port approaches. Six 90 Squadron Stirlings were detailed and Bob's crew were assigned Stirling III, *EF 426*, coded *XY-W* for the occasion. At 21.55 hours on 6 August 1943, the country started receiving the return on its investment in their training when their bomber lifted away from Wratting Common bound for south-western France. Two hours later they were at 10,000 ft over the Bay of Biscay searching for an area coded 'Deodors'. Thick cloud handicapped navigation and Cliff was sorely tested to locate their objective. Adding to their anxiety was the abrupt appearance of a cluster of enemy aircraft — Roy estimated eight — but they were either bombers *en route* to England, or aircraft on a training flight. Had they been fighters, the Stirling would have been in a predicament but, as it was, they felt cheeky enough to loose off a few rounds before the Germans disappeared. Fortune then opened a gap in the clouds and their position was ascertained by recognition of the Ile de Ré. Tug planted their 'vegetable' at three minutes past midnight and the bomber was homeward bound, its crew now blooded.

A fortnight of training flights, air tests and fighter affiliation exercises followed before they were again called to action on 23/24 August 1943. This time it was no cruise to the south of France. Following his success over Hamburg when the first operational use of window con-fused and confounded German defences, Bomber Command's AO, CinC, Sir Arthur Harris, sought to pursue the initiative with a strike against the political and military core that was Berlin, capital of the Reich. 'Window', an innocuous name for strips of tinfoil, each indistinguishable from a bomber to the radar eye, now rendered incoherent the sensitive control essential for night fighters. The attack was anticipated by the Germans and hurried steps taken to compensate for technological blindness. The pattern was being set for the biggest, nocturnal air battle of the war so far. Harris made his decision. From Bomber Command HQ at High Wycombe, the teletype chattered to the various Group Headquarters. Gathering detail, the orders were transmitted to individual stations where Operations Blocks appended further minutiae and instructed squadrons. Station activity set in spate the usual rumours of target selection and air tests were observed by an eavesdropping enemy monitoring the increased radar and radio traffic which preceded a major raid: their predictions were often more accurate than those of the aircrew upon whom they spied.

During the afternoon and early evening, the Stirlings made slaves of technicians tasked with satisfying their demands for oxygen, ammunition, oil, fuel and, of course, bombs. Equipment was tested, film fitted to the night camera, bundles of window loaded — a grooming process proceeding several hundred times over as Bomber Command made ready. Bob's crew would be one of those bound for Berlin, a broadsword of power crashing against the weakening shield of Reich Air Defence, or so it was hoped. Roy Child's feelings were more prosaic when the enormous distance to Berlin was revealed at briefing; he knew that, to survive, they would need not only their training and limited experience, but a benevolent portion of luck. 'Briefing' was something of a misnomer considering the quantity and complexity of information they had to absorb.

Following an introduction by the Station Commander, a series of specialist officers elaborated on each aspect of the raid and principal amongst these was the Intelligence Officer. Berlin was, he advised, code named 'Whitebait' and they, the 'Ravens' of Bomber Command's Main Force would, indeed, be birds of ill omen to the city. For Bob and crew this, their first briefing for a major attack, was typical of others which followed, but a description of it illustrates something of the techniques and terminology they became accustomed to. The attack, they were told, would be by over 700 aircraft in six waves with Zero Hour set at 11.45 pm. Sixteen minutes before this a support attack by ten 'Skylark' Mosquitos would shower window to protect the pathfinders whose role was to mark the target with brilliant, red target indicator flares. This pattern of pyrotechnics continued with 'backers up', 'Old Crows' coming in from Zero plus 1 minute to Z + 39 and maintaining the marking with green target indicators. Supporting the firework display was a further force called 'Recenterers' who tried to ensure the green markers did not drift from the desired Aiming Point and, controlling the entire show, was an aptly named 'Master of Ceremonies' callsigned 'Dagin' whose Mosquito would flit to and fro, advising, guiding and cajoling the Main Force. Les was told to listen for and obey his broadcasts. The Main Force would, it was hoped, be over the target between Z + 2 and Z + 42 and aircraft fitted with

H2S, an early ground-reading radar which showed outlines of built up areas, were told to watch for a distinctively shaped promontory on the north side of Berlin and, from it, take distance and direction to the target area.

Next on stage was the Meteorology Officer with an unenviable role: to predict the vicissitudes of northern European weather over several hundred miles for several hours. At his disposal he had the status reported by weather reconnaissance flights plus predictions from Bomber Command's senior weather wizards. Their calculations were not comforting: bad weather *en route* with icing expected even at lower altitudes, with the target itself clear apart from ground haze to handicap identification. In the event, these conditions significantly disrupted the attack and prevented nearly 25 per cent of the force from bombing their objective. Navigators had their own briefing prior to attending the main session but, none the less, Cliff Mitchell listened attentively to the Navigation Officer describing their route, flak areas, airfields, natural features and the problems they would face with the enemy's success in jamming their navigational radar, GEE. Details of specific interest to Tug were provided by the Bombing Leader as he spoke of loads, detecting decoy targets, dummy markers and the importance of avoiding creepback. Les Griffiths busily scribbled notes as the Signals Officer gave codes, Splasher and Buncher beacon wavelengths and the frequencies for obtaining wind speed and direction broadcasts, vital for navigation. He also had to use the bomber's transmitter to 'Tinsel' — a disruptive method whereby radio operators tuned to German fighter control frequencies and switched on a microphone mounted in one of their

'Sunset and zero hour before the great raid on Berlin . . . One of the crews is just aboard.' So said the Daily Sketch *when front paging this picture on 2 September 1943. Self-consciously posing, 'Tug' Wilson leads the crew, followed by Roy Child and Leslie Griffiths. Bob Rodger is in the rear with Howell Jones and their ground crew chief, Sergeant Arthur Stubbs, nearest camera (J. Munro).*

engine compartments, the resulting cacophony blared into German earphones, frustrating their fighter control. Ed Davany's interest focused on comments from the Engineering Leader: rev settings, fuel loads, range in reserve, etc, etc. The Gunnery Officer followed up with unnecessary pleas for vigilance and the need to keep turrets mobile and prevent freezing, something which occurred to metal and man alike as bombers clawed to higher altitude and lower temperatures. To conclude, Wing Commander Giles summarized the main points and wished his audience well: the rehearsal was over, they now became the cast for the next, deadly act.

The evening sun burnished strips of high cirrus as the ground transports disgorged aircrew by the tall, dark bombers, the menacing silhouettes of which dominated the strangely attired creatures gathering in the shadow of each machine. The crews had acquired the paraphernalia of the airborne warrior but it was not heroic war apparel, more a jumble of scarves, sweaters, jackets and crumpled leather helmets. Bob's crew was no exception: they dressed according to the vagaries of the Stirling's heat-ing system and the draughts prevalent through gaps in its structure. Despite their motley appearance, each was now sharply alert to the occasion and Bob's disciplined external check of their plane expressed some of the tension in their sinews. The occasion was enamelled with some humour but the tension could only be relieved for each man by concentrating on the procedures he had been taught.

Their craft on this occasion was a veteran Mk III Stirling, *EF458, XY-Y*, which had reached 90 via 75 Squadron. As yet, they did not know her temperament but this assembly of over 60,000 parts had to be lifted from *terra firma* without mishap. Clambering through her aluminium hull, each was only too aware of the load carried: two 500 lb medium case, high explosive bombs; forty 30 lb incendiary bombs and 450 4 lb incendiaries.

As the crew settled into their stations, Bob and Ed Davany began the ritual of instilling life into the dormant giant, a duet requiring a careful call and check, which commenced by ensuring that fuel cocks and undercarriage switches were OFF before any power was drawn into the system. Numbers 2 and 4 fuel tanks were turned on and engine controls set with throttles slightly cracked. The mental metronome within each man's head now seemed to crash away each second as Ed primed the fuel system and Bob switched on the ignition and booster coils before pressing the starter for the port outer and gave the instruction 'CONTACT'. Ed worked firmly on the priming pump, transfusing the great Hercules as the propellor juddered stiffly into life. It hesitated, injecting jerky stabs to the airframe then, casting off the lethargy, the engine spoke positively, its rhythmic beat adding to the resonat-

Anxious moments as EF458 prepares to take-off for Berlin (J. Munro).

ing dance of hundreds of other pistons across the aerodrome.

When all motors were running, the pilot and engineer monitored revs and temperatures for any hint of malfunction but *Y-Yorker* seemed content to go. Other Stirlings were already lurching gawkily to their take-off positions flanking each side of the main runway. Bob waved away the chocks and, settling the inners on 1,000 rpm, he used his outer engines to twist the bomber on its ungainly waddle round the perimeter track, constantly watching for obstructions and checking brake pressures. A few minutes later they reached the take-off point, the final check list calls were made and control clearance given. Just after 8.15 pm, Bob ran *Yorker* forward a few feet to straighten her twin tail wheels and stopped with the aeroplane facing down the runway. Brakes were applied and power built up until the bomber shook restlessly. Then, releasing the brakes, he advanced all four throttles, his hand slightly askew to get starboard power advance and counteract torque as the huge machine drove forwards. The eyes of groundcrew and spectators reflected the habitual anxiety experienced in these critical moments of take-off — a Stirling did not readily stop if something went wrong. As speed increased, Bob edged the control column forward, lifting the tail and applying rudder to keep her straight. They had clearly passed 110 mph before he caressed the aircraft skywards: the ravens of Bomber Command were rising.

Roy found the sight awe inspiring. The land fell into darkness but, emerging from the shadows, came bomber upon bomber. It was noisy and already cold as the Stirling joined a flock forming and climbing east. Twenty-one Stirlings left Wratting Common that night and not all would return, but they and the other 727 bombers launched were soon lost to view in the night sky. Occasionally they would bump across the turbulent wake of an unseen aircraft or glimpse a shadow, and the gunners stayed taut for action should a shape prove hostile. One thing they had established and agreed — if any aircraft approached their tail, they would fire, irrespective of whether it looked British or not. Stories circulated of captured aircraft being used and an approach from astern was most unfriendly.

To alleviate the problems caused by window, Luftwaffe tacticians introduced free-roving, single-engined fighters called 'Wild Boar' who would set upon the bombers in the well lit but dangerous vicinity of their target. The close control procedure previously used to guide the traditional, twin-engined night-fighter to its prey was made impossible by window and these aircraft also adopted a new technique called 'Tame Boar'. In this, general guidance on the position and direction of the bomber force was provided by ground control and radio beacons were then used to navigate into the bomber stream. Searchlights and gun-laying radar had also been baffled by window but the former were cleverly instructed to shine at shallow angles along the base of cloud layers so fighters above could spot bombers silhouetted on a soft, luminescent backcloth. In the past, fighters had avoided interception over the target for fear of their own AA barrage, but the guns were now ordered to limit the altitude of fire to 15,000 ft and allow fighters free reign above. Handicapped, the defences may have been, but defeated they were not.

Bob's Stirling had scarcely crossed the

Dutch coast when German controllers at Stade and Doberitz correctly surmised Berlin as the objective and alerted the city's defences. *Yorker* slogged along, striving for an altitude of 15,000 ft and fending off the ice encountered at this height. Her crew were silent and tense as the magnitude of the battle increased: the first victim they saw died in a fashion soon to become horribly commonplace. Routes were designed to avoid major flak concentrations but the channels were often narrow and miscalculation might find them caught in a deadly, silken web of searchlights. Window protection was weakest at the bomber stream's edge and here radar control resumed its effectiveness and flak its accuracy. They watched a bomber struggle to escape the clasp of incandescent fingers but, moments later, it burst, a fulminate star cascading fragments flaming earthwards.

As the distance to Berlin reduced, the cauldron seethed with unholy malevolence and, to *Yorker*'s crew, the spectacle was incredible and unnerving. It was like daylight as the Stirling flew the final few miles to the aiming point. Every sort of coloured light was apparent as flares illuminated the city and thousands of individual fires flickered and began clustering below. The thump of flak buffeted their craft, the repercussions of bombs were felt and hot air simmering skywards caused *Yorker* to undulate as Bob tussled to keep her steady for the run in. Roy vividly remembers Tug's calming influence on the situation as, unperturbed, he settled himself to the Mk XIV bombsight. The noise of their engines drowned all but the most violent emissions from the cacophony outside and the presence of nightfighters was denoted not by noise but by shark-fast shadows and sharp stabs of tracer

as they slashed their victims. Some bombers exploded and vanished, others trailed fiery streamers to oblivion. Sometimes a crew member escaped and his parachute might be glimpsed floating like a dandelion seed through the turbulent, dangerous sky. Roy's night-trained vision registered the awesome spectacle but distraction was dangerous and *Yorker*'s gunners concentrated on searching for fighters while Tug's unhurried voice corrected the Stirling's bomb run.

It was barely a minute to midnight and the green target indicators were clearly visible when Tug, seemingly undisturbed, guided Bob to the aiming point and released their load at 00.02 hours. As their bomber slipped away from Berlin, Roy and Howell had a lingering view of the blazing city, the glow of which was visible for over an hour. The atmosphere on board eased with the diminishing miles home and a sense of relief permeated through the aircraft as a satisfied crew returned the raven to its nest. They were tired yet buoyant with the night's events, eagerly answering the Intelligence Officer's debriefing questions. Hot coffee laced with rum was gratefully taken before the delayed weariness arrived and they went back to rooms left over eight hours earlier. It had been a long night. The Charlottenburg-Wilmersdorf area of Berlin suffered serious damage but the city centre avoided most of the bombs intended for it because the ground haze handicapped visual marking. The Master Bomber had been unable to clearly interpret his H2S signals and had marked six miles to the south-west of the aiming point: most of the bombs fell in this vicinity. Bomber Command lost 56 aircraft and nearly 400 crewmen that night, a reflection of the strength of the German Defences and indicative of the struggle facing Allied airmen as they sought to subjugate the Reich capital.

The crew of Stirling Y-*Yorker* were rapidly developing an affection for the aircraft that had brought them home from Berlin, so they were pleased to take her on a compass test and fighter affiliation on 27 August. This preceded a raid on Nuremburg, the south German city so dear to the Nazi hierarchy. On this mission *Yorker* lifted off at 21.25 hours and continued uneventfully through clear weather to the target area some 3¼ hours later. Again, they observed the unhappy spectacle of bombers, predominantly on the fringes of the stream, being ensnared in searchlights and destroyed by flak or marauding fighters.

The dazzling burst of light which violated their darkness near Nuremburg was as terrifying as it was harsh to their eyes. Roy thought it was a master beam because, within seconds, six more converged to expose *Yorker* for flak and fighter to attack. He never forgot the frightening experience which followed as Bob called for them to hang on and threw the Stirling into a series of violent, evasive actions. Remorselessly, the beams clung to the gyrating bomber and Roy even fired at them in a futile but defiant gesture. Strangely, the flak did not concentrate as venomously as they expected which made them fearful of fighter attack. A belly full of incendiary bombs handicapped *Yorker's* manoeuvrability and Bob just could not squirm out of those lights.

They had already survived this brilliant embrace for longer than most: as Bob dropped into another stomach-churning corkscrew, he called for the crew's agreement to jettison the bombs. They were in a desperate situation and it might help them escape but Bob still assumed final responsibility by ordering Tug to release their load. *Yorker* spilled 784 incendiary bombs from her innards. Whether this placated the defences, or something else doused the power, they never knew, but the lights vanished as suddenly as they had appeared, leaving shaken men grateful for the darkness which concealed their vulnerability. Bob checked his crew — the relief at their escape was unbelievable. The Stirling's engines still thundered reassuringly and they assessed their situation. Feeling guilty about the absence of bombs, they decided they would still cross the target area rather than risk collision by turning against the bomber stream. It was a chastened and wiser crew that returned from Nuremburg, but this incident gave them the feeling they would be a 'lucky' crew having escaped from such a hopeless predicament.

Two days later they carried out an air test and fighter affiliation near Peterborough in readiness for their fourth operation to Munchen Gladbach. The raid was to be carried out by 661 aircraft and Oboe Mosquitos would do the marking. Bomber Command pulled yet another item from its itinerary of deceptive devices and introduced 'Special Tinsel' to jam German high power, high frequency transmissions. This, plus seven to nine-tenths cloud in the target area helped reduce losses and photographic reconnaissance later revealed severe damage in the residential and business district of Rheydt. *Yorker's* contribution was 7,200 lb of incendiaries released at 02.24 hours from 12,000 ft and returning crews reported the fire glow still visible from the Dutch Coast. Bob Rodger found himself more preoccupied with getting the Stirling home after their port outer engine failed and it was five in the morning before the crew nurtured her into Wratting Common, landing on three engines.

90 Squadron achieved the 3 Group record in August for despatching the most sorties and the efficiency of Sergeant Arthur Stubbs and their ground crew was demonstrated when *Yorker* was pronounced ready for the night of 31 August. This may have given some comfort to her crew for the target revealed at briefing was, once more, Berlin. As the Stirlings lifted away from Wratting Common, they could see Eighth Air Force Fortresses landing from a successful raid on Amiens/Glisy airfield and the Americans undoubtedly wished their nocturnal brethren a similarly safe return. Roy felt that it would be an unpleasant night and Les must have sensed it from the significant increase in enemy jamming he encountered. Their GEE set quickly became useless and the looming stratocumulus added further navigational difficulties as it thickened until the tops lay only 1,000 ft below. They crossed the enemy coast north of Texel without mishap, but their apprehension heightened as the first victims succumbed to the defences. The route neared Halberstadt, then approached Berlin from the south-west and they could see that the defences were really putting on a show. Luftwaffe aircraft high overhead had dropped white parachute flares over the bomber stream and Roy could see, stretching ahead, what appeared to be a brilliantly illuminated aerial highway, travelling on which were hundreds of aircraft, many clearly visible. The fighters lurked in the shadows, selected targets and flashed in to attack. Numerous combats were occurring and Cliff left his curtained-off navigation compartment and clambered into the astrodome to assist as an extra observer.

From the mid-upper turret, Roy could see Cliff staring incredulously at the spectacle — he was there about half a minute before he clicked on the intercom and announced that there was no way he could watch what was happening. He had, he added, no idea what it was like and they all realized this was, indeed, the first time he had left his position while in the target area. Whilst not wishing to appear a coward, he explained, he felt more secure with his maps and promptly disappeared from view. Those who had no alternative faced events that thrashed a man's courage — all about were attacks, explosions, searchlights, fires and flares, a battle waging in unnatural light that cast the spectres of hell into the minds of men for the rest of their lives.

Yorker was beginning her run in to the target when a Ju 88 burst from the darkness, eight o'clock high. The Junkers had a formidable array of cannon and machine-guns capable of shredding armour, aluminium and airmen alike but the Stirling's vigilant gunners were prompt in response. At this desperate moment, Howell's turret malfunctioned and although bomber and fighter fired simultaneously, the rear gunner could only fire a few rounds in support of the mid upper's twin .303s. Roy never knew whether he hit the fighter but he may have distracted the pilot sufficiently for him to miss and it whipped by below them, vanishing in the darkness. Tug came on the intercom, obviously unruffled by their narrow escape and his unperturbed voice had a calming influence as he guided Bob in over the target. At 23.48 hours they released their bombs and Bob immediately nosed *Yorker* into a dive for more airspeed to take them from the fury over Berlin. At that moment, Roy felt a knock on the rear of his turret and, looking round, he spotted a hole, about an inch in size, in the perspex but what caused it, he never knew. This was the only damage they sustained and, as they withdrew, the intensity of battle declined although Roy remembers another inexplicable incident which occurred near the French coast.

He and Howell spotted an unidentified aircraft high on the port side and seemingly shadowing them. Such suspicious behaviour brooked no hesitation and, as it edged nearer, both gunners fired. Nothing happened! The stranger slid closer and *Yorker*'s gunners tried again but both sets of Brownings failed, suffering from frozen oil, so Bob took evasive action and sacrificed more height for speed as they fled enemy airspace. Still the other machine persisted in pursuit but did not press any attack and, when the guns thawed out at lower altitude, a few rounds of discouragement were loosed off at him. Having followed them over the sea, he appeared to waggle his wings in some form of gesture and swung back towards Occupied Europe. *Yorker* landed after more than seven and a half hours flying.

Following more training exercises, the next operation was an attack on Mannheim on 5/6 September when Bomber Command was able to report a well concentrated attack by over 600 heavies. Smoke over the target rose nearly as high as *Yorker* and the fires were visible over 100 miles away. The reason for their next mission was a mystery to Roy and it was not until the author studied *Operational Research Section Report B173* in the Public Records Office that the gunner found out why they went to Boulogne. With 'D-Day' in mind, the purpose of the raid was to see how effective night bombing would be against such specific targets as coastal batteries and the attack was conducted in two phases. The first target was at le Portel near Boulogne and Mosquito markers were followed up by heavies including a small contribution from the US Eighth Army Air Force. Phase 2 went in at 22.43 against a second battery near Cap d'Alprech and *Yorker* was amongst the first to bomb. Records show that Tug released 6 x 1,000 lb General Purpose (GP) and 8 x 500 lb GP Bombs at 22.48 hours from 15,000 ft. The crew did not observe any results but, when prints from the camera were developed, their position was plotted as only three-quarters of a mile from the target centre and the bomb chart was favourably endorsed. Sadly, this was the last raid they flew in their favourite *XY-Y*, *EF458*, because they went on leave and, when they returned, *Yorker* had gone down with Sergeant Haynes and crew on 23/24 September during another attack on Mannheim. This caused sorrow to the crew but, again, luck had been with them and they felt confident of their own survival. Stirling replacements were no problem and a new Mark III, *LK380*, was allocated to 90 Squadron on 24 September. The new machine would pick up C Flight's *XY-Y* code but Sergeant Stubbs was later to recall her inauspicious arrival. When touching down from her delivery flight, a primer pipe fractured starting a small engine fire which, although swiftly extinguished, did not get her off to a good start in the Squadron. There existed the feeling that Stirlings produced by Shorts were superior to those manufactured by subcontractors: *EF458* had come from the parent company, whereas this brand new machine was not many hours off the Austin Motor Company's lines at Longbridge.

Newly arrived, Stirling LK380 had an unhappy debut and inauspicious career with 90 Squadron (A. Stubbs).

The anthropomorphis *EF458* engendered did not readily translate to *LK380* and the new machine behaved less comfortably. Their first flight was a thirty-minute air test on 1 October to get accustomed to its manners but they did not take to their new charge and this affected morale because Roy sensed a distinct drop in confidence. They were still unhappy on 3 October when the new bomber was flown for another air test and fighter affiliation but Bob was determined to rally his crew and put *LK380* through some vigorous corkscrews to show it was as good as *EF458*. He even let Cliff take the controls to demonstrate ease of handling but the plane was still not ready for their eighth operation to Kassel so *EH906, L-London,* was used.

The pendulum of success in deception swung to and fro but was with Bomber Command on 3/4 October when a feint by ten Mosquitos over Hanover foxed German fighter controllers into diverting fighters and reduced Main Force losses. Zero hour had been planned for 21.15 hours and *L-London* flew unimpinged over the target fourteen minutes later, by which time the pattern of incendiaries extended from the Thringshausen area in the north to the important Gerhard Fieseler aircraft manufacturing plant in the south which was busy producing early models of the V1. This weapon was planned for Hitler's retaliatory attacks but, that night, the war their fanatical leader created cost the lives of over 5,000 citizens.

The following day, 4 October, Allied

air pressure was maintained when USAAF B-17s hit Frankfurt during the morning. Bomber Command supplemented their effort with the heaviest night raid the city had seen. Senior navigators at 3 Group expressed some concern over the apparent enthusiasm of crews who departed Beachy Head and reached the focal point off the French coast too soon but, after this slight problem, the raid proceeded well with even the weather behaving as predicted, ten-tenths cloud to within forty miles of Frankfurt and clear over the target. Well placed markers encouraged accurate bombing and the docks and harbour facilities suffered severe damage. Bob's crew were wary of the defences but there was less flak than expected and the searchlights, while numerous, wandered aimlessly. *L-London* puffed her way up to 15,000 ft but even this significant height for a Stirling failed to prevent them collecting a 'friendly' incendiary bomb in the wing, undoubtedly dropped by a Lancaster or Halifax from a much safer altitude. Mercifully, it failed to ignite and was only discovered by groundcrew the following morning.

Stirling *LK380* was air tested for twenty minutes on 6 October but her combat debut did not occur with them. On 7/8 October, the new bomber was flown by Sergeant R.J. Phillips and crew on a gardening sortie but she baulked the first fence and returned early with GEE trouble. What was to be the only mission they flew with her, their tenth, was on 8/9 October when, following once more on the heels of a significant Eighth Air Force effort, the RAF attacked Hanover and Bremen. Stirling *LK380* was finally pronounced combat ready and bombed up for the only operational raid she would ever complete. At 10.37 pm the new *Yorker* left Wratting

Common as part of a predominantly Stirling diversionary effort against Bremen while the main force attacked Hanover. Thin cloud hindered the Bremen raid but H2S was used for marking and the green TI glowed through the cloud allowing Tug to sight, but results were unobserved. A few fighters were spotted but the fact that the Stirling's operational ceiling was less than the Halifax or Lancaster proved beneficial on this occasion because the Germans, not knowing the composition of the raid, ordered their fighters to patrol at altitudes Stirlings could not achieve so only three aircraft were lost. The return trip was uneventful and *Yorker* touched down at 03.51 hours.

Later that day, Tug Wilson found a few moments to write home and, heavily underlined at the top of his letter was the number '10'. He began, 'Just a short letter to let you know I am still alive and kicking and as you can see by the number on the top, 10 ops in now'. His stoicism is reflected by his description of Bremen as 'pretty easy' whereas Frankfurt was 'pretty sticky'. Censorship prevented him saying they had flown home with an unexploded bomb lodged in their wing and Tug would not wish to cause anxiety so this RAF understatement sufficed. He could, however, tell the family of a change of address. The Squadron had been expecting a move and, before he had finished writing, it was announced that they would transfer from Wratting Common to make way for 1651 HCU which was shifting from Waterbeach as part of 3 Group's Lancaster conversion plans. The Stirling's front line days were expiring and it was the intention to re-equip with Lancasters. With effect from 13 October, Tug's new address was to be RAF Tuddenham, near Newmarket, and their last flight from Wratting Common was to air test *Yorker* on 12 October.

The following two days were spent ferrying equipment to Tuddenham. Roy remembers the base as consisting of a few fabricated buildings but, surprisingly, the hut the crew shared still existed in 1986. They flew no ops for the rest of that month but took *Yorker* on a number of short trips for bombing and fighter affiliation exercises. At the end of October they went on leave and, for Tug, it was a few precious days with his son, a chance to be free from flak, fighters and fear. Tug's last sight of his lad was from the train heading back to camp — who knows what his thoughts were as he waved farewell. A few days later he wrote home and enclosed some oranges and chocolate, rare gifts in rationed Britain.

Squadron life had its lighter moments and one well supported feature was the liberty bus to Cambridge. Not long after their return from leave, Roy, Tug and the Skipper decided on a few beers so caught the evening bus to town. Later that night, they emerged from the bright, boisterous atmosphere of whatever pub it was and found themselves in damp, foggy streets with zero visibility. The bus driver had to contend with this in addition to blackout conditions so it is little wonder an accident occurred on the way back to camp when they collided with a car. This accident saved Roy Child's life, albeit in a most roundabout way. Thrown forward by the impact, he cracked his chin against the skull of the airman in front but, apart from a slight cut, he thought no more of it and no serious injuries resulted from the mishap. However, the next day he found he had developed a face rash and sores which the camp hospital diagnosed as impetigo, proba-

bly caused by scurf from the scalp of the man in front infecting the cut. They were concerned that an oxygen mask and helmet might irritate and spread the condition so Roy was taken off flying and found his features coated with gentian violet to cure the infection. This remedy was ineffective, so, on the 8th of November, he was asked to spend a night in hospital where regular treatment could be administered. Roy was reluctant to get out of sequence with the crew on operations but, as there was a lull in activities, he felt he might be effectively treated and back before they flew again. That evening, as Roy settled to the attentions of the medical orderlies, Tug replied to a letter received from home. He wanted the family to know he was all right: but by the time his parents received it, their son had been killed.

9 November 1943 was not a significant day in the war — the Red Army recaptured Borodianka and Leonovka, the Eighth Army took Castiglione and what major air operations there were also occurred in Italy. In the UK, East Anglian airfields found themselves facing a misty day but the winter sun was untroubled by cloud and its weak warmth dispersed the vapours and provided visibility suitable for the usual round of air tests and training flights that interspersed operations. 3 Group would carry out 220 affiliation exercises during November and this training had to be thorough. It was often arranged for experienced aircrew to take men from novice crews to impart some of the hard-earned knowledge and Bob Rodger, now in charge of 'C' Flight, felt the opportunity should be taken to help one of the recently arrived crews captained by 21-year-old Flight Sergeant Lees Smith. With Lees were two of his

21-year-old Flight Sergeant Lees Smith sent pictures to his family after gaining the coveted wings (Mrs C. Taylor).

gunners, Flight Sergeant Morley Percival Loyst, RCAF, and Sergeant Gordon George Batten, RAF, who had occupied the rear and mid-upper turrets when they had done their initial, gardening sortie on 22/23 October. Events that day would inextricably link these airmen and it is only fair to recall something about Lees and his gunners for, although they had flown only one operation, their deaths were no less significant.

Lees came from Oldham in Lancashire and had, not surprisingly, gone from school into the cotton industry at the age of fifteen. He maintained his education by evening studies and, when war was declared, had progressed well enough to be offered a 'reserved occu-pation' by his employers. In 1941, Lees joined the Air Training Corps and this organization, sponsoring air-mindedness, encouraged him to enter the RAF so he declined the option of a safe job and enlisted on 1 July 1941. Lees was athletic and had no difficulty passing his aircrew medical at Carding-ton and he also proved to have the intelligence and temperament suitable for pilot training. Like Bob Rodger, Lees crossed the Atlantic but stayed within the Empire, going to Canada as a pupil in the Empire Air Training Scheme. On his arrival at 33 Elementary Flying Training School, Caron, Saskatchewan, in March 1942, Lees found the station facing blizzards and snowdrifts 16 ft deep. The spring thaw brought conditions that suited the Walrus more than the unit's Ansons but the doughty old Avros slithered about both on the ground and when airborne as tyro pilots tested airframe and instructor alike.

Lees marvelled at the beauty of flying and was stunned by the thrill of breaking cloud into the sharp, strong light above. For a young working class lad from Lancashire, life in Canada provided an exciting opportunity to visit places he had only read about and one impressive trip was a visit to the Calgary Stampede. Bronco busting was, in reality, tame compared with the task facing trainee aircrew and several of the boys he knew perished in flying accidents, a sobering reminder that was not compensated for even by Canadian hospitality. A year elapsed and Lees returned to England to continue training with Number 18 (Pilot) Advanced Flying Unit flying Oxfords from Church Lawford, Warwick. In June 1943 he went to 26 OTU at Wing flying Wellingtons and thence to 1651HCU in September and 90 Squadron on 9 October.

Gordon Batten's background was similar to Lees and some affinity occurred between the pilot and the tousle-haired gunner from Croydon. At 22, Gordon was slightly older and had also left a clerical post (in the gas industry) to join the RAF in May 1941. Tuition in air-gunnery took him to Rhodesia and back to 26 OTU where he teamed with Lees. Morley Loyst, the Canadian was nine years older than his pilot and had signed 'for the duration' on 28 July 1942 at the RCAF Recruiting Centre, North Bay, Ontario. A farmer's son, he left school in 1926 and worked on the land for eight years until attracted by higher wages in the nickel industry. This did not satisfy his career aspirations so he joined the police force in 1939 and this facilitated entry to the RCAF. Although he had never flown, he selected 'Flying Duties, Air Gunner'

Above left *Gordon Batten left a clerical post in the gas industry to enlist in May 1941 (Mrs V.E. Batten).*

Above *Canadian Morley Loyst was a fan of the film hero Clark Gable and evidently tried to project a Gable-like image for this photograph (Mrs R. Loyst).*

on his Attestation Paper and, with 20/20 vision in both eyes, he found no problem achieving this goal at Air Gunnery School. This handsome airman fashioned himself on Clark Gable and, as embarkation drew nearer, he and his fiancée, Kay, decided to marry despite the risk he might not return. When he left Canada in May 1943, she was pregnant but Morley never lived to hear of the birth of his son, Brian. His training continued until it merged with Lees Smith when a vacancy occurred in Lees' crew and the Canadian took over the perilous rear turret.

These, then, were nine of the ten airmen who attended a fateful rendezvous that unhappy winter's morning. The tenth, Flight Sergeant Ronald Heald Brown, RAF, was only a few miles away at Newmarket where his Air Fighting Development Unit, Hurricane IV, *KW800*, was being readied for the affiliation exercise. The AFDU operated from Wittering and was principally involved testing new armaments and equipment but another, important role was the provision of a Fighter Affiliation Circus which Bomber Command used for 'enemy' aircraft to attack bombers as related earlier. Pilots with the AFDU were experienced and Flight Sergeant Brown joined in August 1943 after eight months with 1435 Squadron flying Spitfires from Malta. Not only did he participate in the island's defence but he had flown numerous fighter-bomber and rhubarb operations over Sicily as the Allies prodded what Churchill described as 'the soft under-belly of the Axis'. A few days before Sicily was invaded, Flight Sergeant Brown was posted to the AFDU and took up duties which included fighter affiliation sorties.

In the hospital at Tuddenham, Roy Child was restless. He knew the crew were flying an affiliation and did not want to miss it: the flight would be short and any discomfort he might experience was preferable to the tedium of the station sick bay. Following administration of his morning treatment, he decided he would cycle to the aerodrome and catch *Yorker*. On the airfield, Stirling *T-Tommy* had already taken off for an affiliation with Flight Sergeant Brown's Hurricane and the crew of *Yorker* were preparing to board. It was nearly midday and Roy might still make it. Sergeant Stubbs was

contemplating whether to go or not: he could use the opportunity to monitor *Yorker*'s behaviour and Cliff Mitchell had a bad cold so his seat would be spare. In the finish, Cliff chuckled that being thrown about the sky might clear his head so he decided to go and Sergeant Stubbs waved *Yorker* from dispersal before going to the Sergeants' Mess for lunch.

Roy left the hospital and leapt on his cycle: he almost made it and was convinced Skipper saw him pedalling furiously to catch the taxi-ing bomber and, as a joke, hastened *Yorker* away from the panting gunner. Roy guessed the crew found the spectacle of the gunner pursuing his plane very amusing and the defeated airman was left on the runway as *Yorker* lifted off. The drone of *Yorker*'s engines diminished and her dejected mid-upper gunner, left with time on his hands, returned to the hospital. All his life he remained certain of one thing: he should have been on board that bomber. As *Yorker* droned away towards Ely, *T-Tommy* was already having a workout with Brown's Hurricane. The bomber pilot, 'Sandy' Cochrane, thought the fighter was well flown, very active, but did come rather close during the manoeuvres.

Others were at work of a different nature, and none more so than those responsible for the rich, arable land over which *Yorker* now flew as November found fenland farmers and their workfolk busy beet and potato picking. Scarcely any attention was paid to the familiar sight of aircraft manoeuvring overhead but one who did pause for a moment was farm manager Arthur Bedford. He had been supervising the loading of potato wagons in the station yard at Shippea Hill junction but, as lunchtime approached, he wandered over for a word with old Bill Bonnett, landlord of The Railway Tavern. As the two men chatted, the sound of approaching aircraft subordinated the conversation and a Stirling came majestically into view heading south towards Tuddenham. *Yorker*, it would appear, was going home, the powerful beat of her engines reverberating across the open fenland.

Then came the also familiar song of a Rolls Royce Merlin and the two men watched a Hurricane come swooping in from high and behind the bomber in a simulated stern attack. In the next few seconds *Yorker*'s crew would perish, nine brave lives lost in a tragic denouement that the spectators were powerless to prevent. The men up there were of his own age and loved life as he did — for all the years of his own life to follow, Arthur Bedford would never forget the loss of theirs.

Gathering speed, the fighter surged from a dive that took it below the bomber to a swift, powerful climb as if attacking the Stirling's belly. Swept in by momentum, the fighter hurtled towards *Yorker* and then, too late, tried veering away in a tight, climbing turn to starboard. It may be that Flight Sergeant Brown misjudged the turbulence created in the wake of a four-engined heavy bomber and, for a few vital moments, control of the Hurricane was lost. A sharp bang cracked across the open skies as his Hurricane sliced into *Yorker*'s starboard wing and carried on through, shredding debris as it went. A large section of the Stirling's wing was torn off and the bomber was tossed violently on its port side by the impact.

For a brief second, her nose went up in a despairing gesture to the sky but then, to Arthur's horror, she peeled sickeningly round in the opposite direction, away from Tuddenham and entered a steep spiral dive. Bob Rodger and Lees Smith may have had the possibility of escape as both wore seat pack parachutes but they had seven other lives to consider and loyalty to their crew undoubtedly surpassed self-preservation as neither left the doomed bomber. The loss of her wing and aileron control gave them no chance of recovery and, as Arthur Bedford and Bill Bonnett stood, transfixed by events, she plunged into Sedge Fen only a few hundred yards away. There was a huge 'whoomph' of earth towering skywards, then it cascaded back over the site. In less than thirty seconds, *Yorker* had vanished. The Hurricane spluttering and banging, staggered tenaciously higher gaining more precious height and time for its dazed pilot to escape, then it too roared steeply to earth on the far side of the LNER line. By this time Arthur had rushed to his car and, with Eric Bonnett, Bill's nephew, as passenger, they raced to the scene.

A short distance away, on Farthing Road Farm's 13 Acre Field, young Vic Smith had been working with an eight-girl land gang picking potatoes when the collision occurred overhead. To him, the Hurricane seemed to go right through the bomber and bits of plane hung high above before plummeting earthwards. Suddenly, the land workers found their own lives endangered by a rain of wreckage and, panic stricken, they scurried in all directions trying to dodge pieces of debris. Terrified of a large piece plunging towards them, Vic and Violet Butcher, who was pregnant, ran into each other and tumbled over as one of the Hurricane's wheels and undercarriage leg thudded to earth mere feet away. These frantic actions prevented them from seeing *Yorker*'s plight but Vic felt a tremendous thump when the bomber hit the ground and a great, black cloud of earth and smoke erupted skywards where it was observed by the crew of *T-Tommy* who guessed what had happened and radioed Tuddenham. As the clods and debris fell to earth, people noticed, for the first time, a solitary parachute beneath which hung the limp figure of an airman. Mercifully, one life had emerged from the debacle but Flight Sergeant Brown faced a new danger as his descent was clearly towards the railway line and a rapidly approaching train.

Arthur Bedford had raced down the road running parallel with the railway to Sedge Fen and halted at the edge of the field where *Yorker* had fallen but his attention was then drawn to Flight Sergeant Brown's plight as the airman was obviously injured and unable to control his direction or rate of descent. Others were also cognizant of the danger and, to Arthur's relief, someone appeared further along the track and ran towards the oncoming train waving it down with a cloth or handkerchief. Moments later, the pilot hit the railway embankment and his parachute collapsed across the tracks, sagging over telegraph wires on the far side. So near was the train that the engine crew were among those who ran to assist and they found the pilot alive but suffering concussion and a fractured arm.

A short distance away, the appalling scene where *Yorker* had crashed made it tragically self-evident that any thought of rescue was pointless. Arthur stayed long enough to give his account to an RAF officer but the incident had shaken him and he was relieved to depart. He paused at Farthing Drove bridge which was blocked by the largest piece of *Yorker* now extant, the severed section of starboard wing. It had fallen on the narrow hump-back bridge, completely blocking the road and Arthur estimated its size as between twelve and sixteen feet. A group of men were busy trying to clear the road but no further assistance was needed so Arthur continued home, still unable to shake from his mind the speed of events and his own impotency as an eye witness to a disaster.

By now, the authorities were in charge of the crash site and the grisly task of clearing up began. *Yorker* had made a huge crater lipped with disgorged soil and surrounded by fragments from the disintegrated bomber. Parts of the wreckage were ablaze but the high water table was filling the hole causing steam to merge with the black, acrid smoke and generating a malevolent hissing interspersed with the popple of exploding ammunition. With the first RAF personnel to arrive from Mildenhall was Aircraftsman Henry Binns who had been on Crash Call and was one of those manning the emergency tender when it raced to Sedge Fen. On arrival, they found a local appliance had reached the scene and *Yorker* was a mess of smouldering fragments. Aircraftsman Binns was one of those detailed to guard the site and use foam extinguishers to control wreckage which re-ignited. To deter the inevitable sightseers, they were given a sten gun apiece and, during his eight days of duty on Sedge Fen, he did find it necessary to display the weapon to discourage the persistent souvenir hunters. A more unenviable role was that faced by Leading Aircraftsman Frank Fuller — he was given the grisly task of searching the mud and foam covered debris for remains of the crew and their identity discs. Of nine on *Yorker*, only the Skipper was recognizable, the rest would be forever known only unto God.

Roy Child had been playing cards with some other patients when they heard an explosion but they assumed that a German nuisance raider had eluded the defences and bombed an airfield nearby. When news of *Yorker*'s loss reached Tuddenham, it was initially thought Roy had been on board but her groundcrew knew he had returned to the hospital and one of them broke the news to him. Roy was heartbroken. No one who has not shared the close relationship of a good aircrew will understand the depth of the bond, and the emotions that flooded his being that afternoon would linger the rest of his life. His crew were dead and he stood unharmed — he was inconsolable, convinced that, had the Skipper stopped and let him on board, the actions of the plane would have been different. The young gunner was distraught, shaken with grief, and undeserved feelings of guilt wove into his personality, never to be entirely assuaged.

The following morning, when it was obvious none of the crew had survived, Wing Commander Giles authorized the dispatch of telegrams to the next-of-kin, and that received by Tug Wilson's mother typifies the stark reality of such telegrams: 'Deeply regret to inform you that your son, Sergeant Robert Wilson, lost his life on November 9th 1943 as the result of aircraft accident. Letter follows. Please accept my profound sympathy.' Later that day, a further telegram advised funeral arrangements and procedures for obtaining a railway warrant, but it did not end there for, on the 11th the RAF advised that his body had not been recovered and a further blow occurred the following day when it was disclosed that his body was unidentifiable. The funeral for *Yorker*'s brave boys was to be at 2.00 pm in Beck Row

Cemetery on Saturday 13 November. Bob Rodger's parents courageously allowed the remains of their son to be interred with his crew and kept to themselves the fact that he, alone, had been identified as solace to the other families. The splendid spirit of this family was further demonstrated when Roy Child learned that the Skipper had left £100 to be divided amongst his crew or their next of kin.

One gesture Roy could make was to be at the front of the funeral party and, on a grey, cloud-laden day, an RAF lorry pulled the funeral bier to the parish church of St John, Beck Row, near Mildenhall. Three coffins, each draped with the Union Flag, were borne solemnly to their graves in a sad and moving ceremony. Later that afternoon, Roy accompanied relatives to Shippea Hill Station to catch the train home but he did not reveal that the crash site was visible from the railway platform. He had been there earlier and was stunned by the complete destruction of *Yorker* — the only part he recognized was an engine laying alongside the crater. Even as the grieving families waited for the train, the grim task of extricating the crew continued and another body, again unidentifiable, was found a few days later. Some months after the RAF left the site, a fifth unidentifiable body was discovered and interred at St John's in the spring of 1944. These five graves contained all that had been found of *Yorker*'s nine-man crew.

Roy had been badly shaken by the loss of his crew and felt unable to remain with 90 Squadron so he applied for a transfer to 7 (Pathfinder) Squadron at Oakington. There he crewed with Squadron Leader Davis and participated in the bitter, winter war Bomber Command waged against Germany. Berlin

Behind the RAF chaplain, Roy Child leads as a pall bearer for the burial of his crew, 'Known unto God' (J. Munro).

was revisited as were Stettin, Brunswick and other targets. On the night of 19/20 February 1944, his Lancaster was shot down *en route* to Leipzig and three of the crew were killed. Roy became a prisoner-of-war and had numerous further adventures, themselves worthy of a book, before his release at the end of hostilities. The transition to peace was not easy and the scars, while not physical, were there none the less. He became successful in banking but never forgot the feeling that God had granted him additional time for life; time for a life denied his comrades.

As the years elapsed, people in the vicinity of Sedge Fen forgot the loss of Stirling *Y-Yorker*. The site was backfilled with shingle and household refuse and the immediate topography was altered by the removal of hedges and the nearby Cross Bank, built to prevent flooding but made redundant by land drainage. Thirty-two years later, the exact location where *Yorker* lay buried was impossible to discern without metal detectors. Lodge Farm changed hands and the new residents, Mr and Mrs Stanley Parr knew only that a bomber had crashed in what had become known as 'the aeroplane field'. Across the now British Railways track, on Plantation Farm, Flight Sergeant Brown's Hurricane proved a little more troublesome and, during the late '40s and early '50s, it kept snagging the plough until exasperated farmworkers dug and chopped away some of the wreckage before taking the unorthodox measure of pouring acid in the hole to dissolve what remained. Thereafter, the Hurricane disappeared and would not be found again for several decades.

In June 1974, I heard of a bomber buried near Lakenheath and enquiries resulted in a meeting with Horace Thompson, a retired farmworker, who recalled the collision but thought it involved a Spitfire and Lancaster. Horace introduced me to Stanley Parr who had taken over the farm since the war and he related how, although he did not know its identity, the field where the bomber was buried had become known as 'the aeroplane field'. Mrs Parr was enthusiastic when I suggested recovering the bomber and produced a shoe box containing fragments she had collected. Naturally, Mr Parr was concerned about people digging on his land, but I explained that we had considerable experience and always removed topsoil first, to replace it on conclusion of the dig. This ensured that subsoil polluted with aviation fuel was not placed on the surface of arable land. Recovery that year was impracticable, but plans were laid to remove it following the 1975 harvest and, in April 1975, further investigation led me to another farm worker, Bill Morley, who felt sure the bomber was not a Lancaster but a Stirling, so my application to the Ministry of Defence for permission to recover stated 'Stirling'. In later years, merely stating the type would be insufficient but aviation archaeology was less widespread and incidents like 'Bird Dog' related in Chapter Seven had not enforced the provision of more data to ensure the safety of recovery groups. Accordingly, the MOD gave permission on 9 July and, as was customary, I invited a team of enthusiasts prepared to share the costs of hiring a digger.

During the early morning of Saturday 30 August, this group gathered at 'The Railway Tavern' without, of course, realizing that this was the spot from which Arthur Bedford had witnessed the ill-fated bomber's last moments nearly 32 years before. The site lay in the corner of a field on Sedge Fen, close to what had once been the Cross Bank flood barrier and we were told that soil from the bank had been used to backfill the crater leaving a small mound over the site. Harry Hall, our digger driver, was instructed to remove this and clear a wide band of topsoil two or three feet deep so, for over an hour, the machine was employed on this unexciting but important task. Several fragments emerged during this scraping and I experienced some anxiety in case this was all that remained: it would not have been the first time lengthy preparations yielded little more than a bucketful of scrap.

These doubts were dispelled by strong detector readings from the new level cleared by the machine and we began hand digging test holes to establish how much deeper the bulk of wreckage lay. The rich, black soil was excellent to work in and allowed several narrow but firm sided shafts each penetrating over three feet deep and, at the bottom of one of these, we received a fright. One of the team, George Vyse, came across a sinister, dark cylinder bearing some writing, the first discernible letters being, alarmingly, 'EXP...' I immediately stopped the digger to minimize vibrations and went to investigate. Lying on my stomach, I twisted my head into the

Saturday 30 August 1975 and the remains of Yorker emerge from beneath harvest stubble. George Vyse explains the discovery to a young spectator.

shaft and, as my eyes adjusted to the gloom, I could see a canister but was unable to identify it. There was also an electrical wire protruding from the soil next to it so, in case it was from some malevolent circuitry, I was careful not to disturb it as I gently brushed earth from the cylinder. Its length could not be determined but I gauged the circumference as over twelve inches, it could be a small bomb and, small or not, laying on it was not a healthy pastime. The casing felt suspicious but I did not want to alert the authorities unnecessarily so, with a rapidly increasing pulse rate, I eased more soil from around the object. Everyone stood well back and I must have appeared incongruous as I lay, head and shoulders stuck down a hole in the ground and, if they could hear, muttering numerous expletives to ease the tension.

I was reluctant to halt the dig until positive our find was hostile and, at the back of my mind, I felt there was something familiar about it. Calling for a cloth, I began nursing away earth adhering to the lettering and more letters emerged, 'EXPLO...NS'. This puzzled me, the grammar made no sense for a bomb. Then it registered. Fools that we were. An oxygen bottle! Being accustomed to American sites, the British style, wire-bound oxygen cylinder had thrown us. It was black and stencilled on the side was a warning: 'USE NO OIL OR GREASE. THEY CAUSE EXPLOSIONS'. A reminder to personnel on the reaction caused by mixing oil or grease with oxygen. Given the confidence to do it, removing the culprit took only seconds and excavations could proceed.

Local opinion told us the bomber must be 30 ft down but this proved an over-estimation. At six feet the digger

snagged heavy sections of wing structure and Harry adeptly manipulated parts from the crater. Sadly the bomber was thoroughly smashed and the debris emerging was of little interest, although all were amazed at the shiny condition of the aluminium. With more and more items appearing, the men became slaves to the machine, hurriedly clearing the fragments it disgorged but maintaining a vigilant eye for items of interest and positive identification. That it was a Stirling was confirmed by twin tail wheels and, as the machine probed deeper, the vapour of high octane fuel lay heavily in the atmosphere. Ruptured and torn fuel tanks were dragged to the surface followed by one of the Stirling's enormous wheels. Then the first battered, mud-encased Hercules VI engine was discovered. Jumbled in the debris nearby were the remains of its propeller,

the sheer force of impact evident by the appearance of the now detached blades, one of which had been split and torn back like a peeled banana.

We were now over ten feet down and water seeping into the crater created a quagmire for those working below. Large items were easily spotted, but smaller artefacts are no less interesting and careful sifting yielded the camera lens, rudder pedals, a broken fountain pen, a small aeroplane-styled pencil sharpener and numerous other items but, unfortunately, no serial number. By mid afternoon, a large, black scar had been gouged in the harvest stubble and, at the field's edge, stretched a long pile of debris. A crash site conference decided to start earlier the next day and hire another machine to double our digging capacity and reduce the time needed to backfill and replace topsoil. This action

Above *Bob Rodger would have advanced these throttles askew to avoid propeller torque swinging the giant bomber on take-off.*

Above left *Ron Buxton works on a seam of debris below the infill used to bury a bomber 32 years earlier.*

Right *Morley Loyst's RCAF cap badge was found in the wreckage.*

was effective and we quickly removed two more engines and tons of smashed Stirling, amongst which we found panels bearing the serial *LK380*. Having disinterred the giant bomber, various aviation museums, including the RAF Museum, came to collect items to represent an extinct type and, when research revealed it, the story of her gallant crew. The ammunition found was

Above *One of the battered Hercules engines retrieved from 15 ft underground.*

Below *Concluding the 1975 excavations, the author studies shattered remnants of a proud machine.*

handed to the police as were all except one of the machine-guns which was retained for restoration.

Establishing the serial number yielded the basic facts surrounding the loss of *LK380* and further information was gleaned from 90 Squadron's Operational Record Book in the Public Records Office but that was as far as research proceeded until I started writing this book. *LK380* was a dig worth including but I lacked knowledge about her crew. Official records provided facts, not feeling, and I needed more than a stark list of nine names. Where they were buried might tell me something and I could photograph the graves so, in 1982, I contacted the Commonwealth War Graves Commission who informed me that the Services had not advised them where the crew were interred, but all were commemorated on the Runnymede Memorial. From the Memorial Register, I learned their home towns and decided to contact local newspapers appealing for information.

First to respond was the *Forfar Dispatch* who contacted Bob Rodger's sister Eileen. This was followed by *The Coventry Evening Telegraph* who located Tug's son, Peter, and helped me establish contact with the late Jim Munro, secretary of 90 Bomber Squadron Association. Jim's help was invaluable and he introduced me to Roy Child whose initial anger over disturbing what he felt was a war grave turned to support when he recognized the motivation was to ensure that *Yorker*'s crew would be remembered. I had learned where they were buried and was saddened that the Church contained no reference to the five headstones each poignantly epitaphed 'An Airman of the 1939-45 war'. My activities became the catalyst for an idea cherished by Roy and Peter

Peter Wilson, the little boy who received the oranges, grew up without a father but proud of his memory.

Wilson, to establish a memorial for *Yorker*'s crew in the church so visitors would relate the headstones to nine brave airmen. I had presented Roy with a propeller blade from *Yorker* and this provided an ideal symbol on which to mount a plaque dedicated to the crew. The deep and enduring feelings Roy held for his comrades were demonstrated by his devotion to this task but, while he and Peter worked towards the realization of this project, matters developed at the crash site, not only of *Yorker* but Flight Sergeant Brown's lost Hurricane.

Derek Brown, a member of the

Anglian Aeronautical Preservation Society (AAPS), had heard of *Yorker* from his brothers who, as children, played rafts using one of her fuel tanks which fell in a dyke away from the main body of wreckage. They also remembered one of the engines had been cast further over and embedded in the fen where it was left by the RAF recovery unit and they felt it must have avoided detection during our excavations 32 years later. The AAPS had not been formed in 1975 so the engines we retrieved were in other museums but Derek felt the story of *Yorker* should also be commemorated in the AAPS collection and began searching for the missing Hercules. Several visits to the site were made. Then, in August 1983, he located the tip of a propeller blade standing vertically in the soil and obviously attached to bulkier wreckage below. Luckily, I met Derek that summer and was delighted when he invited me to join the recovery planned for 5 November 1983, almost exactly forty years after the crash.

Conditions that Saturday morning were bleak and inhospitable matching my own sombre thoughts. *Yorker* had become so personal that I felt deeply a sense of loss and tragedy. If I felt it, how much deeper must be the emotions of Roy and Peter. Roy was convinced things would have been different if he had boarded *Yorker* that far off morning. Peter's father had perished on this very spot, the Dad who sent him oranges, whose courage was a source of pride, but what a price such pride had cost. My thoughts were disturbed by others arriving and soon the scene had been transformed by activity. The first significant find was a single propeller blade followed by sections of wing structure and an integral fuel tank identified by a maker's plate as 'starboard outer'. It was obvious

this area had been undisturbed since the crash, and I was amazed at how much the 1975 recovery had missed. At six feet we found a supercharger and, from the soil nearby, protruded a propeller blade still attached to the boss. Behind this, we located the last of *Yorker*'s engines, a badly battered starboard outer. By midday the remaining major items from *Yorker* had been loaded on a trailer destined for the AAPS storage sheds and our thoughts turned to locating Brown's Hurricane and completing the story.

The field into which the Hurricane fell had been enlarged and descriptions of the location varied significantly, so many hours were wasted searching in, as it emerged, entirely the wrong area. Dan Engle of the AAPS then had the idea of publishing an appeal in the local press for as many eyewitnesses as possible, and then arranging a meeting on site for a consensus on the location. By 9 February 1984, Dan had ten eyewitnesses, several of whom agreed to meet us at Plantation Farm on the 18th. Amongst these was Walter Ingle who had been driving a tractor on Decoy Farm; he remembered hearing the bang even over the tractor's engine and recalled sunlight flashing off the fighter's wings as it fell. Eric Bonnett was carting beet on Plantation Farm, the bang startled him and the awesome sight of a huge bomber spiralling earthwards was one he would never forget. As the eyewitnesses spoke to one another, forgotten facts were remembered and we soon narrowed the search area to one of manageable proportions. The first clue was a fragment of perspex on the surface. Then my detector gave a strong, positive emission — it had to be the Hurricane. Everyone gathered as we began digging. A few inches down, we found pieces of the fighter's battery and

Forty-three years later, the crew hut they shared stands derelict at Tuddenham.

fragments of aluminium, all easily removed. Then, at a depth of just over two feet, we came across fuselage structure still attached to heavier wreckage below. Having located our fighter, we found ourselves racing against time to effect its recovery. Contact with the landowners revealed their plans to install drains, and we were told that we had only one opportunity to remove it for once the drains were in, the land could not be disturbed. To maximize land utilization, harvesting the carrot crop would immediately be followed by fitting the drains. We had to fit the dig between these events and our team was put on standby while the Ministry of Defence was contacted to urge their consent.

Luckily, events coincided and on 10 March, AAPS members met at the Railway Tavern with eyewitnesses and a retinue from the media. Roy Child arrived. His story was central to events and he found himself being interviewed about his feelings and the now well-advanced plans for a memorial to his crew. He was their representative, the only man alive who knew the full story of their courage. Excavations commenced with the removal of topsoil, soon revealing wreckage indicating that the fighter had crashed the right way up at an angle of 60 degrees. Items from the cockpit were uppermost but many had been removed or destroyed when the acid was poured in. We expected to find the engine straight in, nose down, but discovered the fighter had broken forward of the cockpit, slewing the engine to one side.

Harry Hall, the Hymac driver, had worked on the Stirling and other sites, and was sufficiently experienced at assessing the situation to make a crater

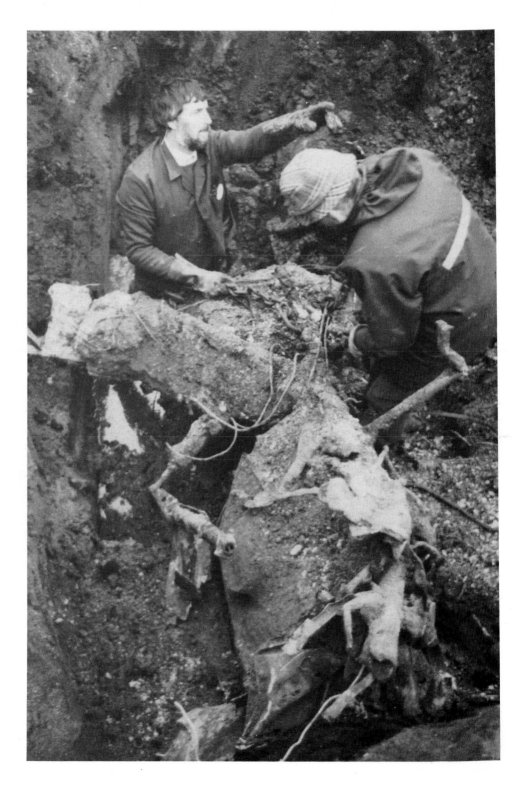

large enough to manoeuvre in. Members of the recovery team worked kneeling on top of the wreckage, carefully removing items from the cockpit. In this way, small artefacts such as an intact spare gunsight bulb were not broken or missed. The wings outboard of the centre section had gone, but the fixings remained and, when all small, loose items had been cleared, we shackled chains to the wing root and lifted it out along with the radiator airscoop and one wheel of the undercarriage still retracted in its housing. Pieces of the shattered, wooden-bladed Rotol propeller had been found at all depths and the boss had broken off the engine some twelve feet down and lay alongside. This was removed, leaving only the engine, now identified as a Merlin XX number *351203E*, to tackle. The bulkhead between cockpit and engine was extricated providing access to remove the carburettors, but the Merlin itself was not going to surrender easily as suction gripped it, frustrating the first direct lift attempt. We decided to loosen it, so wooden stanchions were inserted alongside for protection from the digger bucket and the engine was nudged on to its side, then hoisted free using a strong, nylon sling. For a few minutes, the Merlin was airborne again, the television cameras whirred and the jubilant diggers posed with their trophy before it was lowered to earth.

For Roy, fulfilment came on 6 May 1984 with the culmination of the project he and Peter Wilson had devoted many hours to — the dedication service for the memorial to those who perished on *Yorker*. Over 200 attended, including representatives from Canada, Australia, the RAF, USAF, relatives, friends and those who had been involved in recovering the aircraft. The Reverend Gordon Green supported the idea throughout and conducted the service, so it is fitting to close this chapter with his words:

'Although many years on from that tragic day, surviving relatives and friends must take comfort from the fact that their loved-ones' names will be recorded in the Church, as well as on official records and in their hearts. Not least of all, this is an occasion in which Roy Child is able to recognize, in a lovely way, his crew-mates: all that they meant to him in camaraderie and friendship during hours of action over enemy occupied territory and in leisure hours. Roy and Peter Wilson . . . have done so much to see that these men should be named, and we thank them. . . Most important of all — I see this dedication service as a graphic way of reminding us all that we, as well as the nine young men killed on that day, are "known unto God".'

Left *10 March 1984. Derek Brown directs removal of Hurricane KW800 while another AAPS member shackles the centre section for lifting.*

VERA'S VISIT TO LUDHAM

The need for manoeuvrability meant that most successful day fighters of World War 2 were single-engined machines but several air forces developed twin-engined fighters designed to encompass dogfighting ability enhanced with the safety of another motor. An innovative configuration of this philosophy was Lockheed's P-38 Lightning, a beautiful design and extremely advanced for 1939 when the prototype flew. A conventional fuselage was eliminated and the cockpit was designed into the main aerofoil centre section between twin Allison engines. Booms housing superchargers and main undercarriage extended aft from each engine to integral twin rudders linked by a one piece tailplane and single elevator. Projecting aggressively forward from the cockpit was a shark-like snout housing four .50 calibre machine-guns and a 20mm cannon. Tricycle undercarriages, normal now, were uncommon and the P-38's nose-wheel tucked neatly into a fairing below the cockpit. Dimensions were large for a single seater: 52 ft wingspan; 37 ft 10 in long and a weight of 16,000 lb on the combat versions.

By mid 1943, proponents of the unescorted bomber theory had learned the fallacy of this strategy in flame-torn skies and the bitter statistics of lost aircraft. The need for fighter protection was paramount to prevent the ultimate defeat of daylight strategic bombing and the P-38 was one of those chosen for urgent development as a long range escort fighter. From the original XP38 stemmed variants with increased range, power, performance and pilot protection. In September 1942, the P-38H version flew and 601 were ordered for assembly beginning March 1943. Production pressed ahead with series improvements being denoted by suffixing the basic model reference until the P-38H-5 was rolling out of the Burbank, California plant. One of these passed on to Army Air Force inventory on 6 August 1943, and cost the US Government $98,990. Four months later it would be scrap, scattered in the streets of a town over 5,000 miles away. Before that happened, it would be personified in the female gender and acquire both name and reputation but, for now, the olive drab and grey fighter was distinguishable from its kin only by serial number *42-67053*.

War is avaricious and, a week after acceptance by the Army Air Force, our P-38 was ferried to Newark and then partly dissembled and cocooned for its freighter journey across the Atlantic. Surviving Hitler's seawolves, it was one of a batch off-loaded in the Mersey and taken to Lockheed's factory at Speke near Liverpool for re-assembly. Lockheed's Chief Test Pilot, C.H. Wilson, flew '053 on 15 September and pronounced it combat ready. The P-38H then gained the minor distinction of being the first of its model allocated to the 55th Fighter Group based on a

Pictured during her early days at Nuthampstead, 42-67053 has yet to gain nose-art, markings and lucky reputation (K.J. Sorace/M. Olmsted).

recently-constructed airbase dwarfing the Hertfordshire hamlet of Nuthampstead. It was 21 September when the six-week-old fighter touched down at Station 131, Nuthampstead. The 55th comprised three squadrons, the 38th, 338th and 343rd, each of which coded its planes with squadron letters and an individual radio call letter. Aircraft 42-67053 was assigned to the 343rd and carried, in white, on its booms, their letters, 'CY' to one side of the national insignia with the radio call letter 'L' on the other.

Vociferous demands for the Lightning came from all war theatres thus forcing the pace of introduction. Wartime exigency meant units learned as they went but not without cost and problems became apparent early in its career when instances occurred of P-38's failing to pull out of dives. The trouble was eventually established as inherent in the twin boom design — it was found that a vacuum was created aft of the centre sec-tion, affecting elevator operation. The solution was to use the trim tabs, almost like airbrakes, but several pilots died before this was recognized.

Against this background, the 55th began working up to combat commanded by Lieutenant Colonel Frank James who, incidentally, had been the first 55th pilot to fly '053 on its arrival. James ordered an exhausting training programme and Nuthampstead residents quickly grew accustomed to the fledglings flexing their wings: they would pioneer the P-38 into combat against the experienced Luftwaffe. One of the pilots receiving this discipline was the 343rd's Lieutenant James Gilbride and, on 10 October, he was allocated aircraft 42-67053. The Group was only five days away from its first operation and pilots were 'individually assigned' to aircraft. This did not mean that they, alone, would fly a particular ship, but that it would be usual for them to retain that machine, serviceability and furloughs permitting. The benefits of this were practical and morale: practical because aircraft could be slightly tailored for the regular pilot, much as a car-seat is set for its usual driver. The morale benefits came from the pilot's personification of his plane — a trait man demonstrates for engendering machines with character, usually feminine, and this vogue was fashionable in the Eighth Air Force so it was natural for Jimmie Gilbride to christen the plane after his wife. He clearly thought she had the right physical attributes because his Lightning soon sported her scantily clad form posing, Varga fashion, above the name 'Vivacious Vera'.

The first operations flown by the 55th were limited penetrations and sweeps over the enemy coast but their P-38s continued to evince frustrating and sometimes fatal flaws, most frequently engine failure. The cold, moisture-laden climes of Northern Europe had a debilitating effect on Allison engines and, at high altitudes, extremely low temperatures thickened lubricating oil and the engine's life blood circulated reluctantly, causing piston rod bearings to fracture. Added to this problem was the unhappy tendency to haemorrhage precious oil, doubling the consumption from low to high altitude use, but, for the fighter to survive and be effective, it had to be efficient over 20,000 ft. Designed to aid altitude ability, the turbo-superchargers also misbehaved owing to a regulator malady caused by moisture ingressing critical areas then freezing.

Despite these ailments, the 55th had successes and early tangles with the

Door cover from Vivacious Vera *depicts forties' fashion in nose-art, pose and lingerie* (M. Olmsted).

Luftwaffe saw several victory claims with minimal losses, and some of these were most likely attributable to mechanical failure. Events did not always favour the Americans however and the 13 November mission attracted misfortune as the Group fought tenaciously to protect bombers raiding Bremen. Seven P-38s succumbed: five to enemy action and two to either the Luftwaffe or malfunctions, or a combination of both, because a single-engined Lightning was easy prey. *Vera* took care of her pilot and Jimmie Gilbride counted his survival fortunate. On 26 November it was Bremen again with Lieutenant Hiner flying *Vera* and, maybe, she did not like the unfamiliar touch because one of her Allisons packed up over the Zuider Zee and Hiner had to coax her home on one engine.

Three days later she was still unserviceable and Jimmie Gilbride took another machine when the 55th provided escort on yet another bash at Bremen: 38 Lightnings took off but Luftwaffe controllers, skilfully positioning their fighters to attack near the Dutch coast, forced the 55th to jettison their drop tanks for combat manoeuvrability, a move which consequently reduced their endurance. No less than 85 Me 109s intercepted the Americans and a fierce dogfight ensued with the 55th taking a beating: seven of them were lost. One of the casualties was Jimmie Gilbride. He might have escaped but bravely turned back to help others in trouble and was shot down into the sea near Koekange where his body was later washed ashore.

The following day, 30 November, saw a much reduced effort from the 55th, they mustered only twenty and even this number was bolstered by P-38s from their sister Group, the 20th. *Vivacious*

Vera was flown by Lieutenant Stanton and the mission was a hazardous journey to escort bombers raiding industrial targets in Solingen. Technical troubles again dogged *Vera* when one of her engines failed over the Ruhr but she maintained her reputation as a lucky ship bringing her pilot back a harrowing 250 miles to Nuthampstead.

By 12 December, *Vera's* ailments had been rectified and she was assigned to Lieutenant Hugh J. Goudelock. Like Jimmie Gilbride, Hugh Goudelock was married and, coincidentally, he preferred to be known as Jim. He trusted that his own wife, Sybil, would not mind his flying a ship named after another man's wife but, in the event, it was to be only a brief affair. The following day, 13 December, the Eighth made a major attack on the North German port of Kiel. Nine Combat Wings of B-17s and B-24s were involved with the 55th and other fighter groups providing support. For Jim Goudelock, the day began uneventfully: 'like any other cold and dreary winter day in England'. At briefing, he learned that Lieutenant Colonel Frank B. James would lead 41 ships from Nuthampstead and, at 10.29, the assembled group took an easterly course to rendezvous with their 'big friends'. They crossed the North Sea to make landfall at Friedrichskoog and, a few minutes later, sighted five Ju 88s. A section of the 343rd was detached and the skirmish ended with Lieutenants Buttke and Hiner sharing a Junkers though the remainder escaped.

Two hours after leaving Nuthampstead, the 55th met the bombers south of Neumunster and divided into two elements, one at 29,000 ft with top cover at 30,000. Opposition had been light but the bomber crews were comforted by the twin contrails from each P-38 as the

Jim Goudelock in the cockpit of a P-38 (J. Goudelock).

group weaved a characteristic 'S' pattern overhead. Below the bombers stretched an enormous, unbroken sweep of 10/10 cloud which, although contributing to the Luftwaffe's absence, meant that bombing would be on Path Finder Force (PFF). Using, this technique meant that bombers would rely on the radar image provided by the target on a scope in the Lead Ship whose crew co-ordinated the formation's bomb release. The technique was still being developed but the Kiel attack was very successful and an informant in the town reported that bombs descending on a target the populace knew to be invisible from the air, produced a terrifying effect. Significant damage was incurred in the town centre and harbour district including the shipyards of Deutsche Werke, Kiel.

Radar was not, however, a prerogative of the Allies and the German 'Wuerzburg' series radar was very effective controlling anti-aircraft fire through the overcast as an increasingly intense bar-

rage proved. Flak hit at least one P-38 causing minor damage and Jim saw bursts bracketing the bombers. To this day, he feels flak caused *Vera*'s demise but it may have been the familiar gremlin of mechanical failure. Shrapnel or malfunction, the effect proved disastrous: without warning, *Vera* flipped over to port and Jim suddenly found himself almost inverted. Abrupt loss of acceleration on one side with power on the other caused the P-38 to roll — four days earlier, this very situation had killed one of the group's best pilots when he ran out of sky. Luckily, Jim had the altitude.

Training and experience governed his reflex reactions: the sharpness and direction of bank indicated loss of the port engine and tumbling oil pressure confirmed it. His immediate task was regaining control so he reduced power on the starboard Allison while applying rudder to correct the yaw. As the P-38 levelled off, Jim moved the port engine mixture control to idle cut-off and then feathered the propeller: this turned the now useless blades of the Curtiss-Electric edge on to the slipstream for minimum drag. *Vera* was now doing as she was told and he wound on starboard rudder trim to alleviate the pressure on his foot. His fall from formation alarmed his fellow pilots and, having regained control, he contacted the leader of his Flight, Lieutenant Ken Sorace, to outline his predicament.

The situation was very uncomfortable: Nuthampstead lay over 400 miles distant and, on a single engine, the range of the P-38 was reduced. In addition, loss of the port engine was particularly critical as it drove the generator providing electricity for the booster pumps. These were necessary to maintain sufficient fuel pressure at altitude and feed his starboard engine. Furthermore, without booster pumps, he could not draw fuel from his outer wing tanks and calculations of fuel availability, altitude and range buzzed through his mind. Another option occurred as Jim recalled some advice from briefing: if in trouble over the target, neutral Sweden provided an alternative destination. Range to Scandinavia was no problem but attaining that sanctuary meant more time in hostile airspace with ultimate internment and that was not why Jim had gone to war. Before enlisting, in 1942, he had taught mechanics to RAF pilots in Texas and their dedication inspired his own commitment to winning this fight. He could not, he thought tenaciously, contribute much from Sweden and, despite the P-38's record, he had faith in the single-engined ability of *Vera*. She had not failed her previous pilots and was regarded as a 'lucky ship' so, home it would be, although he realized he would

need much of that luck just to clear enemy airspace unharmed.

His vulnerability was recognized by Lieutenant Ken Sorace, and Jim was relieved when Ken's *Pitter Pat* slipped alongside as *Vera* peeled away for home. Ken also called on Lieutenants Paul Dripps and Ernest George as additional support. The three shepherds took station around *Vera* and Jim felt comforted by their presence — he could now concentrate on the logistics of getting home with less fear of attack. As he descended, he knew that loss of the port engine generator placed reliance for all electrical power on the battery and remaining energy was best used transferring fuel from the dead engine so he switched on the fuel crossfeed. Jim deduced that the battery would be flat in about 1 to 1½ hours, then radio communication would cease leaving him lame, deaf and mute. If forced to ditch, the others would alert air sea rescue and transmit for a positional fix although harsh reality told him it would be to no avail as a man could survive only minutes in the water's icy grasp. The risk of interception abated as the enemy coast slid by, unseen below the low, damp blanket now cloaking his new adversary, the North Sea. Jim took *Vera* to 10,000 ft and adjusted power on the starboard Allison to maintain an indicated airspeed of 160 mph, advised in the pilot's manual as the optimum for maximum, single-engine endurance. He had made a risky choice and needed his skill to support the decision but, although skill enhanced chance, the best of pilots needed luck — would the charm of *Vivacious Vera* hold for him?

During each second of every mile, Jim listened apprehensively for any discordant notes from the remaining Allison but it thundered reassuringly, slowly reducing the distance to England. He had crossed the Rubicon, all he could do now was maintain his compass course and pray that Sybil and their ten-month-old son, Jim, would not become war widow and orphan. He knew that the North Sea had drowned many husbands and fathers and regretted what little time his Air Force training had spared for his family before he came overseas. By now the cloud base had broken and glimpses of the sullen, grey swell below made him wonder if he would ever see them again. Emphasizing the point, his starboard engine suddenly spluttered and cut, starved of fuel: the battery was dead. Jim switched off the crossfeed and the mechanical, engine-driven pump picked up fuel supply from the starboard tanks only. His heart, and the Allison both returned to normal. Whatever fuel remained on the port side was now dead weight and, without instrumentation, he had little idea how much was in the starboard tanks. A silent radio stressed his sense of isolation, despite the three P-38s playing mother hen, there was little they could do for him now. Peering down through scattered clouds, he observed a large warship and contemplated ditching nearby — they might reach him before he froze. Then, to his relief, the hazy line of horizon hardened: there it was, the coast. Even a belly landing on the beach was preferable and he willed Vera onwards. Landfall was an achievement and Jim had just nosed Vera into a steeper descent when he saw an airfield about ten miles inland. Vera's luck was holding; Jim hoped there was sufficient fuel and now considered the complications of a single-engined approach.

The pilot's handbook stated that 60 per cent of the Lightning's total drag was created by lowering the landing gear and emphasized that, although altitude could be maintained on one engine with gear down, height could *not* be held with the addition of full flap. The notes warned a pilot on final approach that he was committed when undercarriage and flaps were lowered: a landing had to be made. Standard Operational Procedure was to secure radio permission for an emergency landing but Jim's dead transmitter precluded this — he did not even know which airbase he was approaching. It was, in fact, Ludham Aerodrome in Norfolk which served as a satellite for the nearby fighter station at Coltishall, although it was currently inactive, so Jim's approach risked little interference from other traffic and Lieutenant Sorace had already secured ground clearance. Unfortunately, he could not communicate to advise Jim of a clear pattern.

Having maintained height over the sea, Jim was anxious to lose altitude and land but, ironically, he was now too high and too fast. The diving fighter swept across Ludham at over 300 mph: he would have to go round but would the fuel last? It was safer turning into his good engine so Jim banked right and swung back towards the airfield. At 260 mph, his speed was still excessive, too fast for a normal wheels and flaps down approach but he knew his fuel supply must be desperately low. He would give partial flap to reduce airspeed then lower the gear. By turning off his aileron boost he stiffened the controls but he needed maximum hydraulic power for his flaps and undercarriage. On a single engine, only one hydraulic pump was available to extend his landing gear and it doubled the time: a long half minute before it locked. Vera was now 90° to the runway at 1,800 ft, running sweetly; one more turn, the concrete stretched invitingly. Jim eased the spectacle grip to bank into the final approach. At that instant, the starboard engine quit.

Flying above *Vivacious Vera*, Lieutenant Ernie George was relieved to see his crippled comrade turn on to final approach, then the P-38 simply disappeared and someone in the escort flight exclaimed, 'Oh my God. He's crashed!' They were over a small town and Ernie saw a large cloud of red dust spurt from behind some buildings. His stomach knotted with sympathetic fear, what damnable luck — seconds from a safe touch down — and he watched, helpless with frustration and sickened by the column of dust now ominously blackening.

The town about to have a little more history added to it was the broadland community of Ludham whose past already stemmed back beyond the Dissolution when King Henry VIII had given the manor of Ludham to the Bishop of Norwich after taking possession of the cathedral estates. Situated on what for Norfolk topography was relatively high ground, Ludham lay between the Rivers Thurne, Bure and Ant whose waterways provided reeds for its numerous thatched homes. This terrain suited airbase construction and the 800 inhabitants, like many East Anglians, grew accustomed to their airfield neighbour and witnessed many damaged machines limp to safety. The presence of four Lightnings attracted little attention and the townsfolk were unaware of his predicament as Jim Goudelock coaxed *Vera* in. At the garage, Russell Brooks was supervising munitions work on a small government contract while, across the main street, less martial activities occupied grocer Cyril Thrower managing a normal day's business in his shop. *Vera* was about to impact, literally and

figuratively on both their lives and several others still oblivious of the drama now descending into their community.

The airfield seemed mere fingertips distant when the motor cut but Jim knew he could not glide because his Lightning's aerodynamics were corrupted by the extended undercarriage. He saw the town below and had to avoid other casualties if he could. Speed alone gave some vestige of control and, for it, he deliberately sacrificed height, diving steeply and aiming for the outskirts. There was no clear ground, then — a chance — a slim chance. Behind some buildings he spotted a large tree and, praying it would slow him without proving fatal, Jim went for it. At the last instant, he pulled *Vera*'s nose heavenwards and left events to the Lord. Nose high, the P-38 mushed into the uppermost branches and crunched its way down. The trunk missed the cockpit by inches and went clean through between the booms ripping off the fighter's tail in a burst of branches and aluminium. This snatched *Vera* viciously to earth in the yard of Mr W.K.England, the village butcher, and she tore through an outbuilding creating the spurt of red dust seen by Ernie George in a violent shredding of metal and brick.

Imprisoned in the cockpit, debris boiled around Jim Goudelock but he knew he was still alive: it hurt too much not to be. *Vera* leapt on. A pig-sty, stable and cart house were demolished scattering sheets of corrugated roofing like leaves. None of the buildings were occupied but *Vera* had not finished. Wing wreckage and an engine were deposited in the butcher's garden as she ploughed through while the other powerplant bounded on, vanishing into the rear wall of Mr Thrower's garage and enhancing neither it nor the appearance

Struck by a Lightning. Machine-guns torn from the P-38 are visible, lower right (J. Goudelock).

of his van as it catapulted through closed doors at the other end. The grocer's shop itself formed part of his home and, hearing the crash, Mr Thrower ordered his staff into the cellar, thinking it was an air raid. The house shuddered as *Vera*'s severed tail fell heavily upon the roof while a clattering cacophony heralded the approach of *Vera* herself. Its momentum almost expended, the fighter found enough energy to clout the corner of the grocer's before settling in a narrow passage between the grocer's and the butcher's. Not all the wreckage stopped: one wheel bounced across the street and finished up in a garden several hundred feet away while another heavy piece hurtled through the garage roof without causing injury. Understandably startled by this and the accompanying noise Russell Brooks ran out of the garage to see the mangled remains of an aircraft lying opposite. Flames were spreading from torn fuel tanks towards its pilot, slumped amidst the debris. Jim had been stunned by a gashed forehead but his return to consciousness created a far worse terror when he realized he

could not free his left leg and was trapped in the burning wreckage.

Disregarding his own safety, Russell Brooks raced to the blazing fighter while Cyril Thrower emerged from his battered shop and ran to assist. Dazed and frightened, Jim was deeply grateful when a face appeared through the smoke beside him and Russell helped him undo his parachute harness. This took Russell a few seconds because American parachutes lacked the British quick release mechanism. The seat harness presented less of a problem as it had pulled apart at the hold down bolts but Jim's returning senses indicated no major injuries and incineration was the horror he now feared. Together, the two civilians tried pulling him free but his left foot was pinned by the bent remains of the control quadrant and all three faced increasing peril as ammunition began exploding in the heat. Jim panicked when Russell disappeared from view — were they leaving him? Thank God, no. Russell returned moments later having realized their efforts were useless unless some of the wreckage could be

Most of Vera *came to rest in this narrow alley although one wheel bounded on beyond the parked USAAF Command car (J. Goudelock).*

levered or cut away so he had dashed to his workshop for a crowbar, bolt croppers and fire extinguisher.

For Jim, it was like sitting on the edge of hell as flames crackled and seared nearer over the debris while acrid smoke from burning rubber swirled about choking both him and his rescuers. Russell inserted the crowbar intending to pry Jim free but his efforts brought yells of pain from the pilot whose leg, in the smoke and heat, had been unwittingly used as a fulcrum point. Removing the crowbar, Russell began cutting wreckage away with the bolt croppers but the heat they conducted grew so intense that he dropped them and Jim, in desperate horror of the increasing flames, pleaded for them to hurry even if it meant amputat-

ing his foot. The blaze was intensifying and Cyril had no choice but to leave and warn the women sheltering in his cellar. Russell, choking, scorched and near exhaustion, tried again but it was hopeless. Jim begged not to be left, the fire was engulfing them both, but Russell had no choice and dashed to the butcher's for a meat cleaver: either that or cremation for the hapless pilot.

As he entered the inferno for the third time, other brave help arrived — Robert Utting and another workman employed on the airfield reached the scene. Shielding themselves from the heat, they knew there was time only for one more attempt otherwise the most merciful thing would be to knock Jim out and hack off his leg. If this failed, at least they

Now unrecognizable, the crumpled cockpit section has been dragged from the alley (J. Goudelock).

would not leave a conscious and terrified airman burning to death. Working in unison, they levered and pulled on the twisted quadrant while Russell heaved on the pilot's shoulders. Jim pushed as best he could, concentrating grimly against the pain. His foot moved, just a little, then it drew free leaving behind his sock, shoe and flying boot. Semi-conscious, he slumped into the arms of his rescuers as they hastened clear of the conflagration now threatening Cyril Thrower's home.

When the crash occurred, Mrs Thrower had been nursing their baby son and stooped to protect him as the building shook violently and bricks flew about. She, too, thought it was an air raid but then heard Jim yelling for help.

Moments later, she and her son were also endangered as flames swept up holly trees in the garden and leapt across into the bedroom igniting her curtains and scorching across the beamed ceilings. Cyril tore down the burning curtains and threw them outside but was too late to reach a pile of records on the windowsill which took light and began dripping molten fire. His customers helped and soldiers billeted nearby joined in using water sucked feverishly from the kitchen hand pump to douse the flames. This apparatus was not designed for such energetic use and immediately broke down so water from the butcher's rain butt helped stem the fire and, more in defiance than value, Cyril threw a pail of tea dregs reserved for his plants at it.

Thankfully, the National Fire Service arrived before the flames took serious hold and, despite the devastation of outbuildings, the Thrower's home and shop survived and, luckily, there were no casualties amongst the townsfolk: *Vera's* reputation remained relatively untarnished.

The young Lieutenant, suffering from concussion and shock, had been carried to Russell Brook's garage. Events to him were hazy — all round, he felt kindness and sympathy and that people were caring for him. Someone gently rubbed ointment on his face and he was eased from his flying clothing. Coming to again, he was pleased to see Ken Sorace bending over him, the expression in Ken's eyes was one of disbelief, how could this guy be alive? After seeing the column of red dust, the three Lightnings hastened to land and the pilots sped from the airfield to recover what would surely be the body of their comrade. Ernie George felt it incredible that Goudelock had survived such total destruction of his aircraft. There were fragments scattered everywhere: *Vera's* tail protruded from the roof of a building and the stubs of her wings were embedded in walls either side of a narrow alley in which lay a still-burning wheel well and tyre. An outhouse had been sheared off at the base and its occupants clucked and fluttered amongst the debris, seemingly suffering no other loss than some feathers. The pilots found Jim in a building opposite the crash, sitting on the floor, propped up against a wall with a woman bandaging a nasty gash on his forehead. He was dazed and incoherent but mercifully without major injury and clearly in caring hands as they placed him gently on a stretcher and into a British ambulance.

As the vehicle sped down the High Street, the residents of Ludham continued clearing up. Firemen, using a Climax-engined trailer pump with a system of hoses, took water from the river and prevented flames spreading from fires in wreckage dotted about the town. *Vera's* empennage was extracted from Cyril's roof and a tarpaulin provided temporary repair. The authorities later compensated for all the damage except, by bureaucratic quirk, the repair of his kitchen pump. The sorry remnants of *Vera* were collected by a local scrap merchant and carted ignominiously to the smelter's but one piece, the gun compartment door with its nose art, was salvaged by the 55th and proudly displayed at Nuthampstead annotated with the history of a lucky ship.

Had it not been for the courage of the civilians, the outcome would have been tragic and Major General W.E. Kepner, Officer Commanding VIII Fighter Command was prompt to recognize this. Writing to Cyril Thrower on 19 December 1943, he stated: 'The splendid assistance which you gave a member of my Command, Second Lieutenant Hugh J. Goudelock, on the afternoon of 13 December in rescuing him from a burning airplane has been brought to my attention. I wish to thank you for your part in saving this young officer's life. If it had not been for your quick thinking, your courage and your fine spirit of service above self, which you showed in rescuing another from peril, Lieutenant Goudelock would evidently have burned to death. Your actions and the spirit in which they were undertaken have rendered a real service to my Command, and have done much to seal the splendid relationship with, and respect which its members have for the British people. I thank you with a sense of deepest appreciation.'

Jim Goudelock returned to thank the people of Ludham. L-R: Cyril Thrower, Russell Brooks Sr, Jim Goudelock, Russell Brooks Jr.

Praise of their courage became widespread and culminated in a Commendation from His Majesty King George VI announced in the London Gazette on 4 April 1944 citing Russell Obed Brooks, motor engineer; Iris Kemp, Women's Land Army; Clifford Lamble, tractor driver; Stephen Maylan, telegraphist; Alfred George Osborne, grocer's assistant; James Russell, master butcher; Cyril Albert Thrower, grocer; Robert Wilson Utting, general labourer; Ena Wise, Women's Land Army. Perhaps the most pleasurable expression of gratitude came from Jim Goudelock himself when he returned to Ludham, less spectacularly, in early January 1944, to thank his rescuers for their bravery.

This was the first of numerous visits during the remainder of his service in England and initiated an enduring friendship for the town and its people: 39 years later, in July 1982, Jim and his wife revisited Ludham and it is fitting that his own words conclude the story.

'The village looked much like it did when I left England in the fall of 1945. We visited both Mr and Mrs Brooks, Mr and Mrs Thrower, and a few of the townspeople I had met during my many wartime trips to Ludham. I was able once again to thank two brave Englishmen for giving me an opportunity to return home and raise a family of two fine sons. For this, I will be eternally grateful'.

COLLISION

One of the major hazards facing Allied airmen in the congested East Anglian skies was the risk of collision. A large raid could see more than 800 bombers assembling and later returning to be funnelled into airfield traffic patterns, often in appalling weather. One American bomber group suffered the loss of eight aircraft in collisions before its first casualty to direct enemy action. That there were not more such incidents reflects on the skills of airmen and ground controllers alike, but fate frequently intervened cutting down the most experienced of crews. A tragic example of this flared violently in the cloud-laden skies over Reedham Marshes, Norfolk, on Monday 21 February 1944. Unpublished because of security, witnessed only by one other aircrew, themselves to be shot down three days later, and a few workers on the land below, the episode was soon hidden in the larger pattern of wartime events.

For twenty years remains of the aircraft lay undisturbed. A crater made by one machine could easily be mistaken for a natural pond. The odd, black island in the centre was hardly conspicuous as the remains of a self-sealing fuel tank designed to extinguish penetrating incendiary bullets and feed four thirsty aero engines. True, local marshmen knew of it and the subject might occasionally arise, but they were unaware of the facts and time so distorted the story that it eventually reached my ears as the

rumour of a German aircraft still buried near Reedham. Archaeology is fascinating but in 1964 the concept of it in terms of aviation was unknown — who thinks of aeroplanes being underground? As a Cadet Sergeant in the local Air Training Corps, I was intrigued by the idea of finding parts from famous aircraft. Only later did I realize that the nuts and bolts meant little without the stories they represented.

At sixteen, I lacked the experience and contacts later established but enthusiasm was there and, on a bleak, blustery Sunday in January 1964 four cadets from 469 (Lowestoft) Squadron embarked on a project that would take fourteen years to complete. Verifying the story was our first problem but a call upon Rev Lionel Lawrence at the St John the Baptist Rectory, Reedham, put us on the correct path: that leading to the door of old Bob Burgess. Bob had been born in Seven Mile House on Reedham Marshes during the early 1900s and had spent his entire working life in the area. Retired by 1964, he none the less had energy enough to act as guide for our party, and confirmed the crashed aircraft story, except that there were two planes, not German, but American. They had collided returning from a mission — furthermore, wreckage still lay in the marshes.

Reedham derives its name from the profusion of reeds found in the surrounding fenland and, with the opening in 1833 of the cut linking the Waveney and Yare, plus the Norwich to

January 1964. Paul Clegg struggles with a piece of submerged wreckage on Reedham Marshes (Eastern Counties Newspapers).

Yarmouth railway nine years later, the village became well known to the influx of broadland visitors. They saw the marshland during wide-skied summer months spent cruising leisurely along the waterways. In winter, the land assumed a less enchanting mantle, a desolate, grey, wind-swept perspective of low clouds and snow flurries. Control of the water level is maintained by pumping water from a ditch and dyke drainage system criss-crossing the fens. The unfamiliar easily become lost but the pattern of interconnecting gates and 'leggers' (planks to those outside Norfolk) is well known to men like Bob,

without whom we would never have found the site.

One of the two aircraft had fallen on the edge of Mill Dyke, a main channel several hundred yards long. At first, the scene envinced nothing extraordinary: an ovoid pond about 25 ft long by 15 ft at its widest. Clusters of reeds fringed the banks, separated by areas where cattle trampled muddy access to the water. The pond necked adjoining Mill Dyke and, protruding a few inches above water at this end, was the fuel tank while, nestling in nearby reeds lay a large, aluminium oxygen bottle, still bearing the words, 'Breathing Oxygen'. Chipping at surrounding turf revealed further fragments but the frozen land did not yield easily to the few implements we carried so we decided to return more adequately equipped.

At ATC Headquarters next day, our activities caused considerable interest and a little concern on the part of Squadron Leader I.W. Ebben, our CO. War planes carried weapons and there might be the danger of unexploded ammunition; our next sortie would be supervised. The USAF at Sculthorpe was contacted and, the following weekend, Sergeant Richard J. Wagner, an explosives expert, joined a party of six cadets and a reporter. We found the pond frozen and the land difficult to crack despite pick-axes, forks and spades. On breaking the crust, good progress was made in softer ground below and several items of wreckage came to light including rounds of .5 (half-inch), heavy calibre machine-gun bullets. Sergeant Wagner examined a number of these, explaining how the colour coded annulus signified type: purple for ball, green for armour piercing and so on. He indicated there was little danger providing we behaved sensibly and handed all we found to the authorities. Later that day, the local constable, PC Dowle, was stunned to find a sack of bullets deposited on his desk and we left a perplexed PC seeking his manual on disposal procedures.

So far, all we knew about our aircraft was that it had been an American bomber armed with .5 machine-guns. During World War 2, there were two main such aircraft operated by the United States Army Air Force in East Anglia, the Boeing B-17 Flying Fortress and Consolidated B-24 Liberator. Wreckage indicated a paint scheme of olive drab upper surfaces and light grey underneath, a camouflage pattern applicable to either. According to Bob Burgess, our aircraft had collided during landing but examination of the second site, a quarter mile away on the edge of Decoy Carr, revealed no wreckage extant so our efforts concentrated on the Mill Dyke bomber. Location of the site lay in line with Seething aerodrome, wartime home of the 448th Bombardment Group flying B-24s and we concluded that our find was from this unit. Here, we thought, lay one of over 19,000 Liberators produced but which would only be revealed by research and further excavation.

Our assumption was wrong: our next visit to the site unearthed a fragment stamped Boeing and B-17s had not been based at Seething. True, fewer Flying Fortresses had been manufactured but we still faced a list of more than 12,000. Additional information came on 28 February 1964, in a letter from the Norfolk Constabulary. Police records stated that, on 21 February 1944, a number of Fortresses were returning from a raid when two of the aircraft collided, killing all personnel involved. Not long after I began my researches I received a letter from John T. Rose, a former crane operator with the USAAF 9th Depot Repair Squadron, Honington. A copy of the *Lowestoft Journal* had found its way to Texas and he noticed the feature describing our excavations. As one of the recovery team sent to remove the crew, he remembered the incident and related how they had extricated the bodies but most of the wreckage sank beyond reach.

Throughout 1964 and into 1965, sporadic visits to the site, combined with numerous letters to archivists in England and America, added further pieces to the jig-saw. Recovery of an azimuth mechanism for a chin turret established the type as a B-17G, the most common version produced. This variant carried guns beneath the nose to counteract the Luftwaffe's use of a weak spot in Fortress armament by attacking head on. From the US Army Mortuary System came a letter stating that the aircraft were from the 549th and 550th Squadrons of the 385th Bombardment Group at Great Ashfield, Suffolk. Contact with aviation historian, Roger Freeman, established pilots' names as Pease and Hutchison. The USAF Historical Division supplied the last three digits of both aircraft serial numbers: 963 and 370, but USAAF numbers consisted of six or seven numerals and I needed a full serial to complete my quest for a positive identification. Now I had reduced the possible identity of the Mill Dyke aircraft to only three 'G' model Fortresses with serials ending 370, or 963, while the Decoy Carr B-17, which might be the earlier 'F' variant, could be one of eight Fortresses. Which aircraft we had found eluded me until May 1965, when we had two significant finds at the crash site.

Of the original team, only myself and

Now billowing in the spring breeze, this parachute lay buried for over twenty years.

Cadet Paul Clegg remained, further assistance being drawn from anyone willing to wield a spade and with stomach strong enough to take the stench. Many of the items found had been dragged free after being located by the simple process of groping at arm's length in the stagnant water. Our hoard included oxygen masks, throat mikes, de-icing gear and remains of equipment such as the British Type 62 indicator, a device fitted to American aircraft allowing them use of our electronic, navigational facilities. Lack of finance and heavy equipment limited our attempts, we could only probe with poles into the tantalizing depths of the crater. Metal could be felt and large globules of disturbed fuel would burst in green patches on the water's surface, the aroma hung heavily in the air and discouraged smoking.

We worked eagerly, hoping for some exciting finds — this would be our last visit until more organized recovery operations could be mounted. Our pile of debris grew. Fine weather lowered the water level allowing further access to the crater and deeper penetration in the proximity: in an area previously untouched, we found a remarkably preserved parachute, minus pack, but neatly furled in a bed of clay about a foot beneath the surface. The USAAF salvage units had, in traditional manner, draped the unused parachutes over the remains of the crew and ominous, dark stains in our find denoted the sadness of its service as shroud. Gingerly, we eased the furls free of mud and set it aside to dry. Soon, freshened by the breeze, it billowed and flapped, signifying even more poignantly the misfortune of the plane's crew. The smaller, drogue 'chute had suffered slightly but the manufacturer's name, serial number,

The all-important USAAF serial number is a key to unlock history.

and date of manufacture were legible. Later investigations showed this to be one of the earliest synthetic fibre parachutes produced by the Pioneer Parachute Company Inc of Connecticut. In a subsequent letter, Mr William Bell, the Company President, stated that, just prior to the date this particular 'chute was made, 19 July 1943, supplies of silk had been exhausted and manufacturers switched to the use of nylon. Unlike the disintegrated fibres of a silk 'chute found earlier, the man-made 'chute had survived a 21-year sojourn in the marsh.

While the parachute dried, we continued digging and eventually hauled out a large, battered piece of aluminium alloy which was pulled to the dyke's edge and put through the usual washing process. This procedure was adopted to ensure that every item would be cleaned and meticulously examined for manufacturer's plates, part numbers, or other marks of identification. Traces of writing were discernible so it was carefully rinsed and the mud gently swilled away to expose some black, half inch stencilling. Revealed at last was the proof we sought — faded in places, but still legible was the following information:

A.F. 42-31370
Upper R.H.
Nacelle No.3

Both the RAF and USAAF numbered aircraft panels so that they were returned to the correct machine after servicing. This helped the fiddly task of tightening dzus fasteners and eased work for the maintenance crews. Here we had the remains of an engine cowling panel used on the upper, right-hand side of the starboard inner (No3) engine of Air Force *42-31370*. This coincided with one of the possible serials and a full trace on the aircraft's history became possible.

Hutchison's B-17 following the landing accident in North Africa.

Produced in late 1943, the aircraft was a Boeing B-17G-15-BO assembled at the company's huge Seattle plant near Washington. Aircraft *231370* (the '4' would be for record purposes, both it and the hyphen being dropped so that only six numerals actually appeared in yellow on the bomber's empennage) was ferried over to an airfield in the UK where post-production modifications were embodied and, early in 1944, she arrived at Great Ashfield as a replacement ship. Inclement weather allowed only seventeen missions during the first 42 days of that year and *231370* was not assigned to a regular crew but used by various crews when their own ships were being serviced or repaired. For this reason '370 failed to acquire the nomenclature and graphic nose art often associated with wartime American aircraft.

On Monday 21 February *231370* was allocated to Captain John N. Hutchison, Jr and his crew of 550 Squadron, while their regular ship, *Sleepytime Gal* was on standby. Veterans of 24 missions, they were close to membership of the 'Lucky Bastard Club' for men who reached the haven of 25 missions and completed their tour of duty.

Life had been severe and death flew formation with the bombers many times in the preceding months. Regensburg, Schweinfurt, Emden, Frankfurt and twenty more toll-taking targets had been visited by Hutch and his crew. Several times their Fortress suffered battle damage but limped home to the skilful tending of crew chief, Sergeant August H. Dykstra. They had a narrow escape after the Regensberg shuttle mission to North Africa. Intense combat and high casualties wrote that mission into the history books but Hutch and his crew came through unscathed. As they settled their borrowed bomber, *Sly Fox* on to the PSP at Bone, it blew a tyre and slewed off the runway, axle deep in sand. Too low on gas to go round, and too close to avoid them, the next B-17 sliced the rudder from *Sly Fox* but no one was hurt. Tail gunner, Joe Carpinetti, may have thought the loss of his cherished chocolate bar an even bigger disaster. Coveted and kept cold by altitude, it was a treat Joe anticipated as he sat, exhausted, in the shade of their bomber. As he raised it to his mouth a small Arab child sped past, whipped

it from Joe's grasp and vanished across the hot sand.

That was six, battle-wearying months ago. Today's target looked comparatively easy, a 'milk run' diversionary raid on the Diepholz Aircraft Depot in North West Germany while the main force would penetrate to an aircraft component works in Brunswick. Hutchison's usual bombardier, Ed Gamble, had been ill and his place was to be taken by Clarence Soucek but, during briefing, Gamble asked Soucek to swap as he did not want to miss flying with Hutch on his 25th mission.

Completing a tour was always cele-

The crew of Sly Fox *look relaxed after their desert mishap. L-R: Lt C.G. Curtis; S/Sgt J.A. Catalina; 2/Lt E.J. Gamble; (then) Lt J.N. Hutchison, Jr; S/Sgt J.R. O'Malley; T/Sgt W.J. Dukes; S/Sgt J.J. Carpinetti; S/Sgt J.J. Fulgieri; 2/Lt J.E. Epps. Six of these died at Reedham.*

Photographer 'Bud' Creegan joined Hutchison's crew on that fatal flight (J.C. Ford).

brated and made good morale-boosting publicity. To record the raid and triumphant return to Station 155, the 385th allocated a young but experienced photographer, Sergeant Frank L. Creegan, to fly with the crew, making eleven on board. 'Bud' Creegan's duties as photographer covered all aspects of Group activities but he never shunned the opportunity of filming during a mission and his camera reeled some dramatic scenes in the air war over Europe.

Allied plans were now well advanced to bring the war to ground level in Europe and both the Diepholz and Brunswick missions were connected with a much larger project — the famous, 'Big Week' operations when the RAF and USAAF combined in a series of concerted, round-the-clock bombing operations against the German aircraft industry. It was intended that

these attacks would so reduce the Luftwaffe's strength that it would be impotent during Operation Overlord, the invasion of Europe.

Participating in the raid on Diepholz were 34 385th aircraft and opposition was light as predicted. Fighter attacks were ineffectual and the only casualties suffered by the 385th were Captain Binks and Lieutenant Punches on board the 482nd Group pathfinder B-17 that succumbed, apparently to flak, and was last seen dropping away, still under control, to the rear of the formation. Despite inclement weather, severe damage was inflicted on the enemy aircraft park and, during the return journey, continuing adverse conditions forced the bombers north of their planned route. At 15.37 hours the B-17s were approaching the East Anglian coastline at 8,000 ft. Two minutes later they crossed the coast at

52-43N, 01-41E, just north of Great Yarmouth, descending in preparation for landing. Lieutenant Colonel James McDonald, Group Leader that day, reduced the danger of collision by ordering the descent through cloud in three-ship elements.

Weather conditions were poor — a report for the area indicated cloud at 4,000 ft and clouds up to 3,000 ft thick. As an experienced pilot, Captain Hutchison led one vic of three aircraft. Lieutenant Warren J. Pease and crew of the 549th Squadron flew B-17G 42-37963 off his starboard wing while, on the port side, were Lieutenant John A. Terrace and crew. In a four-engined bomber, the Captain sits in the left-hand, cockpit seat; his co-pilot on the right. Lieutenant Terrace was unable to see the Flight Leader clearly and gave control of the Fortress to Lieutenant Eugene St John, his co-pilot. As they entered cloud, St John had his right wing tucked inside of his leader's left wing and noticed Lieutenant Pease flying a looser position out on Hutchison's starboard side. The crisp, white cloud feathered into wisps over the windscreen, thickening as they submerged from the sharp, blue-and-white world into a grey, shadowy environment.

Each pilot concentrated on his instruments, ignoring the attitude his senses might indicate erroneously, inducing the desire to correct when, in fact, nothing was wrong. Instrument procedure was indoctrinated into all pilots: your feelings lie, your instruments do not. Without horizon, the pilot relies on the

Co-pilot Jack Curtis (left) and Joe Hutchison study briefing notes before take-off (W. Hoagland).

87

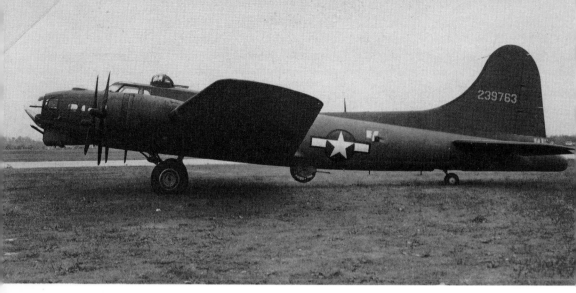

A factory-fresh B-17G Flying Fortress (USAF Official).

symbolic line of his gyro horizon indicator to provide information of his attitude in the lateral and longitudinal planes. This is shown by the position of a miniature aircraft in relation to a gyro-stabilized horizon bar pointer. If the plane entered a spin, the artificial horizon would tumble and force him to rely on his turn-and-slip indicator for information on the direction and degree of spin. What happened on board the Pease ship will never fully be known but it is highly likely that the pilot suffered vertigo. If a pilot loses concentration in such conditions and succumbs to his senses, he could be in serious trouble and could easily exacerbate difficulties by correcting for attitudes existing only in his mind. Once control is lost, a heavy bomber needs altitude and time to recover, particularly if ice has formed on its flying surfaces.

Assuming that Lieutenant Pease suffered vertigo, and it could happen, even to an experienced multi-engine man like himself, his B-17 may have entered a spin within the confines of the cloud and corrective action would be urgently required by both he and co-pilot, Lieutenant Edward B. Brown. During a spin, the artificial horizon would be inoperative and they would rely on the turn-and-slip indicator. The spinning aircraft deflects this needle fully in the direction of spin. Recovery procedure would be to apply full rudder in the opposite direction until the pointer starts to centralize. As this began, rudder would be relaxed and the control yoke moved forward, placing the aircraft in a dive when the indicator centred. Pulling back on the control column would then return the plane to level flight. B-17s were not designed for spinning and the maximum permitted diving speed of a Fortress was 270 mph — beyond this the aircraft increasingly risked structural damage and eventual disintegration. The pilot's manual stipulated that recovery must be 'smooth and gradual' but, if this is what happened with low initial height and altitude rapidly unwinding, both Pease and Brown would have been working to pull their Fortress from its head-long descent and to hell with the manual, within that

Tragic remains of Hutchison's aircraft. Square 'G' denotes 385th Bombardment Group (R. Zorn).

grey 3,000 ft.

When the formation emerged, Lieutenant St John looked right to assure himself of his position. Hutchison's ship was very close and he could see the happy pilot smoking a large cigar: festivities on the Fortress were already under way. Great Ashfield lay only a few minutes ahead following the 'iron beam' — airmen's terminology for the long stretch of railway line that curved out of Great Yarmouth before straightening and heading directly inland, pointing the way home. But something was wrong: there was no B-17 on the starboard side of the Flight. As Gene looked for Lieutenant Pease, the missing B-17 suddenly broke cloud in a very steep dive astern of Hutchison's ship. Their altitude was now less than 1,000 ft. Passing beneath the Flight Leader, Lieutenant Pease pulled up sharply, into the path of the on-coming Fortress. No hope existed — what followed takes longer to read than the events depicted.

The starboard inner propeller (No 3) of Hutchison's ship tore into the spine of the other Fortress, completely sever-

ing its tail section which tumbled earthwards with gunner, Junior M. Falls trapped inside. Debris filled the air and instinctive reaction by St John saved the third bomber as he slammed it into a hard bank to port. The final moments of the two bombers were lost to his view and witnessed only by his ball turret gunner, Staff Sergeant Robert L. Goldsmith and a few workers on the fens below. Continuing upwards, the front two-thirds of the Pease ship looped uncontrollably above Hutchison's stricken bomber before cutting back into it, breaking the Fortress in half. Bob Goldsmith saw two bodies blown out into the sky, but no parachutes, as the shattered remains of '370 spilled earthwards to explode on impact.

The tail-less Pease B-17 descended almost as swiftly but, to Bob Mace and other workmen clearing a dyke near Reedham Rectory, it seemed there were a few seconds of hope. Herbert Mallett, taking posts for gate repairs at Church Farm, Wickhampton, had a similar impression as he sat atop his cart watching the descending B-17 swing 180°

Pictured in February 1944, the wreckage of Pease's B-17 buried on Reedham Marshes (R. Zorn).

towards Freethorpe. Miraculously it was still level and making as if to crash land on the marshes near Decoy Carr. Striking the ground, the B-17 slithered for a distance and exploded as it smashed into the edge of a dyke.

In the moments that followed all that remained of the Flying Fortresses were two water-filled craters surrounded by smouldering debris. The acrid aroma of death drifted across the marshes as soldiers from Halvergate's searchlight unit made their way to the scene. The largest recognizable piece was the tail of Pease's B-17 which straddled the railway near Seven Mile House: inside sat Junior Falls — his watch still ticking — but life had stopped, his body broken internally. Twenty-one young airmen had died in as many seconds.

Captain John N. Hutchison's Crew — 550th Bomb Squadron

Pilot	Hutchison, John N.	Captain
Co-pilot	Curtis, Charles G.	Second Lieutenant
Navigator	Epps, John E.	First Lieutenant
Bombardier	Gamble, Edmond J.	First Lieutenant
Top turret	Kitner, Roy C.	Technical Sergeant
Tail gunner	Carpinetti, Joseph J.	Staff Sergeant
Radio operator	Dukes, William J.	Technical Sergeant
Ball turret	Erhardt, John H.	Staff Sergeant
Left waist gunner	Corgnatti, Emilio M.	Staff Sergeant
Right waist gunner	Bobulsky, Peter Jr.	Staff Sergeant
Photographer	Creegan, Frank L. Jr.	Staff Sergeant

First Lieutenant Warren J. Pease's Crew — 549th Bomb Squadron

Pilot	Pease, Warren J.	First Lieutenant
Co-pilot	Brown, Edward B.	Second Lieutenant
Navigator	Kaplan, Bernard (NMI)	Second Lieutenant
Bombardier	Jenkins, Robert E.	Second Lieutenant
Top turret	Clift, William R.	Technical Sergeant
Radio Operator	Gill, William (NMI) Jr.	Technical Sergeant
Ball turret	Owsley, Franklin C.	Staff Sergeant
Tail gunner	Falls, Junior M.	Staff Sergeant
Left waist gunner	Dickason, Harold E.	Staff Sergeant
Right waist gunner	Bruner, Gail F.	Staff Sergeant

John Rose and the recovery team spent some time extricating the crews for burial at Cambridge but, as related, much of the wreckage was left. In 1944, the B-17 had no historical significance and the daily toll of aircraft falling in East Anglia kept salvage teams busy.

So moving was this story, I felt that the parachute found should be preserved in tribute and it is today kept in a sealed display case in the USAF Museum at Wright-Patterson Air Force Base, Ohio, and seen by nearly 200,000 people a year. I turned my attention to crash sites elsewhere until, in September 1975, we again visited the Hutchison site. Amongst the items found were a small compass used by Lieutenant Epps and the lens from Bud Creegan's camera. The work was arduous, smelly and wet: once again water prevented deep excavation and we withdrew until April 1976 when test holes by Peter Adcock and George Vyse struck heavy wreckage at the Pease site. This site was accessible to heavy equipment and, the following weekend, a JCB was hired and a larger gang called in order to spread the cost.

No crater remained but there was a noticeable depression about 100 yards from the edge of Decoy Carr, a small copse on the edge of the marsh. Cutting through the surface seemed like breaking the skin of cold porridge and we realized how thin was the crust on which stood our machine. However, a JCB achieved in minutes the equivalent of several hours manual labour and had lifting capacity in excess of ten men. Soon, the digger extracted a three-bladed Hamilton propeller, bent but otherwise unharmed and in superb condition. Sifting the mire, we discovered numerous smaller items. Bernard Kaplan's navigational equipment came to light, also an emergency water bottle and various other artefacts all carefully washed in the dyke. A machine-gun with a round jammed in the breech caused concern but Peter Snowling had worked on these before and soon rendered it harmless. The pattern of wreckage spread towards the dyke and it was following this that caused our troubles.

At a depth of 12 ft, the driver located a large chunk that could not be lifted from his original angle of attack and, manoeuvring for a more suitable approach, he put himself uncomfortably close to the back-filled spot from which he removed the propeller. He was on a narrow spit of firm ground with the dyke on one side and a quagmire on the other. Thrusting into the marsh, the machine locked on the buried item and

Above left *April 1976. Bernard Kaplan's navigation computer is found in the wreckage.*

Above *Emergency drinking water was carried as part of the survival kit.*

Left *Donald Buxton with oxygen mask and throat microphone.*

Above right *L-R: Tom Brown, Pete Snowling and George Vyse remove a bullet from the breech of a machine-gun.*

Right *The offending round firmly wedged.*

tussled to pull it clear. Looking like some atavistic carnivore with its victim, the JCB struggled and heaved but the motion put it in danger of sliding into the slough. Too late, the driver realized his predicament and his left wheel slid inexorably into the mud, tilting the machine at an alarming angle and sinking deeper with every movement. In the end, it keeled over to such a degree that fuel settling to one side of his tank starved the engine and the great, yellow beast lay quiet. It took several hours to

winch it free and we deemed it unwise to pursue whatever caused the problem.

For two years we left the sites alone, then, in 1978, Kim Collinson noticed that the East Anglian Real Property Company were operating a large excavator on dyke clearance in the area. A tracked vehicle like this was ideal and Kim approached the General Manager, Robert Steven, who kindly gave permission for his driver, Victor Doughty, to operate the machine on our behalf. On Saturday 1 July, Vic shuffled his

machine across the intervening fenland, skilfully filling and laying boards over the dykes it was necessary to cross. Next day, a soggy Sunday, we found his machine parked beside the Hutchison site. Growling into action, the digger plunged its powerful arm deep into the crater before sweeping easily a load greater than we had moved in fourteen years. In bucket after bucket appeared countless fragments of the once proud Boeing to be sifted for items of historical significance.

From a depth of 10 ft appeared our first important find, a large brass oil cooler originally mounted behind the number one engine. Vic reported contact with a much bigger item and enthusiasm heightened as we hoped that the original recovery crew might have left an engine. Next to emerge was a carburettor, covered in oil but in excellent condition despite three decades buried. Again Vic felt a large piece but it slipped free. We decided to extend beyond where the carburettor had lain and draw

Above *Digger in difficulties: the JCB was winched clear several hours later.*

Below *Duffled against rain and chill, Julie McLachlan is saddened by the twisted, scarred propeller.*

towards the edge, hopefully ensnaring what must be an elusive engine. Cautiously, Vic moved as close as safety permitted, gaining a few inches more reach before extending and dropping the steel claw. The hydraulic arm bent, retracted slightly, then stopped against something solid. More power. Prising this out called for cunning and Victor jiggled the arm back and forth loosening suction and dispensing accumulated mud. Roaring into full power, he wrestled violently causing the entire marsh for yards about to undulate.

We knew we had won when the arm drew remorselessly inwards, nestling its prey against the crater bank. Muddy brown water sloshed noisily away as the cylinder banks of a mighty Wright Cyclone engine broke surface. Cowling panels confirmed this as the No 1 port outer engine. Those many years ago, its powerful song had reverberated across the landscape, now, it stood a silent relic of war. Delving again, we removed the matching propeller, scars on its twisted blades symbolizing the anguish of those final moments when it shredded into the Pease B-17. Further searching revealed little else and our attention turned to clearing the Pease site but the only worthwhile item found was the cause of our 1976 troubles, the remains of another propeller.

The engine and collision-scarred propeller from Hutchison's B-17 are displayed at Parham. Other artefacts can be seen in the Norfolk and Suffolk Aviation Museum, Flixton, and at the 100th Bomb Group Museum, Thorpe Abbotts. These sad relics form part of our historical panoply and serve no purpose left buried and forgotten. Viewing them reminds us of the sacrifice made for peace.

THE SOMERLEYTON MEMORIALS

5

East Anglia's rich aviation history is often commemorated by museums and monuments. The latter, relating to units that served in the region, are most frequently sited near their former airfields. There are, however, a number of memorials dedicated to specific airmen located near where they fell and each reflects a vignette against the broad drama of war. Security prevented revelation of the facts surrounding many of these incidents and the passing years sometimes shade truth into apocrypha. This chapter relates the background of two such memorials, both erected in Suffolk by the then Lord Somerleyton, shortly after the events to which they pay tribute occurred.

The first to be dedicated is located on Home Farm, Somerleyton, and is set in quiet countryside, almost in the hedgerow beside the Flixton bridleway, a little used track between Flixton and Somerleyton. The head-stone shaped memorial stone bears a wreath-enclasped cross below which are the following words:

Remembrance Sunday, 1967. A quiet tribute to the fallen.

> NEAR THIS PLACE
> LT J.BLACK, U.S.N.A.F. PILOT
> AND
> LT T.AIKEN, U.S.N.A.F. NAV-
> GAVE THEIR LIVES IN DEFENCE
> OF THIS COUNTRY
> RETURNING FROM OPERATIONAL
> DUTIES ON NOV - 14 - 1944
> GREATER LOVE HATH NO MAN
> THAN THIS
> THAT A MAN LAY DOWN HIS
> LIFE FOR HIS FRIENDS

As a teenager, I was told that their aircraft had been a Mosquito so, one winter's morning, I cycled out to investigate and find some pieces for my collection. The lanes leading to the memorial were rutted and puddled making progress a slithering business. I found the memorial set in what locals call, 'The Warren', an undulation of farmland rising from Blundeston Marshes. Searching the recently ploughed field, and in nearby hedges, I came across fragments of green and grey-painted plywood, pieces of aluminium and what I foolishly prized as a real trophy, a 20mm cannon shell. Not realizing the moisture on it indicated deteriorating and unstable explosives within, I put it in my saddlebag and bounced happily homewards. The following evening, at an Air Training Corps parade, my stupidity was bluntly berated by Warrant Officer Crisp who explained what the 'weeping' indicated and the assembled squadron learnt that they had a fortunate young fool in their ranks. This ticking-off served its purpose and ingrained in me a respect for crash site ordnance.

Knowing the aircraft was an RAF Mosquito, I was puzzled — why was it being flown by airmen from the United States Navy? The story further intrigued me when I learned it had been destroyed by British guns. How had this tragedy occurred? What went wrong? One elderly rustic related how the Americans had stolen the plane after a party and had to be shot down for being a hazard. I felt this tale to be an injustice to brave men, but what was the truth?

Strangely, the story has its roots in the Pacific theatre of war and the threat Japanese nocturnal air activities posed to United States Naval operations. In mid 1944, Britain had both experience and a technological lead in night fighting to transfer to her American allies. One method of doing this would be for United States Navy aircrew to undergo RAF training procedures and operations. Agreement was reached and USN bureaucracy searched files, selected candidates and cut orders that moved men thousands of miles from the Pacific to the Atlantic theatre of war. Acquiring experience had its price; of ten USN air-men posted to England in June 1944, only four survived. Those chosen, however, did not view life pessimistically and embarked enthusiastically on the first stages of RAF training.

Pilots went to 12(P) AFU at RAF Spitalgate where they trained on the venerable Blenheim, front line retirees of a type which had the distinction of claiming the first airborne radar victory in July 1940. One of the Americans, John Kelly, recalled that the grass airfield was a 'shocking novelty' and they also had to cope with a new language, from 'A to Zed,' not 'Zee'. Cowl flaps became 'cooling gills', propellers were 'airscrews' and manifold pressures were measured not in inches of mercury but as 'boost' of 'pounds-per-square-inch.' British airfield procedures, radio disciplines and air rules also differed: there was plenty to learn. Meanwhile, navigators, or 'Navrads' as they came to be, were taught on the Mark IV AI (Air Interception) radar at RAF Ouston, Newcastle-Upon-Tyne. Hours were spent practising interceptions in doughty, old Ansons but these comparatively slow-motion exercises prepared them for faster aircraft and more complex radar in operational squadrons.

On 1 July 1944, the ten USN airmen assembled in London at the headquarters of US Naval Forces in Europe. Here they formed crews for the next phase of training, on No 35 Course, 51 Operational Training Unit based at RAF Cranfield in Bedfordshire. The pilot/navrad crews were: Lieutenant-Commanders Archibald Sinclair/John H.P. Gould; Lieutenant Everett M. Woodward/Ensign Walter G. Madden; Lieutenant John W. Kelly/Lieutenant Henry T. Martin; Lieutenant Samuel W. Peebles/Ensign Eric R. Grinndal; Lieutenant Joseph F. Black/Lieutenant

Thomas N. Aiken. Six would die before Christmas including Joe Black and Tom Aiken whose story we now focus on.

Joe Black came from Richmond, Virginia. He graduated as a Bachelor of Arts from the university there but pointed his career towards the Navy when he enlisted in the Reserve on 15 October 1940, five days before his 21st birthday. Three months later he terminated his enlistment to accept appointment as an Aviation Cadet and left chilly Virginia for the sunnier climes of Jacksonville Naval Air Station, Florida. Appreciation of the weather was not his purpose. The climate for democracy was approaching a world wide nadir. Europe was already embroiled in a war and tension between Japan and America was increasing. President Roosevelt, recently re-elected for a third term, gave his State of the Union address to Congress on 6 January 1941, declaring that, 'at no previous time has American security been as seriously threatened from without as it is today.' The American giant was being aroused and the declaration of Pacific and Caribbean Defence Zones in February 1941, stimulated naval aircrew training. Further impetus came in May when an American freighter, the *Robin Moor* was torpedoed.

Joe completed his training in August 1941, and became a patrol plane commander on twin-engined PBY flying boats, known as Catalinas to the British. For nearly two years he commanded crews in several patrol squadrons on the American seaboard, protecting shipping against submarines. He then served in the Pacific, still flying PBYs, but on dangerous 'Black Cat' operations searching at night to report incoming Japanese raids. This required skilled instrument fliers and demonstrated to Joe how much the Navy needed night fighters.

Lieutenant Joseph Francis Black, USN (Lord Somerleyton).

Experience gained here undoubtedly led to his selection for training with the RAF and in February 1944 he returned to Florida for a twelve-week conversion to fighters, flying Hellcats at Jacksonville and Vero Beach. This training culminated with an introduction to the De Havilland Mosquito at Eglin Air Force Base but Joe would not get seriously to grips with this legendary aircraft until he arrived in England.

Nine years older than Joe, Tom Aiken was born in Ardmore, Pennsylvania, on 25 April 1909. He was educated in nearby Philadelphia at the Museum School of Industrial Art and was undoubtedly influenced in his choice of military service by the presence of several US Navy installations along the Delaware. On 3 February 1941, Tom enlisted as an air gunner and served

*Lieutenant Thomas Newkirk Aiken, USN
(Lord Somerleyton).*

until 31 March 1943, when he took the oath of office to become a Lieutenant (junior grade). The ensuing months saw him serving in Torpedo Squadron 9 flying Gruman Avengers against the Japanese from the famous carrier, USS *Essex*. For his courage, Tom was awarded an Air Medal, the Gold Star in lieu of a second Air Medal and the Purple Heart. Six months of active service took its toll and, in March 1944, he was detached to the St Simon's Island Naval Radar Training School in Georgia. A few weeks later he was promoted to full Lieutenant and selected for the RAF night fighter programme.

These, then, were two of ten Americans drawn from different hemispheres

of a world at war, the global aspects of which were reflected by the presence of several other nationalities amongst the 48 airmen of Number 35 Course: Britain's colonies had responded to her plight but there were French and Belgian airmen as well. They sought nocturnal combat to lift the darkness that had enveloped their countries and menaced others. The Axis Air Forces, weakened by day, slunk into shadows visible only to the radar eye and these men were training to expose and destroy them. To be effective, the two men in a Mosquito had to harmonize, work as one — the RAF even called the crewing process, 'marriages' and compatibility with mutual trust was essential. Joe Black and Tom Aiken had diverse personalities but there existed that intangible quality which made a good crew. Joe, at 25, was quiet, reserved with a deceptive impression of timidity enhanced by a round, boyish face. Beyond this shyness was a friendliness and strength radiating to others a feeling of trust and reliability, qualities good in a friend and essential for a night fighter pilot. Joe acted as a steadying influence, a counterbalance, for Tom who, although senior in years, was a man of gusto and humour and invariably a boisterous star of pranks at mess parties. He became adept at mimicking the English and would open a conversation with, 'I say, old boy. . .' taking the part with such finesse, that he appeared more English than the RAF officers.

One British taste soon acquired by the Americans was the craving for a pint. Social life at Cranfield consisted of many pub crawls but these were undertaken with methodical planning that bore credit to their military training. It became known to the Course that pubs in the vicinity received their quota of brew on different days. Once, 'Intelligence' had established that a particular inn had received supplies, a maximum effort would be called that evening and the target raided by a horde of thirsty fliers. Much later, a wavy formation of inebriated airmen would cycle back to base, mission accomplished.

From local pubs, at the other end of the social scale, there was an invitation from the Duke of Bedford for the Course to attend a dance at Woburn Abbey. During the evening, Joe Black met Nancy Annan, a Wren working at Bletchley Park on the top-secret 'Ultra' Project, now recognized for the breaking of German codes. Joe was captivated and they met again: Nancy took Joe to London and soon the couple snatched what precious hours they could from the conflict surrounding them. Despite the risks, they fell in love and Joe felt a new purpose in life. After the war, he wanted to become a doctor: he had, in fact, given up medical school to enlist. Joe's medical knowledge may have saved Nancy when she became suddenly ill and he diagnosed acute appendicitis. Hurrying her home to Ely, she was admitted to hospital for an operation which was successful, but the stress of work and illness left her exhausted. She never returned to Bletchley but convalesced and planned their future while Joe continued training at Cranfield.

Social life on the twelve weeks of Course 35 established camaraderie but, in reality, the work was demanding and sometimes dangerous. Their first month began with ground school, some lectures were shared, others separate — pilots to learn about their aircraft, and navigators were taught on the apparatus carried. Crews began to harmonize on the ground; it would be two weeks before they flew together and a month before

Nancy Annan served as a Wren at Bletchley Park (Mrs N. Ballinger).

the British allowed them out after dark. Initially, it was instrument flying, navigation and mock, daylight interceptions before repeating it all at night. Radar was secret; the public read stories of cats' eyes and carrots yet there were medicinal disciplines and crews were taught the basics of the optical system, how the retina received light, methods of improving night vision — to scan, not stare, when searching the night sky, using peripheral vision.

Night vision exercises came in the form of games requiring coordination but played in semi-darkness using white playing pieces. Snooker, skittles, darts and even soccer in a darkened hangar enhanced their confidence while additional support came from vitamin A pills taken daily. What difference they made to the body's natural resource is uncertain but it was recognized that lack of this vitamin induced night blindness. Radar could take them close to the target but visual identification was essential because of the many friendly aircraft abroad at night. True, they carried IFF (Identification, Friend or Foe) transmitters but electronics might fail, or not be switched on, and crews spent hours studying aircraft silhouettes and partially-illuminated models simulating different angles and light conditions.

By this stage of the war Britain had developed a web of night defences, every strand of which was vital and had to be understood. They were shown balloon sites, AA and searchlight batteries and, most important of all, the GCI Station. Britain survived in 1940 because Radio Direction Finding (RDF) positioned Hurricanes and Spitfires to attack the masses of German bombers. By 1944, the British had adopted the American term, 'radar' and refined the method of interception so that any penetration of defences proved costly to the depleted Luftwaffe. GCI stood for 'Ground Controlled Interception' and these stations were long-range eyes for the night fighter. It was their task to manipulate him to an attacking position within range of the on-board AI set. The fighter then stalked its prey until visual contact was made. Co-ordination from GCI to crew, and AI operator to pilot, was essential and became the focus of No 35 Course.

At Spitalgate, Joe had trudged the skies in a dilapidated, twin-engined Blenheim but Cranfield held its more powerful stablemate, the Beaufighter. 51 OTU had a number of these pugnacious twins, early marks retired from operations but ideally suited to scolding recalcitrant airmen for their sins. Survive the Beaufighter, they were told, and you graduated to the glamorous Mosquito, Britain's 'Wooden Wonder'. This ingenious, de Havilland amalgamation of twin Rolls-Royce Merlins and the bold use of a plywood and balsa sandwich construction produced, in a war of leapfrogging development, the fastest, operational aircraft for two years. It was a fighting machine which inspired the men who flew it, a far cry from Joe's lumbering Catalina, but he and Tom had to earn their Mosquito wings.

In the Beaufighter, they learnt to blend actions and responses to a disembodied voice, often female, from the GCI station. The commands had to be unhesitatingly followed and Tom's exuberance vanished as he practised the deadly serious game of intercepting another Beaufighter. Joe had spent hours in night flight simulation on instruments but this was the apotheosis of their being, his single skills were useless if Tom could not get him within range. Dummy interceptions called for every fibre of self discipline. He could see the target but Tom, tucked into the Beaufighter's darkened innards, had only the flashes and flickers of radar images to go by and Joe winced when following instructions he knew would lose the target. Gradually, these occurrences diminished. Tom tracked targets unerringly and Joe grew increasingly proud of his navigator as their successes increased — they became a deadly duo, a night fighter crew. Soon, Joe told Nancy, there would be a real target for their cannons. There would, but it was not exactly the bomber he envisaged.

As No 35 Course proceeded, a new and sinister adversary appeared in the skies over southern England. On 13

June 1944, the first V-1 fell and mankind edged into a new and more terrible era, that of the missile. Allied Intelligence had monitored development of Hitler's first Vergeltungswaffen (Reprisal Weapon) and frequent bombing of launch sites delayed their introduction. Now, with the invasion less than two weeks old, the advent of this weapon, codenamed 'Diver', consumed valuable resources as defences were rapidly redeployed. An eventual establishment of some 2,800 AA guns, 500 searchlights and more than 2,000 balloons were positioned to protect the primary target, London. Air Defence Great Britain (ADGB), formerly Fighter Command, became heavily engaged in the battle against the V-1 and co-operation between the Army and RAF was essential to avoid casualties when both sought the same target. ADGB crews were advised of AA Command's gun zones, the largest of these being the Diver gun box south and east of London to Clacton where a Diver gun strip was created running along the coast to the weaker gun fringe north of the Wash.

Fast though they were, the piston-engined fighters found Doodlebugs difficult to catch and a small target. Powered by a pulse-jet, the V-1 achieved speeds varying from 300 to over 400 mph with altitudes typically between 2-4,000 ft. To attack a V-1, the fighter needed a height advantage and soon the dayfighters, Tempests, Spitfires and Mustangs, created techniques for destroying this fleet but simple foe. Methods involved not only direct gunfire but a style of tipping the V-1 to earth using the fighter's wing tip to disrupt the flying bomb's aerodynamics. Night fighters were less flamboyant and found the task even harder. Collision was a serious risk if more than one night fighter converged behind the same V-1 so some squadrons advised pilots to switch on navigation lights as they closed in. An average 24 hours might see over 100 Doodlebugs launched against London but the countermeasures proved increasingly effective, ultimately destroying the majority. Even so, the campaign killed 5,682 people and took a high psychological toll of war-weary civilians. As the 'buzz bomb summer' turned to autumn, the rate of attack dwindled when the Germans switched their target to continental ports used for Allied supply lines. Hitler's reprisal weapon had a range limitation of 200 miles and the capture of launching sites finally defeated this phase of the attack but the Fuhrer's obsession with target London would not be frustrated and his engineers had another V-1 trick to perform which contributed to the deaths of Joe Black and Tom Aiken.

No 35 Course neared completion and its later stages spilled over from Cranfield to 551 Squadron at RAF Twinwoods Farm, a satellite station now remembered as the airfield from which musician Major Glenn Miller vanished into fog and mystery. The course continued on Beaufighters with advanced AI tactics, air-to-air firing on drogues, and camera gun attacks on other aircraft. Returning to Cranfield, they reached the coveted Mosquito although, at this stage, training versions lacked radar so navrads were taught the sophisticated MkX AI in Wellington airborne classrooms with Hurricanes as targets. All the Americans pressed for operational assignments and, when the course concluded in mid September, these were granted.

The Sinclair/Gould and Woodward/Madden crews went to 456 RAAF

Above *Joe with a 68 Squadron Mosquito* (Mrs N. Ballinger).

Below *He 111 of KG 53 with a V1 mounted below the starboard wing* (H. Hoehler).

Squadron, then flying forward patrols from RAF Ford in Sussex. Joe was pleased to remain nearer Ely with the others who joined 68 (NF) Squadron at Castle Camps in Cambridgeshire. This was one of the RAF's most famous night fighter squadrons and had recently converted from Beaufighters to Mosquitoes. An unusual feature of the unit was its aircrew composition: half were Czechs whose courage and tenacity were renowned. Designed by pilot, Zbysek Necas, an owl on the squadron crest symbolized their activities while the motto 'VZDY PRIPRAVEN' meant 'Always Prepared'. The Americans soon discovered the Czechs were young, hardened veterans of those unforgiving foes — the Nazi enemy and the elements. Hardly had the Americans settled when, at the end of October, the squadron transferred to Coltishall, Norfolk, as a countermeasure to V-1s appearing from the east. This was beyond the range of any ground sites and the advent of Doodlebugs from this direction again demonstrated German ingenuity.

The Allied advance pushed the Wermacht deeper into the continent and over-ran V-1 sites, stifling the planned number of attacks. During the previous year, the German research establishment at Peenemunde developed methods of air launching the V-1. It further pleased them to discover the most suitable platform for the task was the veteran Heinkel 111 bomber, slow, vulnerable but plentiful in the Luftwaffe's inventory. Production tooling was instigated for the He 111H-22 variant which mounted the bomb, offset from the fuselage, under either its port or starboard wing — some H-16s and H-20s were also adapted. Initiating this method of attack in the summer of 1944 was III Gruppe of Kampfgeschwader 3 and this unit later expanded into an entire Kampfgeschwader, reclassified as KG-53. Their air launchings increased during September and October forcing an Allied response by extension of the gun belt and redeployment of fighter squadrons, including 68.

Joe stressed to Nancy how he badly wanted to 'bag a Heinkel' before going home. At the very least, he wanted one of the loathsome robots. Nancy was discharged from the Royal Navy because of her illness and continued recuperating at home. She loved hearing Joe's Navy-grey jeep burble along Market Street to Grove House. Soon, Joe would apply for official permission to marry and was using his influence to ensure she sailed on the same ship when he returned to America.

On 2 November, Joe and Tom flew their first sortie, an anti-diver patrol. No luck — they landed Mosquito HK241 at 07.30. Breakfast, then bed. Five nights later, when they were patrolling in HK348, their friends 'Woodie' Woodward and 'Jerry' Madden disappeared en route to the Continent, nothing was ever found. On Armistice Day, Joe and Tom were airborne until dawn in HK289, WM-K, but still the wily Heinkels eluded them.

Catching the launcher was difficult and dangerous. The Heinkel crew also faced fearful odds and the same remorseless weather as they lumbered low across the North Sea to avoid radar. Near its launch point, the bomber laboured to 1,500-2,000 ft but was so slow, flying at about 110 mph, that an intercepting Mosquito found it impossible to stay behind and risked overshooting or stalling into the sea. At launch height, the He 111 nosed into a shallow dive, gaining enough airspeed to avoid his bomb stalling — the V-1 needed at least 150 mph to have sufficient lift. On release, the Heinkel turned away, diving for the sanctuary of low altitude to scuttle home. This process took less than ten minutes so the opportunities for positioning a night fighter when the bomber bobbed up on the CHL screen were remote. KG 53 lost some 77 aircraft but only sixteen to nightfighters.

The RAF had more success against the V-1 and standing patrols were employed with fighters flying box sectors off the coast. If not under direct GCI control, the Mosquito could 'freelance' in its box for visual or AI contacts. This was the defence threshold and, as mentioned, lining the coast was the gunstrip, extending 10,000 yards seawards, finishing 5,000 yards inland. Army and RAF senior officers agreed regulations governing who had attack priority and procedures for the safety of all air traffic crossing the coast. Rules were circulated telling pilots to fly above 6,000 ft and prohibiting guns from firing on unseen targets over 4,000 ft. Additional precautions were to fly on a track of 300° magnetic or north of this so your intentions did not appear hostile. IFF had to be on and airspeed below 250 mph. The mindless V-1 track was direct so pilots were requested to orbit 15,000 yards from the coast, emphasizing a friendly trace, and they had to contact ground control to warn the guns. On no account was a V-1 to be pursued through the barrage, 'Such action is bound to be disastrous as the AA guns have been authorized NOT to stop engaging a flying bomb owing to the presence of a friendly fighter...'

Early in November, Joe and Nancy became engaged and Joe requested USN consent to marry his British Wren. Nancy was excited yet apprehensive by the prospect of life in America. Joe's family welcomed the news and the USN gave its official blessing on Monday 13

Luftwaffe technicians prepare a V1 (H. Hoehler).

Tom Aiken photographed Kelly and Martin flying WM-H over the Wash. This is believed to be HK344 which crashed at Horstead Hall, Norfolk, on 22 November 1944 killing Sam Peebles and Eric Grinndal. They had destroyed a V1 on 25 October 1944 (J. Kelly).

November 1944. This enabled Nancy to confirm the plans already laid for their wedding the following week. Tragically, there would be no cake, only coffins.

On 14 November RAF Intelligence anticipated a large V-1 attack and night-fighter squadrons were prepared, performing night flying tests, checking aircraft and radar calibration. Joe and Tom flew in 'K-King', *HK289*. Theirs were early names on the crew room blackboard but that persistent enemy, the weather, looked like handicapping their chances of success. The brisk, clear day deteriorated, drizzling miserably into low cloud with rain, sleet and snow showers scudding coastwards.

KG-53 aircrews grudged the same weather: their mass attack planned over forty Heinkels in three waves, but numbers were no consolation if snow-laden clouds deceived you, iced your wings and dragged you into oblivion. V-1s were trollied to waiting Heinkels and ground crews sheltered as best they could while loading the malignant cargoes. As the weak winter sun conceded defeat to darkness, the first incongruous combinations shuffled skywards.

In contrast, Mosquito *HK289* lifted nimbly from Coltishall's wet turf at 18.05 hours and darted eastwards towards the advancing enemy. Joe and Tom became 'Ferro 17', a rapid blip on the master station screens at nearby Neatishead. Reaching his patrol sector, Joe banked the Mosquito into its sentry duty pattern while, unseen and low, the Heinkels stalked towards the camp.

Scout-like signals from Tom's AI searched ahead, their very silence reporting back through the screens he monitored closely. Minutes passed, then a few, fuzzy traces appeared, probably from squalls like those intermittently buffeting 'K-King'. The AI Mk X was unhappy when low: it could image rain showers and lost much of its optimum, ten-mile range. Tom peered anxiously at his set, exchanging few words with either Joe or the forward controller on the coast at RAF Hopton. Joe acknowledged instructions to freelance and the last plot the Mosquito registered was at 18.49 hours, heading east. Their trace vanished as they dived into a pool of hoped-for Heinkels and began hunting. At 19.05, Hopton received their final transmission. They reported no less than twelve contacts but Tom's radar appeared confused by window and he struggled to read the signals. It is doubtful if KG 53 were using Duppel because it offered few benefits at that height and Tom's set may have malfunctioned. We will never know whether the V-1 they finally located was by AI, or a visual from the distinctive, red flash of a released robot igniting. We do know that they pursued a V-1 west, determined to destroy it. Both Americans had seen in London the horror and devastation caused by Doodlebugs penetrating Britain's guard screens. With Merlins howling in anguish, they gradually overhauled the pulsing exhaust flame. Ahead, searchlights probed and a fury of guns pounded shell upon shell against the destructive demons above.

When they entered the gun strip, the bomb was not their responsibility but, if it escaped, how many would suffer? Risking their lives, they hurtled past the safety margin, the V-1 almost in range.

They knew the risks, their mindless opponent risked nothing.

The flurry of V-1 activity attracted spectators to see the searchlights and guns in action. Eleven-year-old Harold Gayfer witnessed the tragedy and it remained a vivid impression: 'I was living at Lound Road, Blundeston and was a keen aircraft enthusiast, well able to recognize most aircraft by the sound of their engines, the Mosquito being no exception. I persuaded my parents to let me go outside as soon as the Mosquito was heard over the coast in the direction of Hopton. The raid alert had been sounded and I hoped to glimpse a flying bomb as many had been coming over the coast. The coastal AA defences opened up and, above the din, the sound of the Mosquito's engines grew louder as it came towards us. It was probably flying at around 2,000 ft, very fast, with its navigation lights on. As it was almost overhead it appeared to be diving and twisting — we followed its path quite clearly by the nav lights. At this precise time, whilst almost overhead, two Very lights came from the aircraft, one red and one green. Shortly after, the aircraft went into a very fast, shallow dive in the direction of Somerleyton, then pulled up into a vertical climb, appeared to loop, then dived vertically into the ground. There was an orange flash, the screaming engines suddenly stopped, some muffled sounds of exploding ammunition and then silence.'

Too late, the guns had ceased. Tom's desperate signal silenced them, but they were not to blame, nor was Joe, only the misfortunes of war. The V-1 flew on unscathed and is thought to have fallen harmlessly near Berkhamsted.

From farms and villages, rescuers struggled along muddy lanes leading to

Home Farm. Air Raid Warden, Mr R.H. Youngs cycled towards the glare — he thought the Mosquito was on fire before it crashed. A hay stack had ignited, increasing the flames beaconing in the darkness and firecracking cannon shells threatened those early on the scene. From Lowestoft, the NFS were summoned and their tender took ages struggling along rutty bridleways to douse the flames. In the darkness, no one was certain that the crew were dead and rescuers hoped that the last agonizing surge skywards might have enabled them to escape. The lower hatch door was found some distance from the crash indicating that an escape had been attempted but any hope was expunged by the discovery of two charred corpses, Tom still clutching the Very pistol.

Nancy was shattered, her life as smashed as Joe's Mosquito and time alone healed the hurt, eased the loss. At the invitation of Joe's parents, she went to America and lived with them before marrying and settling in the USA. At Coltishall, 68 Squadron felt keenly the loss of these popular young Americans. Others who risked the barrage realized how lucky they were. Wing Commander L.J.C. Mitchell and Flight Lieutenant D.L. Cox of 25 Squadron were also shot down in the gun strip that night but baled out safely. Both incidents were subject to Courts of Enquiry and lessons learned were incorporated into operational procedures.

68 Squadron, Czechs, English and Americans mustered proudly but sadly for the funeral. Joe's brother, John Black, also attended — he was serving in the USAAF and had hoped to be first in the family to welcome Nancy as kin. It was a grim occasion and Joe's best friend, Sam Peebles, tried to console Nancy. Like Joe, Sam was engaged to an English girl and the couples had become friends. Joe's grave was first in a row of ninety. A week later, Sam Peebles was buried at Joe's feet, first in the next row. His Mosquito lost an engine on take-off and crashed on the lawn of Horstead Hall killing Sam and his navrad, Eric Grinndal.

Six casualties from the indoctrination programme was too much and the Commander of USN Forces in Europe, Admiral Harold R. Stark, ordered their withdrawal. They were needed as instructors and on 7 December the survivors, John Kelly/Tom Martin and Archibald R. Sinclair/John H.P. Gould, left England. The self-sacrifice of Joe and Tom so touched Lord and Lady Somerleyton, on whose estate they perished, that Lord Somerleyton decided to pay tribute to the airmen's courage with a memorial situated where they fell. On 31 December 1944, a Dedication Service was held at Somerleyton Church and the stone was unveiled by the Hon Savile Crossley, now Lord Somerleyton, with this moving address.

'As one of the rising generation, for whom so many lives are being given, I am humbly proud to unveil this Memorial. May it be for us, and for all who come after us, a reminder of those who in their day and generation were not found wanting. May we imitate their faithfulness. May they find the perfect peace.'

These, then, were the events behind the fragments found on my wintry excursion. My initial research appeared in local newspapers, eventually attracting a methodical search for remnants by the Norfolk and Suffolk Aviation Museum. Sweeping the site with detectors, they unearthed numerous pieces, the largest being a propeller boss still bearing spiralled impact scars. An

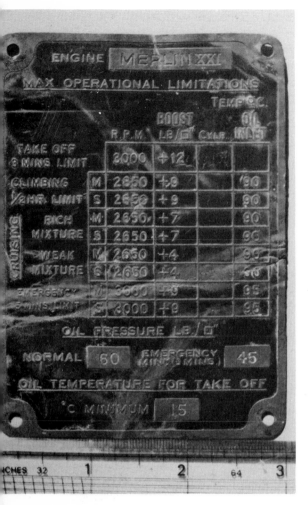

Engine specification plate from Mosquito NF MkXVII, HK289, WM-K.

same design, this stone bears seven names in the following fashion:

NEAR THIS PLACE ON MAY 7TH 1944
1ST LT RALPH W. WRIGHT
LT JACK W. RAPER
LT RICHARD CURRAN
LT CARL A. HERMANN
S/SGT RANDOLPH C. MOORE
ALSO ON 8TH APRIL 1945
LT RUSSELL P. JUDD
F/O LOUIS S. DAVIS
ALL OF THE U.S.A. 8TH ARMY AIR FORCE
GAVE THEIR LIVES IN DEFENCE
OF THIS COUNTRY
GREATER LOVE HATH NO MAN THAN
THIS
THAT A MAN LAY DOWN HIS LIFE
FOR HIS FRIENDS

Those who ponder the events that this stone recalls need to turn round and look in the direction it faces. Across the sloping farmland lies Herringfleet Hall. Walking from the church, along the Blocka Road to the North Lodge and beyond, the observant traveller will notice an area where the trees seem thinner, some appear damaged and the uppermost branches of mature specimens end abruptly with newer growth evident from stunted limbs. The shock suffered by this gentle woodland is also discernible at ground level. Scrape away leaf mould and fragments of aluminium emerge, perhaps a machine-gun bullet or, as in 1968, a 'dog-tag' belonging to one of the airmen. My friend, Simon Woods, and I were searching in the undergrowth when something glinted in sunlight dappling through the trees. Simon picked up a small identity tag and brushed away the remaining soil. Impressed into the metal was a name with some numbers, 'Richard Curran 0703958 T43-44A' and, below the

interesting discovery was a brass engine specification plate for a Merlin XXI presented to the author by Assistant Historian, Bob Collis.

As mentioned, the memorial on Home Farm was dedicated first but the second Somerleyton stone, situated near the gate of the 13th Century church of Ashby St Mary, records two unrelated incidents, one before and one after the deaths of Black and Aiken. Using the

attachment hole, a solitary letter, 'C'. Like all military organizations, the USAAF numbered everything, men included. The prefix 'O' denoted an officer; 'T43-44' indicated anti-tetanus injections; 'A' was blood group and the 'C' represented the Catholic faith.

Seeking information about the circumstances of his death, we returned the dog-tag to the USAF and later received an accident report. From this and subsequent research, I compiled an account of Richard Curran's final flight.

Lieutenant Richard Curran was navigator on B-17G-25-DL, serial *42-38053*, from the 349th Squadron, 100th Bombardment Group — the 'Bloody Hundredth' — based at Thorpe Abbotts near Diss in Norfolk. He and his crew had accumulated over twenty missions by Sunday 7 May 1944. Not all who clambered on board the B-17 had achieved the same number of operations because injuries, illness and furlough could put members of the same crew out of sequence. Tail-gunner, Jack Willburn, was flying his 21st raid but he barely knew one of the waist gunners flying with them. Their regular man was wounded and Staff Sergeant Randolph C. Moore replaced him. Jack never got to know the new gunner but events meant that he would never forget him.

Above *The second memorial at Ashby St Mary.*

Below *Richard Curran's dog tag was found, still lying on the surface 24 years later.*

The day was but six hours old as pilot, Lieutenant Ralph W. Wright, and co-pilot, Jack W. Raper, lifted the B-17 off the runway to join the other Fortresses from their group. On take-off, the tail and waist gunners gathered in the radio room for safety and better weight distribution. Few words were exchanged: the pounding of four struggling Cyclones and their own inner anxieties stifled chatter. Unexpressed relief relaxed the tension as they unstuck, the gear rumbled reassuringly home and the

A picture taken when training in the USA. Standing: L-R: J. Bernard Palmquist; Robert Monto-nado; Pat Madsen; Jack Willburn; Geo McCleary. Kneeling: L-R: Ralph Wright; Jack Raper; Carl Hermann; Richard Curran (J. Bernard Palmquist).

bomber eased steadily upwards. Leaving the radio room, the gunners dispersed to their stations. For Jack, this meant a stooped shuffle aft, swaying to balance as the Fortress gained altitude. His lonely post was 52 ft from the cockpit: he knelt, facing aft, half sitting on a small, padded saddle between two ammunition boxes. Part North American Indian, Jack was small enough to be reasonably comfortable but Berlin was a long way as he connected his heated suit, oxygen supply and checked with

Ralph Wright on the intercom. It was a beautiful spring morning, not a war day, and Jack would have been happier hunting in the hills around his Californian home of Willits. Today, his guns were government issue: California was yesterday's life and tomorrow might not happen.

Undulating through propeller-chewed air, their Fortress and her sisters circled and climbed over Thorpe Abbots, building their mutually protective formation. Plans called for the 100th to fly

Lead Group of the 13th Combat Wing. Seventeen such formations meant that over 900 bombers were bound for Germany. Like Jack, others completed early mission tasks and tried to get comfortable. In the top turret, Technical Sergeant Alden P. Madsen was checking the hydraulic power unit and gun controls. During take-off, he had call-checked airspeed for Wright and monitored fuel gauges during the initial climb. Now, from the dome of his turret, proud of the B-17's back, he had a splendid view of the countryside and the beachy East Anglian coastline. It was 7.00am as the bombers climbed east, into the sun's fresh brilliance. Wright and Raper squinted against needles of light dancing from waves and flashing harshly from the polished perspex of bombers ahead. The sun hurt Pat Madsen's eyes — pressing the power grips of his turret, he hummed round, contented himself that it worked, and swung to face the relief from long shadowed countryside nearly 20,000 ft below.

At that instant, there was a brilliant flash and a second, fiery sun erupted on board the B-17. Stored close to the top turret, it seemed one of the signal flares had exploded, igniting the others. Startled, Pat grabbed for the Co2 extinguisher. In seconds, it was too late, the ferocious, oxygen-fed flames drove him back, beating frantically with the lid off a nearby container.

Moments after the explosion, Wright banked out of formation and headed down, both pilots struggling to see from the smoke-filled cockpit. Radio operator, Technical Sergeant Robert Montonado hurried out a Mayday signal before being driven from his compartment by flames surging out of the rear cockpit section. The B-17 was doomed and Wright rang the bale-out alarm.

Jack Raper stayed, helping fight for control as the crew baled out. All Pat could discern were two forms amid the smoke — the Fortress fell nauseatingly but he managed to pass a parachute to his pilot. Wright would be last to leave and needed every second.

Trapped in the bomber's nose were Richard Curran and Lieutenant Carl A. Hermann, the bombardier. Their exit route meant crawling below the burning flight deck and jumping from the forward hatch. Difficult enough in level flight, frightening in a Fortress twisting earthwards, they ran a gauntlet of flames and searing heat along their escape route. 70 ft aft, Jack Willburn had not, at first, realized that anything was wrong. Little conversation occurred during assembly, the crew were too busy. Over the sea, Wright told him to test fire his guns and the B-17 continued climbing. Next, Jack heard the pilot's urgent command, 'Bale out, bale out, Go!' and the alarm clammered as the aircraft sagged, then fell, faster and faster.

Smoke streamed past Jack's window: he thought the engines were ablaze, but the rear fuselage suddenly filled with acrid, blinding smoke. Snatching his parachute, Jack hastily clipped it on, tugging to feel it was secure as he groped for the small escape hatch below the right stabilizer. Jerking the lever upwards released its hinge pins and the door fell free, according to the training manual. Fumbling for the release, Jack tugged. Nothing happened. Cursing and scared, he kicked furiously at the panel but there was no blast of air or glimpse of freedom, only dark, choking smoke. Blindly, Jack crawled forwards, his senses saying that the falling bomber was going out of control. He had to reach the waist exit but was pinned against fuselage ribbing: 15 ft, over the tail wheel well, towards the exit, felt like fifteen miles. Inch by inch, grasping every fuselage stiffener, Jack fought to survive. In his mind, he wondered how his Mom would feel receiving that ghastly telegram: he had to get out.

Stretching and heaving, Jack reached the exit. It was blocked. Straddled across the opening was Randolph Moore, his parachute streamed outside pinning him helplessly across the doorway. Struggling in semi-darkness to attach it, he must have pulled the 'D' ring prematurely and been sucked across the hatchway, unable to move in or out. Jack tried to help, he really tried. Moore seemed unconscious, jammed in the opening. As the B-17 fell, Jack risked his life straining to free the man he did not know. It was futile. Jack had no choice. The next few moments were his lifetime's nightmares. To escape, Jack crawled over Moore's wedged body. Squeezing free, he tugged the red 'D' ring and the life-giving folds functioned perfectly.

Floating down, Jack saw his B-17 complete two more spirals to explode in some trees, pulsing a blast of hot air skywards, catching him in its path. He surged upwards, terrified his 'chute might collapse but helpless until the draught expended itself. Slowly, his descent resumed and he drifted easily into woodland near the pyre created by his bomber. A civilian appeared and Jack appreciated the man's kindness as he helped the shaking flier discard his parachute. Amazingly, Jack had no burns or broken bones, only bruises — it was too soon for the hurtful, haunting memories that later plagued him. He needed a drink and the helpful stranger took him home to a well-stocked wine cellar. Despite the early hour, Staff Sergeant J.S. Willburn was drunk when they collected him: he had survived.

So had Staff Sergeants J.A. Pontzious, ball turret gunner; Al Bridges, left waist, and Robert Montonado from his radio room. Pontzious had a fractured leg but luckiest of all was Pat Madsen, the last man to jump. Painfully burned, Pat had retreated from the flight deck, groping along the narrow catwalk across the bomb bay. Through the swirling smoke, the shadowy shapes of 500 lb bombs threatened villages below but he could do no more. Pat reached the waist exit still blocked by Moore's body. It was too late to help and he struggled past towards the tail hatch unaware that the release had malfunctioned. Luck was with him, he had no problem and escaped moments before the B-17 scythed into trees and exploded.

Moore's misfortune was seen by others also powerless to help. At Beech Farm, Miss Ivy Prettyman watched the plane descend with, 'something hanging from the back'. Others nearer the scene felt their homes shake as part of the bomb load exploded and a shower of blackened, charred leaves later floated into their gardens. At Herringfleet Hall, Lady Jackson, her family and staff, were fortunate when seven 500 lb bombs tossed from the wreck failed to detonate. Two smashed through the kitchen wall, demolished a section of greenhouse, and landed near the hall itself. Police, Army and American personnel cordoned off the area to deal with the ordnance while a vain search for survivors advanced through the woodland.

Ralph Wright and Jack Raper were never identified, they share a grave in the Cambridge American Cemetery and Memorial. The survivors returned to duty, Jack Willburn finished his missions and went home to lumberjack in the woodlands of Northern California. His emotional scars will never heal: not all

Above *Soldiers clear debris at Herringfleet. Surviving trees still carry scars (100 BG Museum).*

Right *Ralph Wright and Jack Raper share a grave in the Cambridge American Military Cemetery and Memorial at Coton, Cambridgeshire.*

the victims died.

Seven years after we found Richard Curran's dog-tag, the Norfolk and Suffolk Aviation Museum searched the site for items to exhibit. Numerous detector readings occurred as they located fragments of engines, airframe, instruments and, more poignantly, pieces of leather, flying clothing and the remains of an airman's goggles. On 3 August 1975, they discovered a wedding ring inscribed, 'Elizabeth to Jack 11.4.43.' This sad reminder of a brave co-pilot was handed to the police and, as landowner, Lord Somerleyton received a letter of appreciation from the headquarters of the USAF in Washington. The loss of this B-17 is part of the Somerleyton Estate's history.

Perhaps the prettiest feature of the Somerleyton Estate is Fritton Lake, a beautiful, two-mile stretch of water set amid gentle countryside and, nowadays, attracting thousands of visitors to its country park. As they row, sail or fish peacefully in these picturesque surroundings, few realize that the war intruded even here. In 1940, wire hawsers stretched across the lake to deter enemy seaplanes. By 1942, the threat of invasion was changing hands and the lake was requisitioned to train amphibious tank crews. Rumours persist that less-than-amphibious specimens still rest on the lake bed. This may be, but what attracted me was the recorded fact that two P-47 Thunderbolts had crashed into the lake. How exciting it would be to retrieve them! The names of their pilots were on the Ashby stone: Lieutenant Russell P. Judd and Flight Officer Louis S. Davis, III.

Investigating their deaths revealed a little-credited feature of USAAF activities, one which saved many lives — Air Sea Rescue. When the Americans first flew to war, they lacked equipment, expertise and the organization for rescuing airmen from the sea. The small, domestic, pre-war Army Air Corps had little need for this facility and rapid, wartime expansion focused on mainstream activities. Fortunately, the British, fighting from their island since 1939, had considerable experience and immediately made available both operational and training resources to their bold new partners. Necessary and welcome though this was, the Americans quickly realized the importance of augmenting ASR with features tailored to their needs, without duplicating the efficient

service provided by the RAF and the Royal Navy. The anguish of developing ASR falls outside the scope of this book but many grandfathers today are not named on memorials because of the dedication of men like Judd, Davis and numerous others who risked their lives snatching airmen from the life-sapping sea. However, to appreciate what these pilots were doing on that fatal Sunday, so near war's end, we do need to understand ASR techniques at the time.

Understandably, airmen feared the sea and efficient ASR helped morale. What happened when a lonely, frightened young pilot, his engine running rough, pushed button 'B' on his radio and transmitted, 'Mayday, Mayday, Mayday — Carpet 24, one, two, three, four, five . . . five, four, three, two, one'? Carpet 24 is his callsign; the reason for counting 1 to 5 and back was to give rescuers a 'fix' on his position. This was achieved by constant monitoring of the distress frequency, 66.50 megacycles, at widely dispersed, coastal Radio Direction Finding Stations (RDFS). Indiligence on their part might mean the words they heard were the airman's last. Time was life, rapid response imperative. Where was he? On receipt of a signal, each RDFS rotated its aerial to point in the direction from which the transmission sounded strongest. The RDFS each took a compass bearing on the transmission and this was telephoned, on a 'hot line', to the Triangulation Room at the ASR Control Centre, HQ 65th Fighter Wing, in Saffron Walden. The meaning 'triangulation room' becomes clear when what happened to the incoming signal bearing is understood. Centrepiece of the room was a large, circular table, graded with 360 degrees of the compass and superimposed upon a gridded map of the southern North Sea and coastlines. Around the table were men wearing headphones, each holding a string, one end of which was pinned at the location of the RDFS they represented. Responding to instructions from his RDFS, each man aligned this string to represent the direction of broadcast and these imaginary lines stretched out over the North Sea. Where they crossed, a triangle was formed, fixing the position of our lonely pilot. The size of triangle classified the quality of 'fix' and the position was grease-pencilled on the map. This process took about twenty seconds and the flier receives reassurance that he is in capable hands as the duty controller quickly calculates the best course to steer.

Now our pilot is spluttering in the right direction: he may make it, he might go down. The hands of ASR reached to close the gap. Responsibility for this rested with the Duty Control officer (DC), in an ASR Control Booth near the triangulation room but overlooking the main Operations table at 65th Fighter Wing HQ. Preceding any mission, the DC and his Liaison Sergeant checked flight times and routes on the ASR Control Table, a smaller representation of the Operations table, merged with features from the triangulation room map. The DC notified surface vessels of required patrol areas and took similar action with the 5th Emergency Rescue Squadron at Halesworth. Serving with the 5th ERS were Judd and Davis: the part they played will be explained shortly. Other DC duties entailed clearing ASR flights with friendly defences, alerting the D/F Stations and co-ordinating with RAF operations.

The heading broadcast to a distressed aircraft came from the DC. As soon as the plotter registered the fix on his map,

the DC, using a mechanical Craig computer, quickly calculated not only the course given to the crippled aircraft but vectored the nearest launch or amphibious aircraft and 5th ERS spotter patrol to rendezvous.

Callsigned 'Teamwork', pairs of 5th ERS P-47s patrolled mission routes until summoned to a lame duck like, 'Carpet 24'. If he only required escort, they could shepherd him home but, if he jumped or ditched, they carried dinghies and could orbit for a better fix. One P-47 climbed to transmit while the other buzzed encouragingly around the survivor, ready to smoke mark when help appeared. If necessary, both aircraft protected rescue activities — the equipment and origins of these fighters form part of the story leading to the collision over Fritton Lake.

The 5th ERS was an unusual outfit in the Eighth Air Force, a Cinderella, born overseas from operational needs. To exist officially, a unit needed a 'Table of Organization' and such fundamentals stemmed from Washington swathed in red tape which, hopefully, unravelled into a fully-funded unit, recognized by the parent, military bureaucracy. Without a 'TO', the 5th ERS emerged on the wrong side of the blanket but impatient Eighth Air Force leaders needed action and created 'Detachment B, Flight Section, HQ, 65th Fighter Wing' — later sanctioned the 5th ERS. Command of this hybrid they gave to 23-year-old Captain Robert Gerhart, an experienced fighter controller with the tenacity needed to be effective. Gerhart had about ninety enlisted men detached from sixteen different stations; 25 pilots and ground officers were also temporarily assigned. Material for the foundling — trucks, tyres, typewriters — everything — was scrounged from other units.

Even the aircraft were offcasts, a motley collection of retired P-47 Thunderbolts officially declared 'War Weary' and branded such by 'WW' suffixed in yellow on their serial numbers. These letters declared them obsolete, unwanted, but, from their first sortie in May 1944, many fliers were relieved to welcome these 'unwanted' veterans.

Nurturing the 5th ERS during development and providing airfield facilities was the famous 56th Fighter Group. Robert Gerhart was indebted to its CO, Colonel Hubert Zemke, for advice and support before the 5th transferred from Boxted to Halesworth. Like the 5th, the 56th stuck loyally to their beloved Thunderbolts despite the Mustang's longer range but they had the benefit of top-line, operational machines. Gerhart may have preferred the P-51 but it was in such demand he had no choice but to adapt P-47s, not so much beloved but bedevilled. His first task was to modify this collection of 'clunks' for ASR duties. To extend their range, he required drop tanks as well as the ability to externally mount and drop dinghies for survivors. Surface vessels might not see a tiny dinghy in heavy seas so smoke marker bombs were necessary. Escorting cripples or protecting rescue operations meant leaving the P-47s armed but machine guns were heavy. Configuring a worn fighter for all this was like loading a dying donkey and the first take-off was pitiful. Laden with a 108-gallon drop tank and four smoke marker bombs under each wing, plus a twin dinghy pack on fuselage pylons, the poor P-47 wheezed down the runway. An apprehensive pilot pushed for more power from his exhausted nag, she responded by blowing a cylinder and a very subdued airman emerged from the crash. Investigating the reluctance to fly

revealed the primary factor to be the smoke bombs creating a flaps down effect at all speeds. Compromise was necessary and the squadron's engineering section eventually found a solution. The British 'M' type double dinghy pack was split, putting one under each wing and one, 150-gallon drop tank below the fuselage, with smoke markers behind it. Initially, two machine-guns were removed but diminishing enemy strength eventually enabled a reduction to only four guns. Tests proved the adapted P-47 performed satisfactorily. Endorsing their success, the 5th proudly decorated their veterans with distinctive markings which we found on wreckage nearly three decades later. Engine cowlings were highlighted with broad red, white and blue bands, wingtips painted bright yellow and yellow bands flourished on the empennage and tail surfaces. Most aircraft carried on their cowlings a bird motif peering through a telescope to indicate the spotter's function. Some P-47s retained nicknames from former units, others got personalized nose art in the 5th. Official markings were the unit's code letters, '5F' in white on the fuselage with national insignia followed by the individual call letter. A large star-and-bar was repeated on upper and lower mainplanes while standard olive drab and grey adorned all but one aircraft.

From unsteady beginnings, the squadron's achievements grew, aiding airmen who thrust the stake into the evil heart of Hitler's Reich. During early 1945 ASR was averaging 145 homings a month and 21 ditchings or bale outs. By April, the P-47s were bolstered by OA-10 Catalinas and B-17s converted to carry airborne lifeboats. Operations supported on the 8th of that month were attacks on marshalling yards and airfields. Defeat for

Above *This fine study clearly shows 5th ERS markings and equipment carried on their Thunderbolts (USAF).*

Right *Flight Officer Louis S. Davis, III (L.S. Davis II).*

Germany was imminent and airmen thought increasingly of home. Russell Judd had fought with the 356th Fighter Group so the important but less hazardous ASR role increased his chances of returning to his wife, Lillie, and Kentucky's blue grass. That Sunday, he was listed to lead Flight Officer Davis on a routine spotter sortie. Davis, also a southerner, from Athens, Georgia, had barely a quarter of Judd's 1,200 flying hours and was only assigned to the 5th ERS in March so he was anxious for experience. At twenty-years-old, he had an elder brother whose B-17 had been shot down: therefore he recognized how vital his task was even if it lacked premier unit status. Lieutenant Judd might be able to teach him some tactics, if they had time.

It was late morning when the two P-47s taxied out, Judd leading in *Lady Lorelei*, 42-74705, 5F-O, one of the Squadron's original aircraft. Davis was flying *Big Dick II*, 42-76175 coded 5F-D — the similarity in fuselage codes caused problems twenty-six years later. The patrol was uneventful and, near lunchtime, they headed for Halesworth. There was no hurry, plenty of time to work up an appetite with some mock combat and Davis welcomed the chance. Below the two Thunderbolts stretched a cloud layer but it had enough holes not to worry them and the sky above was empty. Powering on, they began a spirited dogfight, engines snarling aggressively in a traditional tail chase.

The sound was noticed by the Peek family having Sunday dinner in their cottage near the lake but aircraft were an everyday occurrence and attracted little attention. Suddenly, there was an alarming change in tone, the engines screeched lower, closer — a terrific crash, then silence. Thirteen-year-old Nevil Colman saw the two fighters playing: they seemed to touch, almost harmlessly, then fall. Losing them momentarily, he caught sight as they plummeted behind the tree line. He winced expecting explosions, but the earth swallowed them silently, nothing happened: only later did he realize they had vanished into Fritton Lake.

Racing to the water's edge, soldiers stationed at Fritton glimpsed wreckage hissing and steaming as it sank. Spreading rapidly across the water were patches of burning fuel and heat, shimmering skywards, blurred the far bank. A few minutes later, Police Sergeant Allison, with three constables and the crew of an Army launch, sped across the water. Reaching the scene, they cut throttle, staring hopelessly at the shrinking flames. Unburnt oil slicked shinily on the water, smearing the launch as it circled cautiously. Hanging in the still air was the stench of high octane fuel and they scraped warily over submerged wreckage but saw no life. Puzzling to the soldiers was the appearance of two bright yellow dinghies, sadly unoccupied.

A call to the Flying Control Centre established that two P-47s were missing from Halesworth. Soldiers and police searched woodland around the lake in case the pilots had jumped but, at only 1,000 ft, the chances were slim and faded in the ensuing dusk. Next morning, personnel from the 5th ERS began the unhappy task of retrieving the bodies. It took nine days to recover Lieutenant Judd and the body of Flight Officer Davis was not found until 7 May, the day before VE Day.

Six months later, in November 1945, the Lowestoft Journal related how members of 469 Squadron, Air Training Corps, sounded the Last Post for those named on the Ashby Memorial. The occasion was a dedication service in Ashby St Mary when Group Captain P. Dunn DFC, AFC, unveiled the tablet. Included in the congregation were Phyliss, Lady Somerleyton: Lord and Lady Somerleyton, local people, and servicemen from British and American forces, men whose own recent experiences were slipping into history, like the losses they commemorated.

Perusing old newspapers provided some information when I began my research. Convinced that two sunken fighters still lay in Fritton Lake, I envisaged almost intact Thunderbolts being lifted ashore. Easier imagined than actioned but chance then put me in touch with the RAF Sub-Aqua Club from Coltishall. Squadron Leader George Taylor was enthusiastic and Lord Somerleyton permitted diving to start on 20 June 1971. Records said the aircraft had crashed off Lake Cottage, near the eastern end and, as the cottage was empty, we were allowed to use its jetty and outhouses for storage if anything was found. To me, that was a nervous 'if' because some reports claimed removal of both aircraft had already occurred — there was only one way to find out!

While divers donned wetsuits, weight belts and bottles, I worried whether the whole exercise was pointless and felt worse when they grumbled about hours wasted the previous week fruitlessly seeking a Spitfire in Barton Broad. Corporal

Brian Ranner was more concerned whether the gas from last night's Guinness would let him sink or not! Jumping from the jetty, they lay cheerfully in the chilly water while, trying to sound confident, I guessed at the direction and distance to submerge. Swimming out in pairs, they reached where I calculated and vanished. Moments later, Leading Aircraftsman Peter Stuckey surfaced, took out his mouthpiece and yelled triumphantly, he had dropped straight on to a torn off tailplane, visible nearby was a jettisoned cockpit canopy. I was ecstatic. Minutes later, our trophies were ashore along with several eels, unhappy over their eviction from the tailplane. No doubt about it, the broad, yellow band was clearly visible — both items lay 12 ft down in a sandy, weed-free area about 70 yards off Lake Cottage boat-

Ken Kelly rows while two divers help pull flotation-bagged wreckage ashore.

A well preserved instrument from the sunken fighter (RAF Coltishall).

house. Visibility was good and, sinking gently to the bottom, divers reported mounds of silt, each concealing pieces of wreckage. Further out, the sand sloped into a strip of deep mud, nearby lay a twisted propeller blade, part of which curled from the lakebed like a sunken tombstone. Had we located one fighter, or the intermingled remains of both?

Unfortunately, such clear conditions were never repeated, the following week it was like swimming in an inkpot with dense algae cutting out the light. Walter Mussett, Lord Somerleyton's Park Manager, lent us a rowing boat to save swimming from the jetty but everything found was by touch. Torchlight increased visibility but it was still less than arm's length as divers groped gently along the lakebed, fearful of disturbing clouds of blinding sediment by their movements. Marking wreckage with polystyrene floats indicated concentrations of debris but my hopes of finding a semi-complete P-47 faded, along with plans to use a 'Jolly Green Giant' helicopter offered by the 67th

Aerospace Rescue and Recovery Squadron, successors to the 5th ERS. Junior Technician, Ken Kelly, cheered me up when he surfaced to announce in his delightful Geordie dialect that he was sitting on a wing and needed help.

He and Pete Stuckey disappeared with more flotation bags: a froth of bubbles said something was happening. Three bags emerged indicating that the wing was free to pull to shallow water, an exhausting task for one pair of oars even with divers playing tugboats. Eventually, we dragged it clear to confirm the badly-smashed remains of a starboard wing, minus guns, ammunition and undercarriage, all ripped out by impact. To do such damage, it must have crashed at terrific speed. There was no evidence to identify which aircraft. Out on the lake again, I examined smaller pieces popped over the gunwale by busy divers. I noted every part number before we rowed ashore to unload and identified some pieces unseen, such as the description of a large, circular item with fins radiating from the centre: this was the supercharger mounted in the rear fuselage.

This required three flotation bags before it broke free of the mud to be dragged ashore and huskied to the storage shed on a homemade sledge. Hardly had we unloaded when the whine of a diving, piston-engined fighter was heard and sore shoulders vanished in our rush along the rickety jetty. A Spitfire roared low overhead, banked steeply and swept in for another pass. Squadron Leader Taylor was then CO of the Battle of Britain Memorial Flight and, returning from an airshow, he diverted to salute the two pilots who perished in Fritton Lake. As the Merlin's nostalgic notes faded in the evening sky, I felt the gesture would have been appreciated.

On 3 July our harvest of debris continued, several chunks of fuselage emerged, some bearing parts of the code letters but, infuriatingly, I could only piece together 5F — and half an 'O' or a 'D'. This frustration continued the following week: nothing we found conclusively identified our machine, but no parts were duplicated meaning that we had only one aircraft. Visibility remained poor but we retrieved two more Curtiss-Electric propeller blades, both engine oil coolers and a bent machine-gun containing a live round in the breech. Pottery and picnic litter proved fascinating, a bottle collector's paradise, but Codd bottles contributed nothing to aircraft identification.

Interest in our activities attracted the media so we were joined by a BBC film crew on 17 July. Eyewitness, Billy Belcher, recounted events and gestured where he thought the second P-47 had plunged because he remembered reeds burning on the opposite shore. Demoralizingly, he said it had been removed and a search yielded only two pieces of aluminium but these might easily have strayed from the scattering of our wreck. To ensure action for the camera, we selected pieces to put back and 'discover' with great, artificial excitement. The cameras departed and we had real excitement when a diver, handwalking along the bottom, groped across a seemingly intact, port wing. This lay further along from the boathouse, indicating the aircraft had been heading west and probably impacted starboard wing first, cartwheeled and disintegrated leaving a trail of debris 400 yards long. How would this prize be lifted and brought ashore? Perhaps we needed the chopper after all. Working in darkness, 17 ft down, divers scraped off the silt and found points to attach all the flotation bags we had. These they filled by removing their mouthpieces and releasing oxygen into the bags but care was essential to avoid the wing shifting suddenly and catching a diver unable to breathe. Co-ordinating this in darkness was risky, but they managed and over 20 ft of mainplane rose steadily to the surface breaking through, wingtip high, in an eerie gesture to its element.

Rowing it ashore proved impossible but Lord Somerleyton generously rode to the rescue in his speedboat which was harnessed to aid the oarsmen. Slowly, this strange procession eased shorewards, divers bobbing in attendance until we beached it alongside the jetty, water streaming from hatches and holes alike. Resplendent on the upper surface was the famous star-and-bar insignia, glistening proudly after all its dark years. We were delighted, but not so pleased, again, were the numerous eels writhing inside when the ammunition access panel was opened. They had nestled happily on some 300 bullets and did not want to leave. Removing eels, ordnance and silt lightened the task of dragging it ashore. Disappointing was the absence

Lord Somerleyton provides assistance to recover the wing.

of guns and undercarriage, again ripped out on impact — the mainspar was also broken but the outer section was almost intact, a superb find. Various part numbers and inspectors' stamps were apparent, even the pencilled comment, 'Sold 10.6.43 Anno' on the wingroot. Would these clues identify the aircraft?

A list of part numbers was despatched to Fairchild-Hiller who had taken over the original manufacturers, Republic Aviation, and they helpfully checked each one but the evidence was confusing. The gun cover assembly was number 1019 of its type and pointed to P-47D-6RE, number *42-74705*, Judd's aircraft, the 941st built circa July 1943. Remembering that American civilians write their dates opposite to the British, the date on the wing meant October 6 1943, which indicated *42-76175*, Davis' machine a P-47D-15RE, delivered in November 1943. During World War 2,

the American military frequently short-formed dates like the British, so '10.6.43' could also mean June. Other part numbers leant towards Judd's fighter but the cockpit canopy had a modified release mechanism fitted to later P-47s, the same model flown by Davis. I was perplexed. Hopefully, proof would still appear but time was short, the divers had devoted several weekends and faced other commitments.

At the end of July, they tried again but weather and diving conditions were appalling, visibility zero. Brian Ranner was groping at arm's length in soft, glutinous mud when he touched a substantial piece of wreckage. Feeling carefully over it, he could discern circular dials, the overall shape was like an instrument panel and bulkhead which carried a callsign plate. Positive identification! Too heavy to lift, Brian needed to mark it but had lost his last float so he surfaced and tried to reference himself before returning to tag it. We never found that panel: even drifting a few feet lost it completely. Diving petered out in August so I had to be content with our discoveries even though the exact aircraft remained a mystery.

That September, items found were exhibited at Coltishall on Battle of Britain Day. I had removed the good outer section of port wing and, after display, this was donated to the USAF Museum. Other items went to regional museums including one which existed at Fritton Lake. Now, at least, the 5th ERS and

its two pilots were more widely recognized, but lack of identification continued to irritate the historian in me.

Five years elapsed until August 1976 brought the opportunity to try again using high technology. Durrant Diving Ltd and Techmation Ltd, both involved in North Sea oil operations, kindly lent personnel and side scan sonar to assist in locating more wreckage and search for the missing second aircraft. Success was limited because sonar signals could not penetrate deeply into the mud and detect buried wreckage. More pieces were found on the lake bed and diver

The P-47's outer wing section is now displayed in the USAF Museum at Wright Patterson AFB in Dayton, Ohio, USA (USAF Museum).

P-47 WING SECTION

ON APRIL 8, 1945, TWO P-47D AIRPLANES OF THE 5th EMERGENCY RESCUE SQUADRON BASED AT HALESWORTH, ENGLAND, COLLIDED IN MIDAIR AND CRASHED INTO FRITTON LAKE NEAR LOWESTOFT, KILLING BOTH PILOTS, 1st RUSSELL P. JUDD AND FLIGHT OFFICER LOUIS S. DAVID III.

ON JUNE 20, 1971, MEMBERS OF THE SUB AQUA CLUB FROM THE RAF BASE AT COLTISHALL RECOVERED FROM 12 FEET OF WATER NUMEROUS PARTS OF ONE OF THE P-47s THAT HAD CRASHED INTO THE LAKE 26 YEARS EARLIER. ONE OF THESE PIECES IS THE WING SECTION ON DISPLAY.

DONATED BY THE SUB AQUA CLUB, COLTISHALL RAF BASE, ENGLAND

Above *August 1976. Side-scan sonar detected the P-47's propeller boss.*

Below *May 1988. Ray Jacobs holds a piece of the spent ammunition ejector system. The East Anglian British Sub Aqua Club plan to use a magnetometer in the hunt for the second P-47.*

Peter Snowling, playing retriever, recovered the propeller boss and further fuselage fragments but no serial number.

Career development took me off scene for several years during which period, Ray Jacobs of the East Anglian British Sub Aqua Club, organized sporadic dives to interest and train club members. Several pieces of tri-coloured cowling were found along with scattered bullets and machine-gun feed tracks. A small, electric generator was dried out and functioned perfectly, but the engine, undercarriage and instrument panel eluded them. No identification appeared, nor was there a trace of the other aircraft. A report, now in my possession, indicates it is still there, an underwater magnetometer is available, the search continues...

Lieutenant Russell P. Judd served with the RAF and then the USAAF 356FG before joining the 5th ERS. Remains of his aircraft still rest in Fritton Lake (Paul J. Trudeau).

APHRODITE

6

As planned, the ageing 'Baby' eased carefully from the runway on its last flight. From above, its white wings contrasted sharply with the verdant countryside and another B-17 appeared to guide the condemned aircraft. Top secret, Project Aphrodite's first attack began.

Over three decades later, the remains of that Baby were discovered, buried in a Suffolk woodland. Investigations by a policeman revealed the secrecy surrounding its death. Off duty, Stewart P. Evans was an experienced aviation historian and credit for unravelling the story and recovering evidence is his. My early involvement was simply that of an extra navvy on one of the toughest digs we tackled but, in 1985, Stewart gave me his material to relate the excavations of 'Baby Eight'. In the roots of that strange dig lie America's early efforts at missile development in response to German, V-weapon supremacy. Ironically, American, post-war achievements owe much to German science but Project Aphrodite was a technological cul-de-sac, a primitive failure compared to Germany's sophisticated robot weaponry.

The advent of the V-1 emphasized Allied inadequacies and Aphrodite was a rapid response, initiated less than two week after the first Doodlebug attack. The concept involved stripping expendable, war-weary, heavy bombers and incorporating a remote control system. Known as 'Babies', these robots would be crammed with explosives and guided to V-weapon launch sites or other suitable targets. Easy in theory, but numerous problems faced the Eighth Air Force Operational Engineering Section who were given responsibility for developing and testing the technique.

The biggest obstacle was radio controlling an explosive-packed, four-engined bomber safely to its objective. Reassuring to the British, and because radio equipment was prone to malfunction, the flights would not be entirely remote-controlled. Volunteer aircrews were tempted from units of the Third Air Division when they learnt that one Aphrodite mission equalled five standard operations and a Distinguished Flying Cross. Before this, however, Colonel Cass S. Hough and his engineers had to experiment.

USSTAF had suggested that 'Azon' could be adapted for remote control: 'Azon' meant azimuth *only* and was a radio control technique incorporating receivers in special fins, on 1,000 lb bombs for guiding their fall in azimuth. Using two of these Azon units, on separate frequencies, evolved into Double-Azon, a method of remote controlling an aircraft with circuits to the autopilot and radio altimeter thus creating the 'Baby', a robot bomber. Fitting its 'Mother' with Double Azon transmitters kept the controlling aircraft high and comparatively safe while directing the flying bomb below.

Spurred by the increase in V-1 attacks, events moved swiftly to prepare the first Mother and Baby. The latter had tur-

Lieutenant John W. Fisher (H. Stone via G. Ward).

rets removed and fared over, and all unnecessary internal fittings were gutted to reduce weight and increase storage capacity. During the evening of Saturday 24 June 1944, flight trials were carried out from Bovingdon. Colonel Hough and Lieutenant-Colonel Key flew the Baby, with Major Henry J. Rand, as controller, in the Mother. Clouds restricted the Mother's height from a planned 20,000 ft, to only 6,000 ft but results were encouraging: the proposal seemed feasible.

Briefed on the tests, General Doolittle called a meeting the following Monday at 8th AF HQ where he delegated operational implementation to General Earle E. Partridge's Third Air Division. Conversion of a further ten robots was already underway, with plans for up to 65. Additional B-24 aircrew, with three Mother ships, were assigned from the Azon-experienced 458th Bomb Group at Horsham St Faith, near Norwich. Calibration of the Azon system was provided by the 458th and they conducted a test loading of empty nitro starch boxes, a task which took ten hours but resolved stowage queries. Pronounced ready for flight testing, the Babies flew to Bovingdon where the original B-17 Mother and B-24s were joined by an adapted 'Droop Snoot' P-38. Some strange, aerial antics ensued as Aphrodite's airmen commenced training.

Speculating on the future, recruits for Aphrodite had left their units for a project about which they knew little, other than it demanded a 'special mission' and a parachute jump. It was so secret that details were given only on a 'need to know' basis with security being emphasized from the moment they arrived. Amongst early trainees was Lieutenant John W. Fisher, a skilled B-17 pilot from the 96th Bomb Group at Snetterton Heath. During training, he teamed with a tall Technical Sergeant, Elmer Most, an expert on Automatic Flight Control Equipment (AFCE), who had served with the 'Bloody Hundredth' before embarking on the Aphrodite adventure. Other bases also lost airmen to Aphrodite's mysterious embrace, but the reality was far from comforting — who, in his right mind, wants to sit in a flying bomb? True, the stripped B-17s were sprightly once airborne, like energetic pensioners, but their ageing structures held a host of serviceability problems, contributing to the task force's transferral to Honington, home of the 1st Strategic Air Depot. Here, mechanics could minister to their ails and make modifications highlighted during tests.

Quite how the geriatric bombers would behave when loaded was still unknown. Calculations by Boeing and USAAF mathematicians worked on what would happen when a B-17, weighing 64,000 pounds, flying at 300 ft, 175 mph, received a signal pushing elevators full down. Officers at Elveden Hall, the headquarters of the Third Air Division, were concerned that abrupt descent might shake loose the explosives, causing premature detonation, or even structural failure of the bomber itself. Major Ralph Hayes had the dubious distinction of evaluating a sand-laden Baby. He reported no serious handicaps on take-off, acceptable, if sluggish, flight characteristics and, simulating dives, a distance from target of 1,000 ft for transmission of the down signal. Mounting a camera in the Baby's nose would improve guidance but this system, code-named 'Block', was itself being developed and

was unavailable for the first mission, so trials focused on resolving other problems. An early decision changed from single to dual range altimeters because robots had to descend from 2,000 to 300 ft and maintain accurate altitude. Later modifications included the installation of smoke pots and a light in the robot's upper fuselage to help the Mother see its Baby. For now, white paint was hastily applied to upper surfaces.

Even with these aids, Aphrodite tacticians already recognized weather as the major obstacle. In addition, while the goddess was desirable, her namesake was not: the idea of airborne relics, constipated by explosives, found little appeal with even the most patriotic base commander, resulting in a military pass-the-parcel. Plans were laid for launching the attack from Woodbridge, nearer the coast, with support remaining at Honington, but this was impracticable and the ground echelon also departed for Woodbridge. Their reception was again subdued, an attitude readily understood when one realizes that this Suffolk airfield was one of the country's busiest emergency airfields and often witnessed cripples losing control as they landed.

Dispersing bombers packed with 20,000 lb of sensitive ordnance, courted calamity but loading for the first mission began on 7 July. Nine robots had nitrostarch, the tenth would test an early napalm mixture designed to burn and suck oxygen from underground bunkers, asphyxiating the occupants.

On 10 July General Partridge inspected progress with Mr Duncan Sandys, the Joint Parliamentary Secretary to the Ministry of Supply and Chairman of the Committee for Countermeasures Against Pilotless Aircraft.

The British political hierarchy found appealing the idea of retaliatory attacks on robots by robots. This gesture was almost realized two days later but weather predictions were not fulfilled. Aphrodite's exposed position was dramatically highlighted on 13 July when a Ju 88 nightfighter of NJG2, lost and low on fuel, landed intact at Woodbridge. A quick squirt of cannon at the loaded drones would be catastrophic and the thought proved very sobering. Next morning, Woodbridge buzzed with rumours about its late night guest and Aphrodite commanders felt both the practical and security risks at Woodbridge were compromised. The Babies were unloaded, tent pegs pulled, and the top secret travellers moved to an airfield which eventually housed them, and their sister, USN project 'Anvil'.

Their new home was AAF Station 140, Fersfield, near Diss in Norfolk which became a satellite of Knettishall, the nearby base for the 388th Bomb Group, commanded by Colonel William B. David. This unit helped Aphrodite's administration and engineering while keeping a suitable distance from the drones. Fretting for clear weather, planners prepared Mission One.

On numerous occasions, crews were alerted, nerves tautened, only to be stood down after the weather ship returned from its reconnaissance. If it was fine in England, clouds frustrated clear targets and the reverse was also true. CAVU (Clear and Visibility

A scare for the Aphrodite Project. Ju 88G-1 4R+UR of 7/NJG2 landed at Woodbridge on 13 July 1944 (R. Zorn).

Unlimited) conditions were vital for controllers to guide their Babies. These delays dismayed airmen anxious to act and John Fisher felt frustrated. He and Elmer spent hours in their Baby while its controls responded eerily to signals from its Mother. Elmer had finely tuned the C1 Autopilot to translate the most delicate touch from Major Rand. In the intervals, between take-off and landing, Fisher felt redundant, unhappy as a passenger, and others sensed this irritation. Frequently John watched while the B-17 descended, 200 feet-per-minute, to 300 ft without his influence. High above, Rand simulated attacks by dipping the Baby's nose towards dummy targets, sometimes alarming its crew. Their task was to watch for other aircraft and override the altimeter if they got too low. Babies reputedly gathered foliage before a frightened jump crew took over: at least on a real mission they would not be subject to remote control buzz jobs, but bailing out had its own anxieties.

Training for the jump included lectures from a paratrooper on controlling descent and how to land and roll to avoid injuries. For practice, they leapt from flat-bed trucks and Elmer's tall frame tumbling across the turf provided some amusement, but the real thing was scary, even with static lines. Suddenly, on 4 August 1944, a slot of perfect weather appeared, the waiting was over.

'V' weapon sites built near the French coast had been chosen as targets: Watten, Wizernes, Mimoyecques and Siracourt. Controllers had studied target folders, viewed low level films and peered at models from every angle. Security meant separate briefings for each Mother crew and Major Rand chewed thoughtfully on his cigar as measures for success were outlined. Four attacks by two task forces were intended, each with two Babies: Rand's role was to tip one on Siracourt, then collect another for Wizernes. Inside the darkened briefing room, a haze of bluish smoke swirled patterns where it caught in shafts of sunlight gleaming through gaps in the drapes. This contrasted with the azure sky, each cloudless minute confirming the reality of Mission One. Emphasizing the importance of the occasion, Generals Partridge and Doolittle arrived to observe officers detailing each phase of attack. To distract the enemy, RAF Bomber Command was pounding other Noball sites and B-17s would hit targets near Ostend. Both USAAF and RAF fighters would be abroad, ensuring that no German aircraft approached the vulnerable task force, while sixteen P-47s provided close escort. Routes had been carefully chosen to avoid known flak installations but risks had to be accepted on the target approaches.

Jump crews did not attend target briefings. Knowledge of the Baby's destination was irrelevant to men whose sole purpose was to set the AFCE, arm the load and abandon the old warplane.

At 11.21 am a Mosquito radio relay aircraft sped from Fersfield to take up position. Thirty minutes later, a 388th B-17, briefed for similar duties, departed into a cloudless sky. Fersfield's skylarks had an hour of uninterrupted broadcasting but their happiness was hardly noticed. Around both Mothers and Babies, olive-overalled mechanics tinkered last minute adjustments.

It was nearing 1.00 pm when Lieutenant J.A. Woodford pushed the No 3 engine switch on Mother 1, a B24J, serial 44-40283. The whine of the starter shrilled to energization and he activated the mesh trigger, watching through the open window on his right shoulder as the propeller's heavy black blades juddered erratically. A stab of flame burst from the exhaust. Smoke spurted aft as the Twin Wasp fired throatily. Woodford's pilot, Captain Wilfred 'Pappy' Tooman eased the mixture control to auto-rich, settling No 3 to a rhythmic beat as the second engine fired. At 1.00 pm precisely, Tooman took off, followed at one minute intervals by the other three Mother ships. No one heard the skylarks now.

John Fisher watched the jeep hurry away from the dispersal pan and turned to inspect his Baby. Undoubtedly, she had seen better days, the clumsily daubed white paint made him squint until he stepped in the shade beneath the B-17's wing. This was an early, Vega built, 'G' model, serial *42-39835*, and had pounded from Polebrook many times with the 351st BG, whose code, *TU-N*, was fading on the fuselage. Upon her nose was the name *Wantta Spar* but her fighting days were almost over. There seemed little point checking an aircraft you intended dumping, but he needed no failures before he parted with it. Completing a visual inspection, the two-man crew heaved themselves into the warm, gloomy interior.

As their eyes adjusted, both airmen would have been understood for baulking the task ahead — stacked in wooden ranks were box upon box of explosives, over 400 of them! Patterned everywhere was explosive primacord and their Double Azon apparatus had individual charges to prevent even the smallest clue surviving. Mingling with the aroma of aviation fuel was pine fragrance from rough hewn shoring, harnessing each stack. Bracing wires sprouted from joints and vanished into shadows, they hoped the ground crew had not wrapped any around exposed control cables. Stumbling was inadvisable and they squeezed cautiously on to the flight deck or what remained of it. While Fisher settled in his seat, Elmer Most had to contend with a crudely, repositioned navigator's stool, replacing the co-pilot's bulkier chair. The stool's pedestal had been horribly deformed by welding extensions on its rear legs and bolting them to the floor. A piece of 2in x 4in planking, crudely fashioned, gave additional support. A hand grip, fixed to the control console, was something to hold on to but improvisation reeked from the flight deck's appearance. Fisher looked at his watch: time to start engines and pray nothing fell off or got stuck.

Forty-five minutes had elapsed since the Mother ships departed, they were climbing to 20,000 ft over their control points. Fisher and Most watched anxiously as Lieutenant Fain Pool and Staff Sergeant Phil Enterline took off in Baby B1, followed by the two navigational Fortresses. Now it was their turn. Idling the two inboard engines, Fisher smoothly governed power from numbers 1 and 4 to taxi their enormous flying bomb on to Fersfield's main runway. *Wantta Spar* sat a few moments while its crew confirmed all engines were healthy, their gauges and needles read correctly, the tail wheel was straight and locked. Cleared by control, power surged on. Brakes released, *Wantta Spar* strove forwards on her last take-off. Her pilot made it a career best, Baby 8 stroked smoothly from the runway, its cargo resonating sympathetically with vibrations transmitted through the airframe. Retracting the undercarriage, Fisher dabbed brakes to stop the wheels rotating and thought forward from the 1.55 pm take-off through the remaining flight plan.

Right on cue, Lieutenant George C. Montgomery's navigational B-17F, *42-*

Above *Navigational B-17 for Fisher was* Tom Paine *an ex-388th veteran seen here at Beccles (Ellough) in April, 1944, after suffering battle damage* (R. Zorn).

Right *The Automatic Flight Control Equipment (AFCE) panel fitted as standard in B-17s and adapted for use with Project Aphrodite* (S.P. Evans).

30793, slid into view. This olive drab, ex-388th veteran, was symbolically named *Tom Paine* after the American hero, born in nearby Thetford. *Tom Paine* led them to Orfordness where Lieutenant Foster Falkenstine's Mother M2, 18,000 ft overhead, could assume control. The difference in altitude created a relative ground speed variation of some 60 mph and Falkenstine needed flaps, high rpm and skilled flying to maintain position. If he overshot the Baby, or had equipment problems, Lieutenant J. Gabler was on standby in Mother 4, a short distance behind. Avoiding barrage balloons near Orfordness, the drone flew south, towards Felixstowe. Its crew were busy, Most had to trim three gyroscopes in the AFCE to maintain stable flight then ensure the Ace altimeter was set to level off at 300 ft. They would jump at 1,800-2,000 ft after which the Baby would automatically descend to 300 ft when signals bounced from the earth's surface triggered the Ace to flatten out.

Above Felixstowe, the jump crew relinquished control to Major Rand and the Azon specialist guided the Baby towards Sudbury. All systems performed satisfactorily except the Ace altimeter which persisted in reading between 200-300 ft although they were at 2,000 ft. This error would deceive the autopilot into climbing. Nothing Elmer did resolved the problem and their orders were to parachute irrespectively. Nearing Sudbury, Fisher told him to prepare for bale out and Most felt the B-17 turn north-east on the penultimate leg of their flight plan. Both airmen had static-lined, Irving T5 Back Packs with an emergency chest pack. At Stowmarket, the Baby edged into a gentle turn for the coast: its crew would leave at Woodbridge.

Elmer released the hatch, slipstream blasted in and the robot's trim altered slightly — later drones had hatches removed and the exit widened as a result of problems on Mission One. They were almost at Woodbridge. Fisher's task was to see the Baby into a gentle descent, arm the explosives and jump. A clock on the instrument panel, set with a ten-minute delay, primed the electronic fusing when he completed the circuit by inserting two jack plugs in a junction box by the exit. This was half of the dual arming system. The other, more physical approach, entailed jerking out a lanyard, also near the exit, which linked to a series of cables and primed a set of contact fuses carefully distributed throughout the load. Activating the clock, Fisher moved quickly from his seat. Dropping to the lower catwalk, he saw Elmer crouching near the exit, Most had clipped on the static line and was poised to leap.

Elmer hesitated, the hatch space projected a moving image of tiny trees nearly 2,000 ft below, a long way down... There was no choice, he dropped into the void but, halfway through the hatch, his backpack wedged in a recess between the catwalk and hatch rim. Elmer dangled helplessly, his lower torso pummelled by a 175 mph slipstream. Fisher saved his life. Reacting instinctively, the pilot kicked the pack free and Most tumbled away as the Baby nosed alarmingly upwards. Something was seriously wrong. The Baby should be gradually descending, not trying to climb. *Tom Paine* was below the robot's port wing and co-pilot, Lieutenant John F. Scott, had closed in for cameramen to record the jump crew's departure. They saw Most go as the Baby nosed upwards. Fisher failed to appear and the Baby levelled off: he probably had control but his predicament was horrific, could he escape before it stalled and spun in? The faulty altimeter created a steep climb, too steep for the load and power. Nothing could be done. Again, the robot climbed, again it levelled. Major Rand sought desperately for reaction to his down transmission, trying to level the aircraft to give Fisher the chance to jump, but Fisher was on his own, courageously fighting the runaway towards the coast. Momentarily, the rogue calmed, perhaps he would jump before it fell out of control? On board *Tom Paine*, the anguished crew willed Fisher's appearance as the robot, with its imprisoned pilot, reared like a frightened stallion. Then the nose arched steeply upwards, propellers flailling uselessly as weight dragged away airspeed. *Tom Paine* was too close and Scott hauled the navigational B-17 away in a hard left turn as Baby 8 stalled. Sliding sidewards, to its left, the despairing bomber fell to disaster, carrying John Fisher in with its ghastly burden. At 2.31 pm, it exploded in Watling Wood, Sudbourne Park, Suffolk.

The blast was enormous, rolling thunderously for fully twenty seconds in two distinct detonations. *Tom Paine* was lucky, its crew felt a huge push on the underside of their aircraft and tail gunner, John Guirgerich, was dazed by the shock waves, but their fleeing bomber escaped.

Elmer Most felt the explosion but was unaware of what had befallen his pilot. The static line had whiplashed, striking the back of his head, leaving a slight wound to the scalp then, moments later, he braced for landing. Gathering his breath, Elmer realized what had happened but revealed nothing to the curious civilians who found him near Chillesford. To protect Aphrodite, he told the police he was eighth of a nine man crew to bale out. Their Flying Fortress was returning from a raid and the pilot was heading it seawards before parachuting. Prior to his descent, the police had received reports of parachutists and a search found two airmen, the others were thought to have landed in another district. The police were unaware that the second airman, Lieutenant Fain Pool, came from a different bomber. Pool heard the explosion and thought his own robot had crashed but Baby 1 was en route to target. Far above the police search for non-existent airmen Major Rand requested a second Baby and the war continued.

Even further away, Pool's Baby was being steered by the Mother ship for Watten but its mission had failed over England. Staff Sergeant Enterline had not been able to set any down elevator. Frustrated, he was ordered out near Martlesham, followed by Pool whose descent police confused with Fisher's B-17. Enterline's frustration was shared by the Mother crew who reached Watten but got no response trying to dump their unwanted Baby. The backup Mother also failed and a farcical situation ensued with the Baby being paraded around Watten as target practice for its flak batteries. Finally, a hit by coastal guns near Gravelines put all concerned out of their misery.

Two robots gone, one pilot dead, targets unscathed. Hardly encouraging. Major Rand tried again at Wizernes but the only cloud for miles floated over his dump point and the Baby overshot by 700 ft. Last chance for Mission One, Baby 5, nearly succumbed to British AA gunners near Dover. Fortunately, their shooting was on par with their recognition and the robot flew on to Mimoyecques. Nearing the target,

Second Lieutenant Glenn Hargis realized the Baby was too high and his hasty response inadvertently tripped the dump switch. A huge explosion 500 yards short was impressive but unrewarding and the disconsolate airmen headed for Fersfield to assess the operation.

At Station 140, Lieutenant Colonel Roy Forrest USAAF, Commanding Officer of the Army project, watched Foster Falkenstine's B-17 land. It was 6.30 pm, Mission One was over. A jeep collected the Mother crew and they joined other participants waiting to review the day's events with senior officers. The atmosphere was gloomy. Apart from Fisher's loss, two of the jump crew were hospitalized by parachute problems —

the T5 back pack needed modifications; wearing the T3 chest 'chute was cumbersome. Minor injuries occurred because the exit was not wide enough for a large man wearing two parachutes, and opening the hatch induced trim problems. Instructions were issued to remove the door, fit wind deflectors and widen the exit along with a request to the Irving Parachute Company for chute alterations. The list of problems continued: even with high visibility paint, controllers had difficulty seeing the robot: smoke canisters and a bright, red light in the upper fuselage eventually alleviated that problem. Lack of television was a major handicap; four robots on one day was too ambitious; the Ace altimeter definitely required modifica-

The crater was a steep-sided pit, 25 x 31 ft in diameter. Lying at the far end is a section of undercarriage and tyre recovered 31 years later (S.P. Evans/USAF).

The blast from the explosion destroyed trees within a radius of 110 ft from the crater and damaged more beyond (S.P. Evans/USAF).

tions and, fundamentally, Double Azon was inadequate.

The more sophisticated 'Castor' system and the USN's similar, FM control methods superseded Double Azon following another failure on 6 August. In truth, none of the results achieved by remote control met expectations and historians adjudged the programme a failure although the fliers' bravery merits recognition. The fact that Joseph P. Kennedy Jr died in a Navy drone on 12 August ensured greater historical interest in the project. Kennedy's B-24 exploded at 2,000 ft near Blyburgh killing the former ambassador's son and his co-pilot, Wilford 'Bud' Willy. Little of attack value could be gleaned from a mid-air blast but the earlier explosion in Watling Wood might provide knowledge about target damage potential. The day before Kennedy's death, Air Commodore P. Huskinson, President of the Air Armament Board, and Colonel P. Schwartz USSTAF, visited Sudbourne Park. Accompanying them was an ordnance specialist, Dr D.G. Christopherson who wrote a report on the explosion.

The crater in sandy soil was a steep sided pit, 25 ft x 31 ft in diameter containing about three feet of water and surrounded by a secondary, saucer shaped depression approximately 45 ft x 50 ft. Trees suffered total destruction for an average of 110 ft from the main crater's rim, with partial damage extending a further 50 ft and defoliation to 210 ft. Dr Christopherson concluded that the Baby had detonated about 15 ft above ground. Damage to windows and ceilings was appreciable where property lay within 1¼ miles of Watling Wood: minor damage extended over a wide area. Earlier investigations by the USAAF told of total fragmentation of the Baby, the largest pieces extant were chunks of undercarriage, engine remains and a few twisted propeller blades. Of poor Fisher, they found no trace. To his comrades in the 96th, the crater became known as 'Fisher's Lake'.

In 1949 the American Graves Registration Command wrote to the Chief Constable of East Suffolk to establish if Fisher's body had ever been recovered. Police War Reservist W. Green had filed a report on 6 August 1944, saying there was no indication of a crew member crashing with the bomber. Had the

Above *Pete Snowling gropes for a winch attachment point on a heavy piece of hidden wreckage.*

Below *End of a long struggle. Peter Adcock checks progress as the mangled Cyclone is dragged upright during recovery.*

brave pilot been incinerated or would our excavations find his remains for a belated funeral?

On Sunday 23 March 1975, we disturbed the tranquillity of Watling Wood. The intervening years had helped to heal the woodland but such a massive scar would never vanish and we retraced Dr Christopherson's footsteps to see how much had changed. In 1944 the trees destroyed were mostly beech with a few lime and plane: stumps of dead specimens still tombstoned the blast area amid new saplings, mainly silver birch. Around the crater, a young copse had developed and the stagnant pond held the leaf dregs from over thirty autumns. Surveying the site, we realized that it was higher than surrounding woodland and that a natural pond existed lower down: channel to this and we would shift a lot of water thus making the crater more accessible. It worked, water poured from the crater revealing fragments of *Wantta Spar*. Rocker arms; engine valves; gears; peppered pieces of aluminium proved easy pickings but drainage slowed with sludge choking the feed to our ditch.

Dragged from the crater, a squashed oleo leg and section of tyre discarded in 1944.

Wading in, Pete Snowling and I began bucketing out dead foliage while others deepened the gulley. This helped, but the real problem proved to be water in the lower pond levelling to our crater so another trench was cut extending from the pond to a ditch bordering open farmland.

Thousands of gallons gurgled away while we groped in the remaining quagmire. Feeling at arm's length, I touched what I thought was a rubber self-sealing fuel tank but my fingers sensed a tread and the shape of a tyre. Close by, Pete found a section of undercarriage and struggled to attach the winch cable, cutting his hands on hidden shards of metal. Disturbing stagnant water and rotting vegetation stunk, but Pete persisted until he obtained enough grip for Ian Hawkins to wind in a squashed oleo leg. This freed my section of tyre. Using other wreckage underfoot to avoid sinking in the mire, I heaved it to the bank alongside the oleo. Sadly, we reflected on the ravaged appearance of our finds and John Fisher's final flight, the robot taxi-ing out on what was now barely

recognizable as part of its undercarriage.

Our second visit in May 1975 found wading warmer. Busy woodpeckers greeted our arrival but the chatter from our two-stroke pump provided noisy competition. We hoped to simply reopen the drainage scheme to support the pump but this time our enemy proved to be liquified sand flowing from the bank faster than the pump could cope. Peter Adcock found an engine and we concentrated on fighting the sand to expose enough of it for the winch to grip. Behind a makeshift dam, we dug in shifts, pausing only to release those who got stuck. The submerged Cyclone lay almost flat but the stump of a cylinder provided hope for a harness point and Peter looped the chain around it dragging the engine upright. A day was expended removing this pulverized power unit but the story it represented was worth the effort, satisfying our intention of ensuring the death of Lieutenant John W. Fisher was not forgotten.

His remains were not found, he has no grave — the items exhibited at Parham remind visitors of his courage.

BIRD DOG

7

Digging up aircraft can be dangerous. I have already mentioned the risks from ammunition, and anti-tetanus jabs make sense before cavorting in quagmires. When workings are deep, it is wise to monitor cracks developing in the bank and have stepped edges, reducing the risk of collapse. Excavations can become engineering projects, plant hire is expensive and insurance cover may be necessary.

Wreckage readily accessible was usually taken by salvage crews and strenuous efforts made to remove human remains, even if debris was subsequently thrown back. Where no lives were lost and wreckage presented no hazard, why bother retrieving scrap? The attrition of aircraft was recognized and replacements streamed from factories, supported by others returning from repair units. When peace came, the piston-engined warplane had reached the climax of its development and faded into aluminium ingots: jets soared supreme. Three decades later, only the aura remained along with a few isolated examples, some airworthy, others in museums.

What of the airmen? Those who survived had lives to renew, families to raise, memories matured and softened. Some wrote memoirs encouraging an interest in air war history. As one of a post-war generation, I simply thank them for the sacrifice they made to ensure my freedom. To me, those air fleets are as ancient as the Armada. However, unlike formal archaeology, I could contact the past, question airmen, their relatives and eyewitnesses, record a small proportion of stories representing countless examples of courage.

Searching for wreckage in the 1960s needed only enthusiasm and landowner's permission. Growing interest meant that groups formed to share costs and provide a band of skills for research, recovery and preservation. During the 1970s, the Ministry of Defence issued its first 'Notes of Guidance' to recovery groups. These explained the MoD's claim that RAF wrecks remain Crown Property, enemy aircraft were captured property surrendered to the Crown, and the MoD were agents for US Authorities. As related in Chapter 2, consent to excavate was generally forthcoming but in 1979, I was involved in a dig which became a classic. Unfortunately, it resulted in a procedural review within the MoD, the imposition of restrictions leading to licence, even a legal skirmish. The aircraft which caused such controversy 35 years after its demise was a B-24 named *Bird Dog*.

A dozen reasons for subsequent polemics were trollied to *Bird Dog* on her revetment at Attlebridge in the small hours of 13 July 1944. Destined for marshalling yards at Saarbrucken, the twelve olive green 500 lb bombs were winched into position and checked by 466th Bombardment Group armourers. The silver Liberator, a veteran tarnished by combat, sagged with its latest burden. *Bird Dog* had only recently been repaired

Lewd nose-art on Bird Dog *was typical. Armour plate added later covers part of the painting.* (J.H. Woolnough).

and emerged from maintenance to be shuffled from the 784th Squadron, as T9-H, to the 785th, coded 2U-P. Her mission tally exceeded those of the crew to whom she was assigned. This was not unusual, replacement crews often flew older aircraft, even if they had earlier brought a brand new one across the Atlantic.

Second Lieutenant Adam E. Wunderlich and crew commenced training in March 1944, at Gowen AFB, near Boise, Idaho. The syllabus stretched into June when they were entrusted with a factory fresh B-24 at Topeka, Kansas, and ordered to ferry it to Britain. Their route took them to Labrador, across the North Atlantic to Iceland, then south to Wales. Here, their shiny machine vanished to a modification depot while the ten young Americans found them-

selves in Northern Ireland for pre-operational training at a Combat Crew Replacement Centre (CCRC).

Second Lieutenants Robert G. Borst, bombardier, and Milton M. Dobkin, navigator, needed tuition on relevant Eighth Air Force procedures. Wunderlich and co-pilot, Second Lieutenant Russell L. Olson, were taught the latest methods of assembly and RAF flying control disciplines. Staff Sergeant Frank C. Church, radio operator, attended a course on radio equipment and techniques used in the UK. Their engineer, Staff Sergeant Charles E. Thompson, had fewer demands but joined aircraft recognition and gunnery practice with Sergeants Ralph W. Fleming; William C. Myers; Harry R Thomas and William Mallory. Early in July, their theatre indoctrination complete, they left

Ireland for their short stay at Attlebridge.

The 466th welcomed their arrival and quickly slotted them into the 787th Squadron. These were busy days. Since March, the Group had flown 78 missions, many to the toughest targets in Germany. Adam Wunderlich and his crew barely had time to unpack before their first operation, the Group's 79th, to Munich, on 11 July 1944. Flak introduced itself by the violent destruction of bombers and they saw experienced airmen lose this grisly game of chance. Using PFF, bombs were disgorged from the belly of their bomber to fall in the city, they did not see where. Next day, same thing, same place. More Liberators fell, others were seen dragging hopefully towards Switzerland. Two days, two missions, tomorrow was the 13th, again they were scheduled but Robert Borst, at least, would get a break. Orders arrived for him to attend a Dead Reckoning Navigation course for Bombardiers. Changing methods meant the

Crew of Bird Dog. Standing: L-R:- 2/Lt Robert G. Borst, bombadier (not on mission); 2/Lt Milton M. Dobkin, navigator; 2/Lt Adam E. Wunderlich, pilot; 2/Lt Russell L. Olson, co-pilot. Second row: S/Sgt Frank C. Church, radio-operator; Sgt William C. Myers, nose-turret gunner; Sgt Ralph W. Fleming, tail gunner; Sgt William Mallory, ball-turret gunner. Front row: S/Sgt Charles E. Thompson, flight engineer; Sgt Harry R. Thomas, top-turret/waist gunner (R.G. Borst).

bombardier's individual skills were unnecessary on every crew. Bomb release occurred simultaneously with the Lead Crew's bombardier, ships following simply toggled their loads and 'toggliers' needed less training. Many bombardiers were converting to navigators. The crew would tackle Saarbrucken one man short.

Crawling from his cot that morning, Adam Wunderlich cannot have welcomed the mist — not enough to cancel, just enough to make life difficult. Visibility was less than a mile with mist blending horizon into a 10/10 cloud base at 3,000 ft. This enforced a climb out on instruments and some precise pilotage from him and Olson. Overcasts were anathema to airmen especially when 1,000 bombers struggled to assemble in clear skies above. That claustrophobic, groping climb to sunlight held dark terrors of collision, the sweaty fear of vertigo. Wunderlich had only 47 hours instrument flying, mostly on training flights in unladen ships. *Bird Dog*, full of fuel and bombs, would be viciously unforgiving if he lost control. Hitting turbulence from other aircraft could pitch a B-24 into a spin unless its pilots reacted instantly.

To avoid chaos, the Eighth Air Force used many techniques for assembly and the latest had been illustrated at the CCRC in Ireland. Each group had a separate assembly zone with bombers leaving at 45-second intervals on a specific heading for a preset time. Once clear of base, the aircraft turned towards a 'Buncher' radio beacon which transmitted the group's callsign in Morse. On entering the assembly area, each ship flew a reciprocal course using the Buncher signals to hold station as it climbed, hopefully well spaced from those ahead and behind. Breaking free of the overcast, 2nd Air Division units used brightly painted, 'assembly ships' using lights and flares to beckon their flock into formation.

On 13 July the 466th launched 25 aircraft and *Bird Dog* was one of the last to leave at 06.15. Exactly what happened is uncertain. The official report on the loss of *42-95084* states that Wunderlich was on instruments, 'Aircraft went into a spin and crashed. No other information available.' However, 35 years later, we found indications of engine failure and an eyewitness who corroborated this theory.

Farmwork meant an early rise and Mr A. Tovell was milking cows with three other workers at Low Farm, Tunstall, a tiny village east of Norwich. The rattle of pails and morning chatter was undisturbed by the familiar background drone of bombers. Then, cutting into their awareness, they heard a plane in trouble, a loud whining, getting lower, coming closer. Dashing from the cowshed, they searched anxiously skywards, where was it? It seemed frighteningly close, almost on them. Alarmed, unable to hide, they glimpsed its final moments. Spinning from low cloud plummeted a large bomber, one wing ablaze. Diving for cover, they felt the impact as it smashed into the soft, sound-swallowing marshland. Had it happened? An unreal reality transfixed the workmen. Only yards distant, like an alien spacecraft, the fuselage protruded from its grave, steam hissing from hot, sunken engines. Small fires sparkled and flickered in the mist, bright flowers of flame in the grass. Discarded from the wreck lay a twisted propeller: part of the tail unit had been tossed across the meadow while what remained rose heavenwards, like a cross.

Being an ARP Warden, Mr Tovell

hastened to report the crash. Others, approaching the wreck, heard no signs of life — was it empty, had the crew survived? A police constable from Halvergate arrived, followed by some American firemen who hacked through the thin aluminium fuselage skinning. All nine airmen were dead, some bodies were trapped in the submerged nose, three were found near the rear exit but *Bird Dog* had fallen too fast for escape. Boggy terrain prevented heavy equipment reaching the wreck and USAAF personnel spent two weeks removing victims. Mrs Willimott provided lodgings for two guards and remembers being shown a control column cut from the cockpit. *Bird Dog* was chopped apart on site to extricate her crew and they were buried at Cambridge with full military honours.

Tunstall residents knew that the engines had been left. For several years, work horses traversing the site sank knee deep, but improved drainage firmed the surface and the exact whereabouts became indistinguishable.

In February 1977, Kim Collinson initiated our recovery process. Living in nearby Cantley, Kim researched local sites, interviewing eyewitnesses and checking if wreckage remained. The precise location was forgotten but Kim contacted Pete Snowling and they took Pete's magnetometer over the meadow. This does not register aluminium clearly but responds dramatically to ferrous metals and, over *Bird Dog*, the needle slammed against the end stop. Word spread excitedly amongst the digging fraternity but many problems needed to be resolved before the Liberator could be salvaged.

Landowner Mr Robert More expressed understandable reluctance to having heavy machinery traipsing across the meadow but agreed to discuss it with his farm managers. Marsh digs frequently yield superb finds so *Bird Dog* was worth pursuing and negotiations continued. Reference addresses were provided for farmers on whose land we had worked. An offer to rent the site was made but Ron Buxton and Pete Snowling finally reached a legally drafted agreement undertaking to make good damage to land, crops, buildings, livestock etc. Additionally, we would reinstate the marsh, re-seed and erect a stockproof fence around the site. Insurance cover of £1,000,000 was arranged and the recovery team incurred all costs. Mr More would sign on the morning of the dig only if satisfied with our plans and equipment.

Compared to this, consent from the Ministry of Defence was comparatively simple and we hired a Hy-Mac digger for Saturday 6 October 1979. Costs would be spread amongst individuals with extra contributions from local museums. Months of discussion and planning were almost over. Had we known what lurked beneath that innocent meadow, we would not have been so enthusiastic.

To avoid a convoy of cars attracting attention, we met some distance away and shared cars to the site, worrying on our journey whether Mr More would sign the agreement. We met him leading a column of farm machinery near Tunstall Hall and tried to look respectable while documents were exchanged. In the event, Mr More proved helpful and supportive throughout the operation. People prepared to fund the project and behave responsibly were obviously in earnest and he wished us well as the farm contingent squeezed past.

On site, my first task was to photograph the meadow and record its predig appearance. *Bird Dog* had crashed on the edge of the marshes, 30 ft from the nearest dyke. Pete Snowling had aligned the location from the Church of St Peter and St Paul at Tunstall. This forethought proved invaluable for our first problem was that wet grass disturbed detector signals, producing constant, but useless readings. We reverted to basic probing until several solid thuds indicated buried metal. Sun, warming the meadow, drew forth grey wraiths from the marsh, swirling about our ankles and conversation was subdued as we imagined that early morning mist a long time ago.

The snarl of a diesel heralded the mechanical digger lurching through the gate. Beneath the grass, we felt the marsh wobble as it drew nearer. Time to start. Already the aroma of aviation fuel seeped from our probe holes, the smell of a promising dig. Peeling back the first layer of turf, we sighted a heavy black, self-sealing fuel tank and the remains of a wing, less than 4 ft down. Excitement crackled through the group like static discharge. Discovery of a propeller, its two remaining blades in feathered position renewed the charge but we quietened when we realized that feathered blades possibly symbolized the doomed crew.

Had *Bird Dog*, struggling to climb, hidden in cloud, suffered an engine failure and fire? Dangerous moments, desperate actions to avert loss of control: Wunderlich and Olson, inexperienced on instruments, may have faced an overwhelming emergency rather than the tragically simple case of lost control.

At this moment, we had an engine failure ourselves for the digger broke down. Recovery ceased while the mechanically apt in our midst whipped off access panels and a fervent discourse

ensued about fuel feed systems. For an hour, they poked, prodded, undid, adjusted, tightened and tried until, at last, the dumb diesel responded. The broken carcass of a Pratt and Whitney Twin Wasp was dragged from the peat, No 1 engine, followed quickly by No 2 with a bent but unfeathered propeller.

Moving over, we began retrieving items from the forward fuselage. Heavy flak jackets were hauled clear. Made from stout canvas, they had dozens of overlapping steel plates inside and acted like armour to prevent bullet and shrapnel penetration. Two tabs enabled quick release and those found had been discarded as gunners tried to escape. Next emerged an unopened parachute, the first of several, this one still packed with its red rip-cord handle intact. Others were drawn from dark, brown peat in

John Flanagan demonstrates the size of the weighty flak-jacket worn by gunners.

Strips of aluminium foil glisten in the mud. American 'Chaff' (British 'Window') was dispensed from aircraft to upset enemy radar.

streams of white nylon. Laying them to dry, their folds soon billowed, sail like, in the breeze — so clean, so sadly unused.

Each dollop of mud, descending from the bucket, held finds and we strove hard to clear wreckage before the next load. Our plan was to stack and sort later. Countless, small pieces were thrown clear, delicate items gently set aside, large chunks manhandled away. The best method of discovery was to clamber in the mud until your feet contacted metal, then, using one foot as a lever, try to prise it loose, balancing on your spade. Failing this, you dug it out. Suction made movements ponderous, it was filthy but enthralling work. Children of the jet age, we learnt much about equipment and construction of this bygone bomber. A smashed, TU-6-B tuner unit had valves, not transis-

tors, the calibration record card still attached to its battered face. Antique circuit diagrams emerged, not a microchip in sight, as we dragged equipment from Frank Church's radio compartment, moving towards the cockpit.

Spilling from the mud were myriad glistening strips of tinfoil from bundles of chaff intended to deceive Saarbrucken's flak. Bent machine-guns from the top turret, ammunition, chunks of armoured glass and plating. The contents of *Bird Dog* were a jumbled time capsule, a buried inventory of Eighth Air Force equipment. Oxygen masks, flak helmets, throat microphones, instruments — parts from the bomber's systems, later to be catalogued, cleaned and exhibited.

Our workings were 25 ft long, about 15 ft wide and over 6 ft deep. Conditions in the bottom were soggy but lacked a great depth of water so visible wreckage was selected for extraction rather than dragging blindly through. Not everything could be seen: at 12.15 the machine thumped into something solid and part of the bank fell away. Protruding from the side was the nose of a 500 lb bomb! Instantly, I waved the digger to shut down. The silence was deafening as we stared disbelievingly at the offending article. Workers on the fringe of activity sensed something amiss and 'Bomb' was whispered around nervously. Martin Thompson had the misfortune to be nearest so he was 'volunteered' for a closer look. There seemed little doubt but we did not want to summon a Bomb Disposal unit for an oxygen cylinder, or part of the undercarriage. Nervously, Martin slid gently into the crater, picking carefully towards the bomb. At first, he started scraping earth away with his spade but, realizing this might be injudicious, began gently wiping it clean. No doubt now. A frighteningly obscene, 500 pounder, large as death, as unhealthy as the day they loaded it.

Ceasing work, a semi-dignified exit ensued: 200 yards away, we realized we had forgotten Ian Hawkins. Handicapped since he was the victim of an assault, Ian was confined to a wheelchair but his tongue had lost none of its sting and the invectives heaped upon us lightened the atmosphere. We were worried about what would happen: would the authorities clamp down on us? How had the bomb been overlooked in 1944?

Tunstall village phone box was occupied for the next hour contacting EOD (Explosive Ordnance Disposal) and awaiting their reply. Next, the police were advised and the local constable duly arrived, theoretically to take charge but admitting he knew less than we did.

At least he fended off the merely curious. We did not advise the media, they sniffed it from the police incident log and a notebook-bearing reporter tried to catch reluctant diggers. Most of the recovery team went, it was pointless all of us waiting for the RAF.

Late afternoon, an RAF Transit van from No 2 EOD Unit, Wittering, arrived. Pete and I introduced ourselves to Flight Sergeant Dave Andrews and Junior Technician Ken Ogier, apologizing for the inconvenience. Dave Andrews cheerfully told us it was better than being bored and wanted to see the culprit straight away. We had marked the bomb's position but, peering into the crater, there was no sign of it, the brute had sunk.

Now I had qualms about it being a bomb at all. How embarrassing to fuss for an oxygen bottle. On the other hand, what if it was delayed action, set for six hours? Maybe clouting it activated the timer. . . how long to go? Five minutes. The thought prickled down my spine. I shuddered, it was silly to dwell on being blasted in a thousand directions. Get a grip, there's work to do. Taking buckets into the hole, Pete and I slung out enough water for Dave Andrews to grope at arm's length. Nervously, we watched as he grunted, probing deeper, outstretched fingers seeking contact with our malignant discovery. Got it! Looking up, Dave nodded — a nose fused, 500 lb HE. I was not sure whether to be pleased or terrified.

Next morning, our pump chattered enthusiastically but made little impression on the depth of water. Flight Sergeant Andrews, assuming control, soon realized the problem and contracted our machine to dig a sump and drain water from the bomb's position. Minutes later, we saw it again, luckily resting with the suspension lugs uppermost. Shackling a chain through the lugs and around the bucket, Dave Andrews prepared to lift and ordered all non-essential workers off site. Now came a problem, how to remove civilians yet operate the excavator. Junior Technician Ogier received a crash course on Hy-Mac controls but Dave still needed help in the crater. Roy Baker had been operating the pump and proving generally useful so he bravely remained as the rest of us retreated.

From a safe distance, we heard the Hy-Mac tussling with its burden as Ken wrestled with unfamiliar controls. Instead of easing gently free, the bomb suddenly popped out, rising swiftly from the crater to swing alarmingly overhead. Scary seconds elapsed before it settled and Ken lowered it slowly to one side. Just then, Dave Andrews made an awful discovery. Visible in the cavity created was another bomb!

Rather than risk an amateur in the Hy-Mac, Charles Robb, the driver, agreed to remove number two. Roy Baker was secretly relieved and helped harness it, noticing as he did, some rope, apparently left by the wartime recovery crew. Perhaps these had been too deep and part of the load was abandoned. Skilfully manipulated, the Hy-Mac coped easily and the second bomb hoisted smoothly, exposing yet another with its fins broken off.

Incredulously, we realized *Bird Dog* might have on board a full contingent of ten or twelve 500 lb bombs. Flight Sergeant Andrews was concerned, wondering whether he should halt and call for support. In Roy's opinion, delay would allow flooding, soil would subside, hiding the deadly cache, and removal become harder. While conditions were favourable, work should continue, under EOD control, but using the enthusiasts to help clear wreckage. Flight Sergeant Andrews warned that the bombs had been subject to impact, fire and ageing — we also had to be wary in case the load contained examples of sensitive, anti-personnel fusing. Those found so far had both nose and tail fuses but the arming wires, fitted to prevent fuse vanes rotating, were still attached. On release, the arming wires pulled free allowing fuse vanes to rotate and prime the bomb.

We understood involvement was at our own risk but felt responsible and willing to share in making the site safe. Mr More planned to drain the meadow and might have cut through the site with disastrous results. Soon, six bombs sat atop the meadow, rocking gently as the Hy-Mac trundled by. One had had its tail fuse ripped out on impact, most had lost their fins but all the casings were intact, no dangerous cracks. Although they remained roughly in their original stowage pattern, some had turned, and locating suspension lugs meant digging between them by hand. Wreckage, carried in by their weight, was compressed amidst the bombs and Flight Sergeant Andrews pulled out a canvas hold-all, squashed but intact. Pete Snowling unzipped it. Inside was a set of flying apparel: trousers; fur-lined anorak; gloves; helmet; goggles and spare lens; headphones; towel, even a blue woollen balaclava knitted by ladies of the American Red Cross. Later, when it dried, the name 'Frank C. Church' was revealed stencilled near the zip. The next item I found epitomised the tragedy of lost tomorrows every time a plane plunged earthwards.

Searching mud removed from the crater, I spotted the soggy, crumpled remains of a small photograph album. Gently prising it open, I could see family

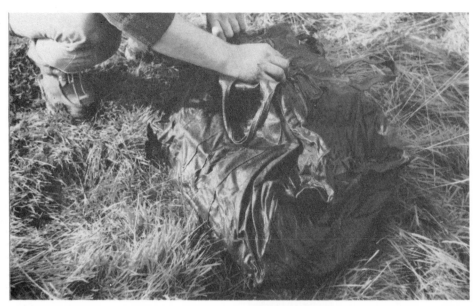

Left *Frank Church's kit-bag from the wreck about to be opened for the first time since July 1944.*

Below left *Well preserved contents of the bag included this Type B-15 jacket thought to belong to Frank C. Church. Now in 100th BG Museum.*

Right *Spoof identity card for the Myers' pet dog.*

Below *In a Kansas yard, the toddler whose photograph was buried in a Norfolk marsh for 35 years. She grew up in the peace her father earned.*

Below right *A picture to comfort the home-sick aviator.*

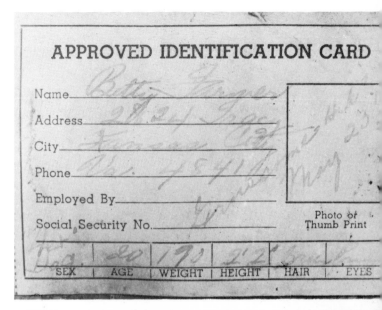

APPROVED IDENTIFICATION CARD

Name

Address

City

Phone

Employed By

Social Security No.

Photo of Thumb Print

SEX	AGE	WEIGHT	HEIGHT	HAIR	EYES

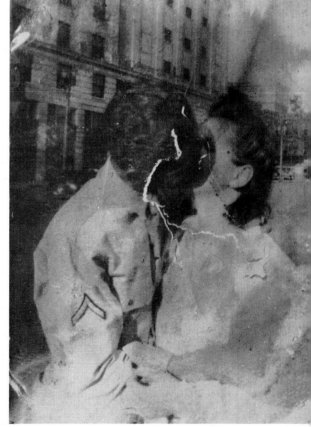

153

Preserved in peat, this photograph makes a powerful statement on the tragedy that befell Bird Dog and many of her kin.

pictures and an identity card. Washing it carefully, I read the name, 'Betty Myers, 2824 Tracy, Kansas City' followed by a phone number. Across the card was a strange comment, 'Gruesome Huh? May 23!' For a moment, I was puzzled, not a nice thing to say — perhaps a private joke. Then I noticed the line at the bottom, it described a 'Pet Dog', twenty-years-old, weighing 190 lbs, 2 ft 2 in high, brown hair and pink eyes. With this touching insight were pictures which created an overwhelming sadness.

Gazing at a young airman's yesterdays, I felt the nearness of my own tears as I realized the enormity of his loss. There, in a Kansas yard, was a toddler with her trike. She would never really have known her father, he never had the tomorrows he deserved with his daughter. Another picture, happy moments, a street in Kansas City, the flier kisses his wife, a scene captured to comfort him through dark days ahead. Although I felt an intruder into a dead man's memories, I also felt I had to ensure he was remembered. What were we doing this for, if not to remind people of the sacrifice made by so many young men and their families? War was no glory, not when you saw Myers' father looking at you from a photograph long buried in the wreckage of his son's bomber. If nothing else, the idea of relating this story sprang from that glimpse of a lost airman's family. How else could I express my feelings or prove the serious purpose behind my activities?

Those struggling in the crater were knee deep in mud that stuck like brown porridge: a bucket team slung the slodgy mixture clear for the digger to scoop out. Risking the machine too near the bombs was unwise. By early afternoon, ten bombs had been retrieved and probing found no evidence of others so the EOD and police took a break while we continued clearing debris. The bomb load was unknown at this time so we assumed that all had been found. No sooner had the RAF team departed than we located number eleven, cast away from the main batch and over 15 ft deep. A dilemma. If we waited, the crater's sides would slide in for water was already pouring in from surrounding marshland. Another worry, the load would certainly have been twelve, not eleven. Hesitation might bury the last two so, copying EOD, we shackled our trophy and eased it free. Sure enough, a twelfth rested behind and we worked swiftly to catch it before the sagging bank collapsed. When EOD returned, they had a neat dozen to deal with.

Flight Sergeant Andrews explained that defusing was too dangerous with bombs so old: tiny particles of explosive crystals might have formed in the fuse thread and unscrewing it risked detonation. Transporting them to a military range was also risky. Destruction on site threatened nearby pig pens so Mr More was asked where he would like the odd duckpond or two. Choosing a spot where blast risk was minimal meant moving them along the marsh and entailed a major exercise for civil and military authorities.

On Monday 8 October we made national news. Roadblocks were established on the main A-47 and smaller roads leading to Tunstall. The Norwich — Great Yarmouth railway line was closed for each detonation. Locally, police went from house to house warning of blast effect and advising windows be opened. Even the low flying cells at West Drayton and Rudloe Manor were cautioned. Travelling to Tunstall, I was stopped by police at Halvergate. As I explained my involvement, there was a sharp bang and blast rustled through the trees, one had been dealt with, the sound was heard over ten miles away. On site, Dave Andrews explained the procedure.

A trench had been dug for the bomb with two other trenches to help absorb blast. On each bomb, EOD packed nearly 2 lb of PE4 plastic explosive and a detonator, from which ran a *very* long length of Cordtez. Dave Andrews lit it like an enormous firework. Jumping into a waiting police Landrover, he sped away. Three minutes then, wallop!

Finding a vantage point overlooking

Now what do I do? A bemused Ken Ogier contemplates the deadly cache.

WHOOMPH! Bomb No 2 rattles windows for miles.

the scene, I prepared my camera. Nearby, a TV crew also waited. Far to our left, on the main road, traffic halted, not long now. Through the telephoto lens, I aligned on a small green pumphouse, just off centre from the anticipated blast point. Lower down the viewfinder, I saw the Landrover speed bumpily away. It seemed ages, then the TV crew began counting. Five-four-three-two-one. WHOOMPH! A great, black mass of earth heaved heavenwards, the sound and blast punching past. From far-flung shrapnel, spurts of dust peppered the field in front and our proximity was emphasized when a piece went zinging overhead. One startled spectator jumped into a bramble bush. If this was one bomb, what must an air raid have been like?

Later, Dave Andrews gave me a large piece of casing with viciously sharp edges. Shrapnel was currency amongst wartime schoolboys whose successors continued the custom when the area reopened. Before then, EOD had ten more to deal with and took until Tuesday evening when the last bomb vanished violently. Now for the aftermath and inevitable questions.

Fortunately, EOD praised our conduct. Less welcome were three complaints of damage and an enormous bomb crater, grown from each detonation. Equally unfortunate, an inarticulate member of our team, bullied by the media, spoke unwisely, so I then acted as spokesman to stress the serious purpose of our work, its contribution to aviation history. Regretably, damage in both senses, had been done. During November, the Ministry of Defence wrote to all aircraft recovery groups stating that a great deal of media attention had been directed at the subject. 'One result of this has been that the general public has become more aware of the dangers involved...particularly with regard to unexploded bombs.' Permissions previously granted were withdrawn, re-application was made necessary and more stringent checks promised before consent could be given. Press coverage was double edged. To remind the 'general public' of the debt owed to airmen, the media were important and finding bombs certainly attracted attention. It also prompted questions about ordnance being left and whether there was sufficient research before giving consent to dig. Under the new rules, this would not happen. We had no desire to clout 500 lb bombs with excavator buckets and would have proceeded very cautiously had ordnance been suspected. Arguably, we were rendering a service by clearing sites in a responsible manner: the answer lay in improved co-ordination between groups and the MoD. In later years, this happened, but repercussions from *Bird Dog* took time to settle.

Six months after the dig, a letter arrived from MoD Claims Commission seeking reimbursement of £257.35, compensation against a damage claim. True, we had insurance but the problem needed professional handling. My solicitor and friend, Eric Mingay, contested the case and the Claims Commission eventually withdrew, accepting that EOD had taken responsibility for events from the moment they arrived. The decision to detonate and site chosen were outside our control. We had followed the *Notes of Guidance* and been commended by EOD, damage was not our liability, the bombs should not have been overlooked for 35 years. The controversy surrounding *Bird Dog* settled, but the fuss had thwarted our purpose, much of the wreckage still lay buried.

In 1985, we asked Mr More for permission to clear the site. Anxious to drain the field, he readily agreed and, in August, we returned with a new Ford 4 x 4 hired from Tom Banham. His skill was essential, the area was still a soggy

trap for the unwary. In 1979, we worked from the port side into the fuselage but the starboard wing had been abandoned. Calculating the position of No 3 engine, we found it only 5 ft deep. Next came a large section of starboard wing followed by No 4 supercharger lying just below the surface. The fourth Twin Wasp and propeller offered little resistance, only two blades were still attached to the Hamilton Standard but, even after 41 years, traces of red paint remained on the boss. *Bird Dog* was

1985, the No 3 Pratt and Whitney R1830 Twin Wasp emerges from its long sojourn.

It was a Ford! Automobile plants were sub-contracted to manufacture aircraft during World War 2. This plate was attached to the remains of a seat.

Found in the debris, a Planters Nut and Chocolate Co salted peanut tin.

AAF Identity Card belonging to Frank C. Church.

almost over, slowly we began backfilling, searching for items overlooked.

As before, sifting yielded smaller tokens of Eighth Air Force history. An identification plate gave Ford's construction number, 3329. The aircraft was one of over 18,000 Liberator variants produced by different manufacturers but few survived, so *Bird Dog* represented a species almost extinct. A lighter, historical note was a crushed Planter's Salted Peanuts tin, either from the wreck or discarded during recovery efforts.

There was no doubt about the badly-damaged remains of a wallet. Carefully opened, it revealed photographs and fragments of documents relating to Frank C. Church, the radio operator. His AAF identity card was there with thumb print and signature; a medical record showing dates of injections; even a card relating, ironically, to Federal Old Age Insurance. A list of equipment issued to him tied in with the kit bag found in 1979. All the wallet's contents reeked of aviation fuel and the photographs were in poor condition but I quickly copied them before exposure hastened degradation. These poignant, family snaps reached across four decades, humbling we of later generations. When the site again lay level and the roar of the machine ceased, we reflected with quiet gratitude on the young warriors of *Bird Dog*. We tried to thank them.

Buried four decades, this picture must have been treasured by Frank Church. In 1985, it emphasized the purpose of aviation archaeology.

DEATH OF A DORNIER

In June 1941, Germany invaded Russia. The subsequent drain on the Reich's resources proved severe. Britain had prepared for another Blitzkreig but the Luftwaffe was depleted supporting Russian operations.

A year later the majority of the German bomber strength was still embattled around Stalingrad and in the Caucasus. Comparatively few aircraft were available to attack Britain and more were squandered during the infamous 'Baedeker' raids. Infuriated by the RAF's increasing potency, Hitler raged about using the Baedeker tourist guidebook and eliminating cities of historical merit. These pointless plans were implemented during the spring of 1942 and places like Bath, York, Exeter and Norwich suffered, but the attacks sapped the Luftwaffe's weakening strength for little military benefit.

Permanent damage to the Luftwaffe's roots was incurred when it withdrew experienced crews from training organizations, degrading an essential resource. These crews were irreplacable and one succumbed to the commanding officer of Britain's first Mosquito nightfighter squadron. Facing increasingly sophisticated night defences, the courage of this German crew deserves acknowledgement. Their demise typifies nocturnal air combat in 1942 and the recovery of their bomber in 1981 enabled representation of their story in British aviation museums.

Realizing that aircraft lost on 'Baedeker' reprisals contributed little to reducing Allied power, the Luftwaffe reverted to small scale operations, still forcing the British to maintain significant defences for a minimum German investment. If precise, military targets could be hit, this was a wiser use of diminishing strength.

Details of such a target were drawn from the files of *Kampfgeschwader 2* at Eindhoven on 22 August 1942. No more than a handful of aircraft would be used. During the early evening, Oberleutnant Hans Walter Wolff had instructions for the attack from his *Gruppenkommandeur* and, as acting *Staffelkapitan* of 6/KG2, he was to brief the aircrews. Concerned about time, Hans gathered them in a small hut near their waiting Dorniers. Pointing to a large scale map of Cambridge, he highlighted the Unicam factory in Arbury Road — a small factory making precision, optical equipment for guns and submarines. Hopefully, the delicate, engineering apparatus would be vulnerable to their 500 kg HE bombs. Hans referenced the target to a nearby LNER bridge over the Cam, it would show prominently in the moonlight. Hans' own observer, *Unteroffizier* Edward Nieser could be relied upon. He had flown with Hans during their period as an instruction crew from December 1941 until July 1942. *Unteroffizier* Willi Schlegel and *Unteroffizier* Anton Mang, radio operator and flight engineer respectively, were also with Hans at KG2's training school near Achmer but high losses

8

161

Oberleutnant *Hans Wolff, second from left, with his Dornier crew* (Mrs R. Wolff via C.H. Goss).

forced their return to combat. At 29, Wolff was seven years older than his crew but his love of flying and pre-war airline experience with 'Deutsche Lufthansa' earned their respect and confidence. They certainly needed it: in January KG2 had had 88 aircraft, they now numbered less than thirty but, despite this, their morale was good as they prepared for take-off.

That night, they were using a Dornier 217E-4, *Werk Nr. 1152*. Minimizing searchlight reflection and night visibility, the Dornier was painted black beneath with dark green upper surfaces. On the narrow fuselage appeared its coding, U5+LP, again in black except for the blood red 'L'. Camouflage helped

but Hans knew British radar would see them anyway and he must vary height and direction to confuse controllers.

The twin, BMW 801C engines pounded noisily as Hans climbed from the Dutch coast. Anton Mang checked fuel consumption, relaxing a little once the motors settled and the bomber's system read satisfactorily on gauges and meters. Willi Schlegel listened for signals conveying weather information and monitored progress on the *Knickebein* radio beam. Over the North Sea it helped navigation but British interference weakened its reliability as a guide to the target. Edward Nieser knew exactly where they were, his route took them to the English coast at Orford

162

Ness with the Rivers Ore and Alde silvering their distinctive moonlit patterns through the dark countryside.

Helpful in appearance, moonlight was also treacherous, a friend of the stalking nightfighter. Happily, there was some cloud cover and Hans eased the Dornier into a shallow dive, grateful for the patches of protection.

A few miles behind, Wing Commander R.G. Slade cursed the same clouds as his Mosquito submerged. His radar operator, Pilot Officer Philip Truscott, hung determinedly on to the flickering green trace. Firing on unseen targets was forbidden, there was too much friendly traffic about, so he had to coax them close enough for a visual as soon as they broke cloud. This patrol had not been easy.

Gordon Slade and Philip Truscott left Castle Camps at 20.53 hours, flying their all-black Mosquito II, *DD612*. As CO of 157 Squadron, Wing Commander Slade felt keenly the frustration of fruitless patrols using the superb new nightfighter his Squadron had introduced to operations. Galling was the fact that 151 Squadron beat them to the first Mosquito victory and continued to score while success eluded 157.

The initial stages of this patrol offered little encouragement. Flight Lieutenant Parnell at GCI Trimley Heath positioned them 25 miles off Southwold where they might catch a minelayer. For several minutes, it looked like another disappointing night then the GCI station reported an incoming raid, the crew of *DD612* were cheered to hear that Trimley had a customer for them.

An aircraft emitting no IFF, presumably hostile, was approaching Orford. Parnell told the Mosquito to vector 120° and reduce height from 14,000 to 10,000 ft, the target was about twelve miles away. Studying the blips, Trimley warned Slade to prepare for a starboard turn on to 280°. As the Mosquito banked, an AI contact emerged from ground return, hard on their port side. Urging his Mosquito into a tighter turn, Gordon was relieved as Truscott retained their contact, 3,000 ft away. Then, instead of the distance closing, it opened to 6,000 ft and they realized that they had unwittingly hauled round in front of their target. In 1942, radar was imprecise and operators learned from signal behaviour. Sliding starboard, the Mosquito sought to shed distance and pull in behind but the AI trace vanished. Anxiously, Gordon Slade appealed to Trimley for help but Parnell's team had their hands full with four contacts near *DD612*, one of which was friendly. Trying to sort something from the confusion, GCI moved them starboard in 20° segments, Truscott's narrow-beamed AI Mk V pencilling ahead. No luck. Calculating his opponent's intentions, Gordon suggested they were going the wrong way and began moving left in 20° stages. Trimley were perplexed, unable to determine from four traces, which was *DD612*. Then, skimming from ground return, 10,000 ft away, came an AI contact. They were closing too fast: above... dead ahead; slow down, or speed underneath it.

Hurriedly, Gordon Slade lowered his undercarriage, effectively dragging away airspeed and stabilizing contact at 7,000 ft. Whoever it was made their task no easier and swung into a right turn. Responding, Slade skidded his Mosquito to avoid slithering past. On board the Dornier, Hans Wolff straightened out, resuming his westerly course and a steady dive through comforting clouds.

Philip Truscott followed his quarry,

straining to hold station behind and below. Gaining confidence, he quietly advised his pilot to close in, the Mosquito's cannon were set to 'Fire'. Edging upwards, they almost levelled with their adversary, creeping nearer. For several minutes, they bumped along in cloud, patiently holding at 3,000 ft range. Still in cloud, a game of blind man's buff with two blind men. Who would see first? The Mosquito's four .303 machine guns and four 20 mm cannon could deal a severe punch but the Dornier was not helpless. Armed with both dorsal and ventral MG131 machine-guns, a Do217 could thwart a stern attack. Two lateral MG15s gave extra protection and a potent, forward-firing 15 mm MG151 was available to Hans. Not much larger than a Mosquito, there existed a Do217 nightfighter variant — this combat was no foregone conclusion.

U5+LP emerged from cloud. Ahead was another large black cloud bank, ideal for concealment. Running straight was risky: Hans jinked into a port turn, held it for a minute, then swung towards the nearest cloud face, still diving for extra speed.

DD612 emerged from cloud. Gordon Slade powered on the Merlins to close up. Combat had to be in this heavenly valley. Using the earth's dark shadow, he crept nearer, the trace obligingly moved but where was it visually? Got it! Ahead 1,500 ft, and 500 ft above, just where it was supposed to be, he saw a silhouette. What was it? In answer, the other aircraft conveniently turned left displaying twin rudders: a Dornier. DD612 followed easily through the turn and moved directly beneath to confirm. Gordon Slade wanted no mistakes.

Craning his neck, the Mosquito pilot stared upwards through his canopy for a superb plan view of a Dornier 217: two great, underslung radial engines, a seemingly large, typically German crew area, all bunched forwards behind a perspex nose. As men, he wished them no harm but, in addition to its personnel, the bomber carried 2,000 malicious kilograms intended for British citizens.

Time to act. The Dornier scurried towards clouds ahead. Gordon Slade fell in behind and peered at it through his gunsight, adjusting it for improved accuracy. Closing in, he saw two thin arcs of exhaust flame on each engine. Coolly, head pressed firmly into the radar set's vizor, Truscott called the reducing range: 900 ft...800...700. The intended victim seemed oblivious of the poised dagger.

At 600 ft distance, Hans Wolff half rolled vigorously to starboard. Gordon Slade fired immediately, keeping the Dornier in his sights and rolling with it. A three-second burst of cannon fire hit the bomber's port side and centre section. An enormous shower of sparks shot out and the bomber plummeted away, too fast for a deflection shot. The silhouette was swallowed into earth shadow then, strangely, some dim lights appeared, apparently on the bomber's wingtips, as if someone had accidentally knocked on the formation lights. A faint glow came from the dropping Dornier with more sparks trailing like a fading firework behind it.

Hans' instinctive reaction was to shake off their tormentor. U5+LP had been badly damaged but his abrupt half roll and dive avoided crew casualties as they fled earthwards. Hans held the dive, curving left to out-manoeuvre their attacker. Hopes of home diminished with the brightening flames from their port engine and the Dornier shuddered alarmingly: control was increasingly difficult and Hans eased from the dive.

They had been caught unawares and were lucky to be alive but, he thought, they might have shaken off the night-fighter. Hans was right, for now. Mosquito *DD612* was diving steeply in pursuit, following the half roll and left turn. Gordon Slade lost sight of the bomber but Truscott's radar eye held on remorselessly, steadying at 4,500 ft. Both machines continued diving, the Mosquito unable to close on the fleeing Dornier before the blip vanished into ground return. Swinging into a wide circle, Slade sought help from Trimley then, as they orbitted, three bursts

of flame splashed from the darkness to their north. Their victory was still uncertain for the bomber might only have jettisoned its load.

It had. Struggling for control, Hans ordered the bombs to be dumped. Two fell near Hall Farm, Tannington, one failing to explode, the other harmlessly cratering a field. Seconds later, two more burst near Worlingworth, slightly damaging a house. Hans, holding vain thoughts of home, dragged the protesting Dornier on to an easterly heading but fuel from punctured port tanks ignited and flames ate viciously into the

Gordon Slade (right) pictured post-war with record-breaking pilot, Peter Twiss (Bob Collis/ N & SAM).

wing. No use: the Dornier was doomed. Ordering his crew out, Hans fought to hold it steady. Fire was destroying control linkages and he needed all his skills. At 2,000 ft, he was alone: time to go. Leaving U5+LP to a fiery finale, he leapt clear and joined his crew, descending gently through the warm, night sky near Stradbroke.

Hans' empty bomber swung west of its own volition, the dive increased and the sound of an aircraft screeching to destruction carried far over farmland below. At 22.50 hours, U5+LP exploded in a cornfield at Lodge Farm, Worlingworth, the glare bonfiring the darkness for miles.

Hans landed safely nearby, hoping that his crew were as lucky. Unclipping his 'chute, he set off to surrender, glad to be alive but apprehensive about captivity. En route, he startled a farmer by asking directions to the nearest police station and was soon in custody. His early moments as a prisoner-of-war were lightened by hospitality from the British police, kindly providing welcome tea and biscuits. Concern for his crew turned to relief as, one by one, they were caught. Last to be captured was Anton Mang who hid out until daylight. For them, the war was over.

Next day, Wing Commander Slade visited the field where U5+LP had disintegrated and burnt out: a machine-gun was taken to join the Squadron's trophies. British intelligence picked over the pieces but gleaned nothing new from the debris.

Following routine interrogation, the Dornier's crew went to English PoW camps and then to Canada. Over four years later, Hans was released to rejoin his family. Willi Schlegel also returned home but died in an accident soon after. Mang and Nieser had to gather their lives together, as so many did, in a struggling, defeated Germany. Having been well treated by the Canadians, Hans felt that the younger country offered better prospects and in 1952 he emigrated with his wife and two sons. Eight years later, his daughter was born and the Wolff family became truly part of a newer nation. Following a three-year illness, the ex-Dornier pilot died on 12 April 1980.

Sadly, Pilot Officer Truscott perished on a 'Serrate' sortie during September 1944, but Wing Commander Slade survived to become a Group Captain and in 1946 became Chief Test Pilot for Fairey Aviation. Ten years later, he organized a new World Absolute Speed Record when Peter Twiss flew the Fairey Delta 2 at 1,132 mph. Following a successful career with Fairey, he retired in 1977 and died on 7 October 1981. Had he lived, he would have been keenly interested in the excavations of Dornier U5+LP which commenced just eleven days later.

The Dornier's demise became part of Worlingworth folklore yet, strangely, the water-filled crater attracted scant attention from local people. Nine years after the crash, some pieces were removed and dumped into a nearby rubbish pit. A bulldozer levelled the site and it disappeared into part of a larger field when hedges were removed and ditches filled. A nearby barn was demolished and by 1981, the exact site was forgotten.

That October the Norfolk and Suffolk Aviation Museum asked landowner, Mark Horvath, for permission to excavate. He showed great interest and helped find the site. On 11 October, a hand dig was organized and the rubbish tip relocated but it yielded none of the wreckage reportedly dumped. Searching for the main point of impact

166

Anglia Television made a programme about N & SAM activities including footage of the Dornier excavations. Museum members John Crowe and Terry Spruce assembled a composite engine from the remains of two. The camera crew wait while debris is cleared to excavate the first BMW 801C.

produced a spread of fragments but clues appeared where the strata of sandy subsoil had been disturbed. Digging into this produced corroded aluminium, the remains of a spectacle, machine-gun magazine and parts of the machine gun itself.

A week later Anglia Television accompanied the N&SAM as part of a documentary film about the museum's activities. Carefully clearing topsoil, a BMW 801C was located and removed with remains of an undercarriage leg, wheel and bent mudguard. Following the Dornier's main spar, items from the compacted fuselage emerged including the medical kit. Bandages had somehow survived the conflagration along with bone-saw, tweezers, safety pins, syringe and spare needles. Evidence of combat was dramatically demonstrated by the discovery of a British cannon shell amidst the debris. Sifted from the detritus of *U5+LP* were oxygen bottles, crew

Medical kit survived the blaze.

Identification plate: 'Dornier 217E-4 W.Nr 1152 Dornier-Werke G.m.b.H. Friedrichshafen'.

seats, armour plating and the crumpled cockpit control console. Completing the task came the removal of the second BMW from a depth of 12 ft.

During the 1981/2 winter the N&SAM sorted, identified and cleaned four tons of wreckage. Generously, parts were distributed to other museums and, perhaps more importantly, items were given to the families of Hans Wolff and Gordon Slade. The death of a Dornier illustrated enmity between nations. Four decades later, presenting mementoes from it to the airmen's families furthered reconciliation and friendship

SPITFIRE

9

'Nobby' Hargreaves settled as comfortably as possible into the bucket seat of Spitfire P9548. Being over 6 ft tall, he still found the familiar cockpit cramped and it seemed worse at night. Tucking his maps into the mapcase, he felt confident that the route he had pencilled in would be no problem. From Bibury, he had drawn a line to Bristol, across the Severn to Cardiff, then along the Welsh coast to Swansea. A few miles on, overfly RAF Pembrey, turn right and home over the valleys of south Wales, Stroud and back to Bibury. These intentions were subject to interference by the weather, mechanical trouble and, of course, the Germans. Having tried many times, Nobby knew his chances of finding the enemy at night, using a Spitfire, were slim.

Brilliant daylight interceptors, the Spitfires and Hurricanes of Fighter Command were gradually defeating the Luftwaffe. It was 27 August 1940 and the Battle of Britain was nearing its climax. Already, the Germans knew that their bombers could not effectively penetrate British airspace unescorted and the Me 109 lacked the range to escort bombers attacking targets deeper in Britain. Nocturnally, it was different: Heinkels, Dorniers and Junkers ranged far, suffering relatively small losses despite the heroic efforts from AA defences and an inadequately-equipped nightfighter force. AI was in its infancy, the Beaufighter about to enter service, the Mosquito had yet to fly. Stalwart Blenheims, backed by day fighters, tried their best but losses inflicted were barely worth casualties and accidents sustained, especially amongst weary Spitfire pilots.

92 Squadron had fought gallantly during the Dunkirk debacle. Nobby had flown patrols under Flight Lieutenant Stanford Tuck, later one of the RAF's leading pilots. The spirit of the Squadron was typical of the times, there was an irreverence towards bureaucratic authority and a desire to crack the arrogance of their opponents. That they were engaged in a war defending the free world was known but not debated in scholarly terms. They lived, fought and died with more mundane matters on their young minds. The loss of friends hurt but grief had to be suppressed and boisterous behaviour became their release valve, even when their CO, Roger Bushell, went down.

Only a few weeks earlier, Bushell had taken Nobby for some dual instruction in a Miles Master and Nobby venerated this, 'old man' of nearly thirty. Bushell survived being shot down but was murdered by the Gestapo after organizing the 'Great Escape' from Stalag Luft III at Sagan in 1944. In bitter combat, 92 avenged the loss of their CO but Nobby, like those who survived, aged on the experience.

At 21, Pilot Officer Frederick Norman Hargreaves was a veteran for many friends had died defending Dunkirk. During a short leave from Pembrey, where the Squadron was sent for they understand the helplessness felt when a friend's Spitfire spun earthwards, his screams ripping through your headphones? The remorseful young man who had shot a sparrow with his Webley air pistol now blasted at men with machine-guns. The difference was that, unlike the bird, these men were not innocent, nor defenceless — they had rampaged across Europe and now sat cockily across the Channel, waiting to goose-step over.

By day, German access was punishingly denied over southern England while 92 Squadron fumed in the quieter west country. Their turn would come. For the moment they fought sporadic daylight actions and flew many, 'cats eyes' patrols at night. In darkness they struggled to defend cities like Bristol and Cardiff and even the approaches to Nobby's home city of Manchester.

Spreading its resources, 92 moved 'A' Flight to Bibury in the Cotswolds, on 18 August and a Ju 88 welcomed their arrival two days later by bombing the airfield. This raider paid for his impudence when Spitfires caught him but at night frustrated pilots frequently returned with gunport seals intact, if they returned at all. Navigation over a blacked-out Britain was difficult and, in bad weather, dangerous, so patrols were restricted to nights with favourable forecasts. Even in good conditions, the Spitfire's narrow-tracked undercarriage and restricted landing visibility handicapped effectiveness. Pilots could be dazzled by their own exhaust flames, although cowling blinkers, fitted in the line of vision, between exhaust glare and cockpit, helped. Nobby appreciated this modification on *P9548* as he climbed away from Bibury.

He did not appreciate the weather he flew into. Soon, buffeted in clouds, sum-

One of 'The Few', Pilot Officer Frederick Norman Hargreaves in formal pose (H. Gabbott).

replenishment and recuperation, Nobby visited his former office at Threlfalls Brewery, Salford. He had been a stocktakers clerk before enlisting. It seemed, and was, lifetimes ago. His, 'Tuck' type of slim moustache aged his appearance, but his character had also changed. Gone was the youth his colleagues remembered. Nobby laughed and jested with them but his eyes reflected the horror of sights unmentioned. How could mer static crackling in his headphones, Nobby was lost. When ground was visible, no landmarks registered and his fuel gauge drained with every lost mile. The eerie luminescence of his instruments seemed to scoff at his inadequacy. Where was he? Descending too low to search held terrifying prospects, the Brecon Beacons rose over 2,000 ft, ready to snatch him into their rocky, unforgiving peaks. Trimming for maximum range, Nobby desperately sought a landmark but unremitting clouds flashed only tantalizing glimpses of unfamiliar terrain and as the fuel diminished his misery increased. Even at its most economical, the Merlin sang thirstily and his fuel was soon perilously low. Nobby had no alternative but to join the caterpillar club: Spitfire *P9548* it appeared, had fought the elements and lost.

Preparing to bale out, he disconnected the R/T lead and slid open the canopy. It seemed that the threatening darkness surged in with the eddies of the slipstream sucked into the cockpit. Somehow, the Spitfire seemed comforting, yet clinging to her was hopeless. Airspeed and altitude were where he wanted them. Time to go. Releasing his harness, Nobby rolled *P9548* smartly on her back and fell neatly away.

Floating through the cloudbase, he was puzzled. Wherever he was, it was not Wales, the countryside was too flat. Moments later, he landed safely to learn that he was at Red House Farm near Blaxhall in *Suffolk*! Soon, the embarrassed flier was collected by a vehicle from Martlesham Heath and undoubtedly met some ribald comments about his navigation.

At least he was safe. The loss of a Spitfire on night operations was not uncommon, but where had *P9548* gone? The East Suffolk Police Daily Situation Report for 28 August, 1940, stated that a Spitfire of, '95 Squadron, Bristol, crashed on the marshes near Blackstone Junction, Marlesford. The aircraft was smashed to pieces, the engine being buried 6 ft in the ground.' This report contained two errors, '95' instead of 92 and, 'Blackstone' instead of Blackstock. Further confusion was created when some accounts listed *P9548* as lost, 'near Bristol', based on the assumption that Nobby planned patrolling that area. For a short period the RAF guarded the wreck, its tail poking forlornly from the marsh but a recovery crew hacked this off and cleared the site and then, as so often happened, its whereabouts were forgotten.

Nobby, too, had other things on his mind. Rejuvenated and fretting for combat, 92 was transferred to Biggin Hill on 8 September. Britain was struggling for survival. That she did owes much to the skill of Air Chief Marshal Dowding, AOC-in-C, Fighter Command. He manipulated his meagre resources to achieve the maximum effect and his policy of holding units back until refreshed allowed exhausted squadrons to retire, often on the edge of annihilation. Now, even these reserves were dwindling. Fighting tenaciously, RAF pilots clawed German aircraft from the skies and the legend of, 'The Few' was born. Nobby Hargreaves, the bank official's son, was one of 'The Few'. His father, who died before the war, would have been proud of him.

In just two weeks operating from Biggin Hill that autumn, 92 Squadron claimed sixteen German aircraft destroyed but five of its pilots perished: one of these was Nobby Hargreaves. During the afternoon of Wednesday 11 September, an enormous phalanx of German bombers, with over 200 escorting fighters, thrust towards London. Over fifteen squadrons of Spitfires and Hurricanes responded and savage combat ensued. Numerically, in terms of aircraft lost, the day belonged to the Germans. Sources differ, but one account lists 31 RAF fighters lost to 26 German aircraft, fighters and bombers. Somewhere, in one of the many scattered combats, Nobby was pounced on by Me 109s. Listed as missing, he is presumed to have crashed in the Channel.

The loss of a former stocktakers clerk would not, individually, influence the course of war. As his mother grieved, the megalomaniac whose single decisions did influence the war, could feel the conquest he desired being wrested from his grasp and Hitler postponed 'Operation Sealion', the invasion of Britain. History relates an epic struggle and it was. History does not relate that Annie Hargreaves lost all three of her children. The name, Frederick Norman Hargreaves on the Runnymede Memorial was the first in a family tragedy. Behind all those names are countless family tragedies and the discovery of a warplane's hulk is cause to reflect on the counterfeit glory of war and the valour of a young airman.

So it was with *P9548*, but she was not easily traced. Instigated by the police report, the search began in the mid 1970s. Local accounts of its whereabouts were contradictory but attention gradually focused on a large meadow near Blackstock Junction. During 1975-80, several searches occurred but not even a rivet appeared despite a local guide showing us the 'exact location'.

Help also came from the USAF when Lieutenant Wilson of the 10th Tactical Reconnaissance Wing (USAFE) flew his Phantom over the purported site and took a series of infra-red photographs.

We hoped these would show heat radiation of the soil and pinpoint the site but there was no sign of it. Then, during the summer of 1981, a visitor to the museum at Parham related how, as a lad, he visited the crash site of a Spitfire, searching for scraps of perspex. Aged twelve, David Hudson was ill with scarlet fever when *P9548* crashed but, as soon as he could, he scuttled off to look at the wreck. Disappointingly, only a pool of oily water remained. David heard that the RAF took what lay on the surface, slung some pieces back, then went to the pub. Other children gathered the scraps, David had to wait 41 years for his souvenir.

In July, David led a cynical party to a long narrow field bordering the River Ore, north of the railway crossing, *not* the pasture we so carefully searched and the USAF photographed! Farmer Martin Greenfields, was growing maize but allowed us on the young crop if we were careful. His plants helped by providing ranks between which I slowly walked, carefully listening for any sound from the C Scope detector. Search conditions were splendid, the soil dark, dry and even so I kept the detector head flat and close to the surface. A slow, methodical search between several lines found nothing leading us to doubt David's reliability. Suddenly, a short, sharp bleep, so small that I lost it. Conscious I had stopped, the other searchers clustered nearer — there it was again, it must be very tiny but any clue would be welcome. Kneeling, I gently brushed soil aside. Shining in the earth, less than an inch deep, lay a small washer with a flake of green paint still adhering. It could have been anything but I *knew* it was Spitfire. Jubilantly, we regarded our trophy as though it were gold. A few inches on, another buzz, stronger this

Above *The tip of a propeller blade increased our excitement.*

Below *Supreme Supermarine, one of aviation's most famous names. Early marks of Spitfire had the maker's name in rudder pedal castings.*

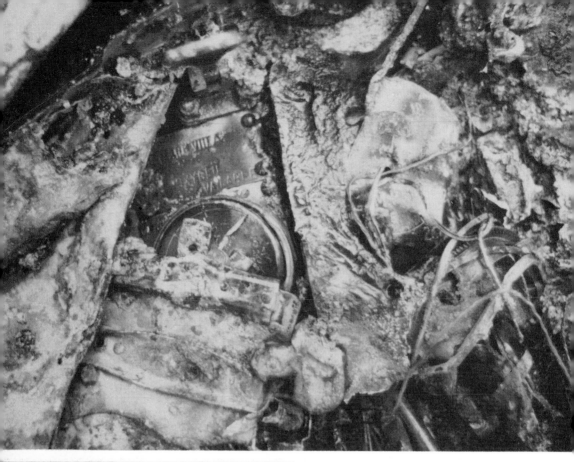

Above *Fire consumed some instruments, others can be discerned in this view of the instrument panel.*

Left *Nigel Beckett and Paul Thrower work in the crater, now about seven feet deep. Nose down, the rear of the Merlin is exposed showing the supercharger housing (left).*

Above right *Supermarine and Rolls-Royce. Arguably the most notable combination in aviation history.*

Right *Protected by being compressed in their aluminium map-case, maps indicated Nobby's planned route. The outward track is the lower of the two.*

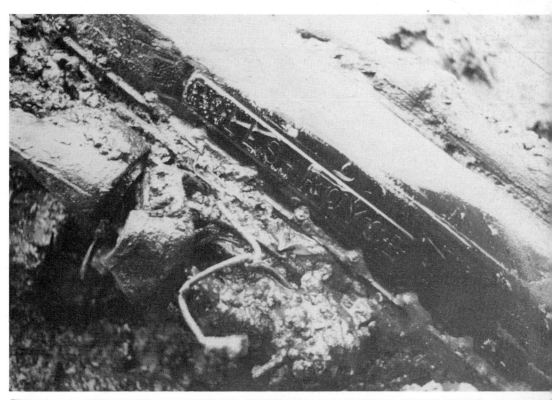

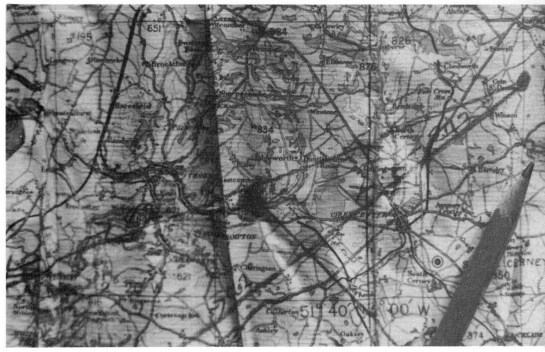

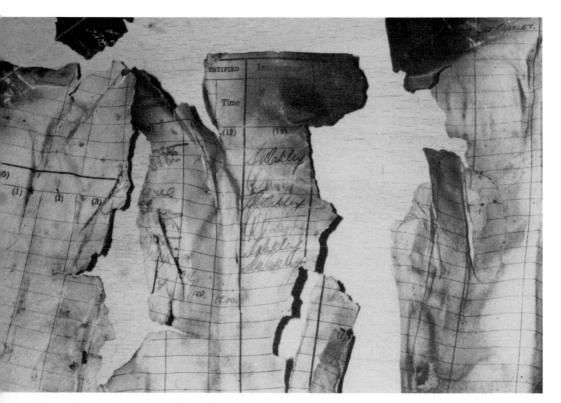

Scorched fragments of the Form 700 revealed some of P9548's career.

time. A .303 case dated 1939. Spitfire P9548 had been rediscovered.

Never has a harvest been so eagerly awaited. At the end of October, the field was clear and I hired a mechanical digger for Saturday 7 November. A few phone calls and a team was organized to share costs. Clearing away topsoil, we located more fragments and proof positive in the form of the Spitfire's modification record plate. Defining the site, we cut deeper and soon plucked out an undercarriage leg lying as though it had been thrown back. Lower down, we exposed the tip of a propeller blade, still rigidly attached to something deeper. Carefully clearing around it, we exposed more debris, obviously from the fuselage behind the cockpit. Pieces of a

Type T1119 radio transmitter/receiver emerged.

Consulting our cutaway diagrams, we noted its position inside the rear fuselage and felt confident that everything forward of this lay below us except the wings which had evidently sheared off. By now, the digger had excavated around the bulk of wreckage leaving an island of Spitfire on which two could perch, gently extracting items from layers of scrunch. P9548 had gone in at 45 degrees and we were now standing on the rear of Nobby's armour plating. Had he not baled out, his remains would have been compressed in a layer only inches thick between the armour plate and engine. P9548 was definitely shorter than her original 29ft 11in length.

Hauling away the armour, we began picking pieces from the concertinaed cockpit. Mud and metal were dropped into large polythene sacks. The control column spade had smashed but the shank was found along with two beautiful rudder pedals cast with that immortal name, 'Supermarine'.

Assuming it had stopped on impact, the clock read 12.37pm, while the airspeed indicator registered 395 mph with engine rpm at 3225. However soft the soil, our Rolls-Royce Merlin was badly smashed. Long ribs of metal mounted outside the cowling on both sides were puzzling, then we realized that these were the anti-exhaust glare blinkers. The Rotol airscrew had broken askew and lay alongside the engine with only one blade still attached. Leaving the propeller as a stepping stone, a chain was wrapped around the Merlin and it lifted as easily as picking a sweet from a packet. A far cry from the slog of Czernin's Hurricane twelve years earlier. A sling was then attached to the propeller and the recovery of P9548 was complete. David Hudson had his souvenir.

Other items were distributed to museums and are exhibited today. Significant amongst these were maps of south-west England and Wales. On the outside was pencilled, 'F.N. Hargreaves, 92 Squadron'. Inside, Nobby had marked his route and callsign, 'Dewdrop'. Being in the metal mapcase and of stout manufacture, they had not burnt. The Form 700 had not survived so well but scorched fragments told us that Sergeant Oakley had taken care of P9548 and she was given a new propeller at Hornchurch on 15 June 1940. Nobby flew her many times but she had hours with other pilots too, including Stanford Tuck.

The Spitfire symbolized a proud period in British history: the shattered remnants we found still had that aura.

THE HUNT FOR 'HERMANN'

10

For nearly 44 years, a German 1000 kg high explosive bomb and three smaller 50 kg HEs slept threateningly in a marsh at Kirton Creek near Felixstowe. In the summer of 1987 RAF EOD and a team of aircraft enthusiasts removed the deadly cache and the Ju 188 which carried it.

As an unflattering gesture to the portly Reichsmarschall Hermann Goering, the SC1000 HE, general purpose bomb became known as a 'Hermann' and our specimen began its journey to England on 15 October 1943. That night, *Kampfgeschwader* 6 sent seven of its newly introduced Ju 188E-1s to attack the UK. Developed from the famous Ju 88, the '188 was an interim measure pending the promise of the Ju 288 but, even so, the new machine had a creditable performance as a high speed, high altitude bomber. What the thinly-spread Luftwaffe now lacked was quantity and the meagre forces deployed faced frightening odds against ever strengthening British AA and night fighter defences. During briefing, crews were told that they would be immune from night fighter attack because of fog over southeast England. Their target was to be north-west London and the *Knickebein* transmitter beams from Den Helder and Boulogne would be set to intersect over the city. They were to come in on the Den Helder signal, make a left turn where the beams met and release their bombs as they straightened out before speeding home.

At KG 6's base, Chievres, 'Hermann' and ten 50 kg bombs were loaded on Ju 188, *3E+FL*, number *260179*, of the Third *Staffel*. To provide sufficient fuel, it was necessary for the loaded bombers to land at Munster/Handorf and only experienced crews were selected because of the risks in landing a laden aircraft. Piloting *3E+FL* was 29-year-old *Hauptmann* Helmut Waldecker, a veteran of early Western Front operations and the compaigns in Greece and Crete. As *Staffelkapitan*, Waldecker deputized for the *Gruppenkommander*, held the *Deutsches Kreuz* in Gold and had achieved 150 missions. He expected to receive the *Ritter Kreuz* and looked forward to the celebrations, but fate decreed his award would be made in the muted circumstances of a PoW camp. Replacing his regular navigator, Waldecker had a young *Obergefreiter*, Waldemar Haupt who had narrowly avoided service on the Russian Front and was now facing his first, and last, operational flight. Other than Haupt, Waldecker had the experience of his usual crew: manning the wireless and electronics was *Unteroffizier* Karl-Heinz Mueller while defence was catered for by *Oberfeldwebel* Julius Hohman.

Whatever the meteorologists said about fog forcing night fighters to stay in bed, Waldecker knew the hazards of operating against England. This was his crew's first mission since transferring from Italy and the need for vigilance needed no emphasis as the BMW 801's powered *3E+FL* into action. Even at this early stage, the plans went wrong. On arrival over Munster/Handorf, the force was separated when controllers told Waldecker and three or four other crews to refuel at Rheine. An impromptu arrangement to rejoin forces was made but when Waldecker's contingent returned to Munster/Handorf, the others had departed for England, thus splitting the attack.

3E+FL gained altitude over the North Sea with Haupt struggling to get a signal from the Den Helder beam which was being jammed by the British. Waldecker weaved and changed height fre-

Hauptman *Helmut Waldecker, holder of the Knight's Cross of the Iron Cross for 150 operational flights* (H. Hoehler).

quently since a straight course was perilous, but his evasive measures did not dim the all-seeing radar eye. Radar was not a prerogative of the Allies, however, and Waldecker's Ju 188 had only recently been fitted with a FuG 216 Neptun R1 tail warning radar. As they climbed, a British night fighter was detected positioning to attack but Waldecker skillfully evaded and continued unscathed. Having thwarted one attack, he knew the fog factor to be nonsense and bright moonlight mocked the idea of secrecy.

At precisely 22.46½, Squadron Leader Guest, controller at Sandwich GCI transmitted to nightfighter F15, 'Starboard 080, Bandit 20 miles.' In the clipped dialogue of r/t conversation, Squadron Leader Maguire of 85 Squadron acknowledged, 'Starboard 080. What Angels?' The hunt was on: Waldecker's bomber had thirteen minutes left. Surviving records detail the action and show that Squadron Leader W.H. Maguire and Flying Officer W.D. Jones left West Malling at 22.15 hours for a routine patrol off Clacton in Mosquito NF XII *VY-E*. Their aircraft carried AI Mk VIIIA radar and packed a bite of four 20 mm cannon but it needed ground radar to facilitate the kill. Sandwich GCI initiated the stalking of Waldecker's bomber but Jones had to find and pursue it on his AI and rules of engagement meant Bill Maguire needed a visual before firing. Understandably, Waldecker behaved erratically and at least seven directional changes occurred as the GCI station positioned Maguire's Mosquito to attack.

Relentlessly, the gap closed. Three times, Sandwich told Maguire to 'Canary' which meant switching on his IFF to embolden the night fighter's radar trace. Finally, Jones got a contact, 2½ miles range, port side and below. Now it was his responsibility to prevent 'Hermann' reaching his destination. Six men were doing their duty — two would soon die. Maguire shed height as Jones nursed nearer.

Almost there — cannon were switched to fire. Closer and closer crept the Mosquito. Whether the Neptun sensed Maguire's approach is not certain but Waldecker suddenly swept into a hard diving turn to port, almost losing his assailant. Deftly however, Maguire curved down, cutting inside the '188. Far below was a layer of cloud but the moonlight above clearly showed pointed wings and black crosses. Maguire recognised a Ju 188, skilfully flown as well. Grimly, the Mosquito hung on as Maguire adjusted his sight for two rings deflection and closed to 250 yards. Now! Four cannon pounded, shaking the Mosquito as it pressed the attack to only 100 yards.

In those milliseconds of distance, the German's fate was sealed. Waldecker felt his aircraft shudder from violent blows on the port side. Shells ripped into the cockpit and the port engine erupted in a fierce banner of torment. Worse still were the crew casualties. Karl-Heinz Mueller was in agony, a shell had blown his left arm off and he suffered head injuries. Julius Hohman fired back but took grievous thigh wounds and lost consciousness. Luckily, Waldecker was uninjured and tried desperately to shake off their tormentor with a tight turn to port. What then happened, he always attributed to sabotage — the control grip came away in his hands! Belgian Resistance had often cut communications to the base and Waldecker had heard of attempts to sabotage aircraft. Staring in disbelief at the severed control column, he was convinced of their

Fateful moment — a splash of flame in the darkness. This still from the gun-camera of Marguire's Mosquito shows the moment when the fate of Waldecker's Ju 188 was sealed (W.D. Jones).

success and equally sure his aircraft was lost. Out of control, the Ju 188 straightened momentarily, then pulled a vigorous, nose up turn to the right, losing height. Flames from the burning BMW gave Maguire a beacon and Waldecker's bomber was doomed. Following the Ju 188, Maguire fired again and went right in to 100 yards smashing pieces from the '188. This stoked up the fire raging within. The German bomber seemed to fall out of the sky, flaming earthwards. Inside, its crew were fighting for their lives.

Waldecker ordered them to bale out and helped Waldemar Haupt with the unconscious Hohman and poor Mueller, both bleeding profusely. Haupt had an injured knee but he and his pilot managed to push their comrades through the escape hatch, operating their parachutes as they fell clear. Then Haupt jumped and Waldecker leapt for his life as the plane began breaking up. At 22.59½, Squadron Leader Maguire transmitted, 'He's going down, curse him.' Already, Sandwich had another customer.

Far below, people heard the combat. AA guns in the region had been bark-

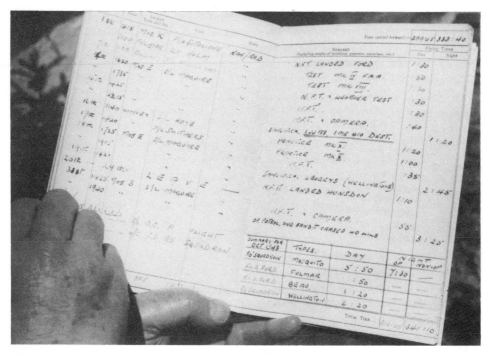

Flying Officer W.D. Jones recorded two combats that night. After destroying Waldecker's Ju 188, they shot down an Me 410 into the sea.

ing angrily and the distinctive drone of a 'Jerry' was detected between salvoes of gunfire. Then came the sound of another plane, the rattle of cannon fire and the swelling scream of tormented engines. The whist drive at Waldringfield was abandoned as players went out to see what was happening. Mrs Read of Kirton recalled seeing a parachute caught in the searchlights. There was a tremendous flash and explosion from the direction of Church Farm and the night seemed quiet again.

In Kirton village, Police Constable David Johnson hurried from his home to the crash site near Kirton Creek. The aircraft had exploded and was completely shattered, leaving a crater approximately 25ft by 5ft. Fortunately, there were no injuries or damage and the policeman found evidence to prove it

was German, but there was no trace of the crew. Placing a guard of Special Constables and Air Raid Wardens, the Constable made his way to Hemley Hall when he heard that three German airmen had landed. Waldecker and Haupt were safe, poor Julius Hohman was found dead. Karl Heinz Mueller was missing and, at 4.00 am on 16 October, Lieutenant J.W.F. Causton led members of the Newbourn and Hemley Platoon, Home Guard, on a search. For five hours, the area was combed without success then a report came in that the mutilated body of a German airman, still in his parachute, had been found by a Land Army girl in Thicket Field, Church Farm. The policeman later reported that the left arm was missing and there were severe head wounds. A pool of blood against the head indicated that Mueller was alive when he alighted but was too weak to get help, the efforts of Waldecker and Haupt had been in vain. Haupt received an operation on his knee and made a full recovery, eventually going to a PoW camp in Indiana, USA. Waldecker went to another camp for officers and received confirmation of his *Ritter Kreuz* on 22 November 1943, still convinced that his downfall was primarily sabotage. Perhaps the wreckage of his bomber held clues.

Flight Lieutenant Ella, RAF, examined the remains and confirmed it as a Ju 188, the first of its type to fall on the mainland. In his opinion, the aircraft was carrying at least one bomb which exploded at the time of the crash. Little did he realize that only part of the load had detonated, the rest lay hidden in the crater. Unaware of Waldecker's theory, RAF Intelligence could glean little from the site apart from the discovery of a new machine-gun mount and, four days later, a Maintenance Unit bulldozed it in burying Hermann for the next 44 years. Local inhabitants collected souvenirs, some of which proved dangerous as young Thomas Pickering discovered when he was injured tampering with a bullet. John Watling kept a flare-pistol and four cartridges in a leather case until his father found out. Gradually, most trophies were discarded, people moved and even the exact location of the crash slipped into imprecise memory.

It was 1972 when I visited Kirton to obtain eyewitness accounts and heard that most of the plane lay buried. Again, years passed, and the introduction of the 'Protection of Military Remains Act, 1986' meant that my activities when I revisited the site that year would need to be on a more formal basis. Firstly, permission to excavate was gained from the landowner, Mr Michael Paul and MoD wisely granted a licence only on condition that Explosives and Ordnance Disposal (EOD) were present. Records indicated that the bomb load had exploded but Mr S.B. Bryant of S10 (Air) introduced this caveat to our activities: there would be no repetition of *Bird Dog*. At this time we had not pin-pointed the site and our magnetometer chose the moment to go unserviceable. The East Anglians were in trouble so a plea went up north for the use of a Fisher TW5 M. Scope. Alan Downing with Mike and Rob Cookman from Typhoon International generously provided support and equipment to locate the buried bomber.

I would also like to record the superb co-operation we received from the MoD and the RAF EOD from Wittering. They are busy people and the earliest slot on their task board was 4 July 1987. This was a beautiful day so Sergeant Steve Burgess could bask in his deck-chair while monitoring activities. A short briefing was held alerting all to the hazards of ordnance and to question, not touch, if anything suspicious appeared.

Prentice Plant Hire had been sympathetic on the rate charged and provided a JCB 860, capable of reaching over 25 ft and tracked for maximum support on the marsh. Events proved we needed it. Rather than rush and miss interesting artefacts, the pace of excavation was controlled and the spoil sifted to recover small items. Early finds were sections of Kutonase cable cutter, wing structure and parts of a BMW engine denoting it had smashed on its way under. Soon we had a sizeable hole and were pulling out more interesting items including the tool kit, maps and first aid equipment. Steve Burgess was collecting

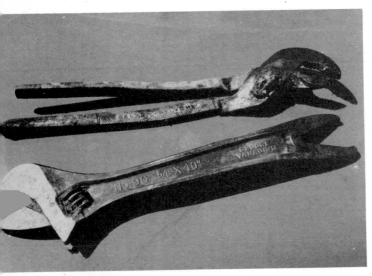

Left *British-made tools, perhaps captured during the BEF's retreat in 1940.*

Right *50 kg of German explosives destined for English soil finally gets there.*

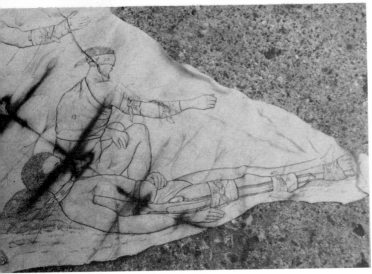

Left *Detail from one of the bandages. Note old-fashioned style of musket.*

numerous cannon shells, some seemingly in mint condition. At 13.26 hours, a scoop of grey clay was swept cleanly from the crater to reveal one 50 kg bomb. Nobby, the digger driver, promptly baled out! Reactions elsewhere ranged from prosaic to profane and Nobby sheepishly emerged from behind his machine. RAF EOD now took charge and excavations ceased while Steve called in his support team from weekend standby.

Later that afternoon, Flight Lieutenant Alan Swan and Senior Aircraftsman Andrew Priest arrived. Our SC 50 kg was in excellent condition, had an ELAZ 25 fuse, no rust, and still wore all its batch markings, but appearances can be deceptive and no chances would be taken, the bomb would be detonated. To reduce the blast, it was placed in a trench dug some distance from the crater. A pound of plastic explosive was slapped on the nose and body of the cas-

ing. Detonation would be by electric charge and the RAF positioned themselves behind a sturdy oak. Non essential personnel were removed to a safe distance and guards mounted to prevent people approaching.

Minutes passed, telephoto lens wavered, then the radio crackled, 'Take Cover.... Take Cover'. Seconds later, there was a flash, a sharp bang and a plume of soil spurted skywards. The noise was startling, even when expected and the explosion had a distinctive crack, seeming louder than the 500 lb bombs in 1979. As we stood up, earth and fragments showered into nearby shrubbery and one piece of shrapnel burnt the first fingers to touch it. Like wartime schoolboys, others eagerly scooped up these jagged souvenirs — the end of an exciting day and our 4th of July firecracker took some beating.

About 1½ tons of Ju 188 were removed but more wreckage remained. Could we get at it? Again, support from the authorities was excellent. No one knew whether other bombs lay in the wreckage so permission to continue was given but under close EOD supervision:

Steve would have to relinquish his deck-chair. If any more bombs appeared, we would cease and the RAF take over. On Sunday, caution was our watchword and every bucket of debris was scrutinized. A host of interesting items emerged — more documents; the dinghy and equipment; a propeller and engine; even packets of cigarettes. Other items would need a technical manual to identify. The second bomb needed no identification — same as yesterday only Nobby stayed in his cab this time.

Keeping our activities secret was difficult given the noise we made. Sunday was not to be peaceful either — but Steve Burgess tried to crack the casing on this one with a linear cutting charge, a strip of specifically shaped lead, filled with plastic explosive and taped on the bomb's casing. In a controlled explosion it was designed to split the bomb so the contents could be burnt off harmlessly. As related in chapter seven, removing fuses is too dangerous. Unfortunately, the controlled explosion failed and complete destruction was necessary, a repeat of the previous day's performance and the end of our dig, so we thought.

Above *Taken to be official documents, these pages turned out to be from a paperback novel!*

Left *Towel and razor carried by one of the crew in case he landed away from his home airfield.*

For safety, the site was partially filled and fenced off. Despite requests to the contrary, a radio station had given away the location and we wanted no injuries sustained by souvenir hunters falling in a 25 ft deep crater. EOD were convinced other bombs were extant and the condition of items found prompted their belief that the 1000 kg 'Hermann' was still in the marsh. Reaching him might be a major project and their calendar prevented further work until mid-August.

Phase two of this project was strictly under RAF control but the author was given permission to attend. In charge of the five-man team was Flight Sergeant Colin Gillick. Their task was to retrieve 'Hermann' but doing so meant removing wreckage and local museums were delighted to learn they could have any debris which emerged. The East

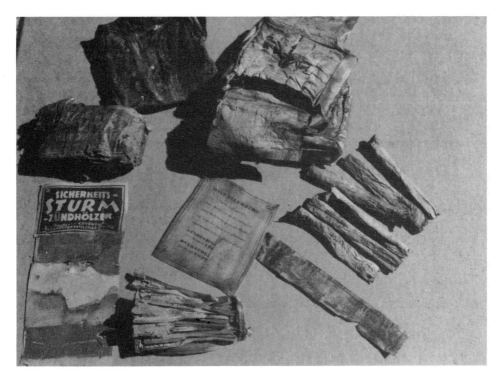

Cigarettes, coupons and matches were found as part of the dinghy kit. Norwich City archivists treated all paperwork and other perishable items.

Anglian Aircraft Research Group happily provided a lorry to aid distribution.

Unlike earlier operations on the site, bad weather handicapped the task and the RAF's JCB proved inadequate so Prentice Plant's brand new Komatsu PC50LC digger was hired. This machine was tracked for marsh work and could lift 3 tons but finding 'Hermann' still proved difficult. Metal detectors could not distinguish him from the mass of other wreckage and the possibility of seven more 50 kg bombs. The first crater had been kept at 30 ft in diameter but early attempts with the JCB expanded this and even the Komatsu had to be careful where it stood as pouring rain made slippage into the crater a frequent hazard. On 26 August, nine days after arriving on site, another 50 kg emerged,

jumbled amidst remains of the second BMW 801A. Later that afternoon, 15 ft down and to one side of the enlarged crater, part of an ominously large cylinder was uncovered. 'Hermann' had been found! Soon the nose was revealed pointing skywards but rain and darkness drew activities to a close. The two airmen on duty that night had a very sinister companion nearby and undoubtedly hoped he would continue sleeping, despite being disturbed.

Next day, he had gone! A massive landslip had occurred burying the bomb and depressing our spirits. For several hours, we strived to clear clay which kept sliding in. This process removed an undercarriage leg and tyre, ironically made by Dunlop. Of 'Hermann', there was no sign and the Komatsu had

Above *A linear cutting charge intended to crack the casing failed and this 50 kg bomb had to be completely destroyed.*

Below *Tyre from Junkers 188 made by Dunlop's German factory.*

difficulty finding firm terrain within reach. The afternoon was well advanced before we found 'Hermann' again — the weight of clay sliding in had turned and pushed him to the most inaccessible part of the crater.

Next day, several attempts were made to drag the bomb clear but each failed because the straps slipped off the smooth casing and a makeshift arrangement of wooden splints for chains to bite on fared no better. Colin Gillick's team had no alternative but the slog of many hours manual digging to reveal enough of 'Hermann' to harness. This task was eased by placing a 'Dutch Ring' over the bomb. 'Dutch Rings' are circles of aluminium, one metre deep, which can be stacked creating a tube to work in.

Fortunately the weather improved and the land dried out so, by Sunday 30 August all was ready for another attempt. This time the Komatsu got close enough for a direct lift. Time was running out for the project and Wing Commander Keith Hopkins arrived to review the situation. The first effort was an embarrassing failure, 'Hermann' stubbornly shrugged off his harness and barely moved. Cursing, Colin Gillick slithered into the mire, refitted the chains and adjusted the wooden spacers concocted to spread the load. Try again. Strangely, the fact that we were struggling with a device designed to blow us over several hundred acres did not induce any noticeable fear although I have to confess the possibility of instant extinction crossed my mind. Apprehension was vented by cursing the bomb's continued resistance, then to our amazement, he lifted free. He was several feet up when the chains slipped, everyone flinched, but the harness held and 'Her-

Very gently, Hermann is eased from his resting place: 15 ft up, the chains slipped!

Tired but triumphant. Part of the successful EOD team with 'Hermann'. L-R F/Sgt Colin Gillick; SA Gary Stockwell; LAC Andrew Smith; SAC Adrian McKinstry.

mann' landed gently on the surface. Now came a jubilant photo session, hunters with the tiger. EOD deserved the real credit but you could not prevent the diggers getting in on the act and we were even more excited when the RAF generously allowed us to continue excavating. Happily, no more bombs appeared as the site was thoroughly turned over to extract the remaining wreckage. No evidence of sabotage emerged so Waldecker's conviction is unproven. Nor did we find anything to support the story that a fifth

man, a spy, was on board — this story continues in local legend. Waldecker died in 1966 but contact with Haupt in 1988 drew no admission of any clandestine purposes in their mission. Like all stories, it embellishes the yarn.

On Bank Holiday Monday 31 August Flight Sergeant Gillick began the serious business of washing out the explosive. A blast barrier was built around 'Hermann' but villagers were warned to keep their windows open. The fuze pocket had been damaged but the fuze was identified as an ELAZ 25B and markings on the case denoted a filling of Ammonium Nitrate/TNT/Aluminium powder. Of concern was the possibility that 'Hermann' was fitted with a ZUS 40 anti-disturbance device so, apart from the likelihood of damage, this was a good reason to leave the fuze alone and concentrate on trepanning through the casing. To do this, a cutting head was attached and the Flight Sergeant retired behind a second blast barrier built as far away as the remote controls allowed. The trepanner cut two neat holes in the casing, one for washing head entry and the other for liquified explosive to exit safely into a container. When the powder filling had been removed, it was found that the nose section had a cast filling and a decision was made to steam this out, an operation lasting several hours and, once commenced, one that had to continue uninterrupted. Although the exploder pocket had not been deactivated, 'Hermann' was now comparatively harmless and transported to RAF Wittering. There, the delicate fuze mechanism was trepanned at each extremity and the complete exploder tube removed for X ray to see if a ZUS 40 had been implanted but none was found. This exercise tested skills and equipment that had not been used in anger for a long time but the knowledge gained must be useful as the older generation of Bomb Disposal men retire. The fact is that World War 2 has left a dangerous legacy of unexploded bombs, some plotted, others not, and the experience gained recovering and taming 'Hermann' is invaluable.

Today, Hermann's husk is a proud trophy at RAF Wittering and several

May 1988. Bill Jones with a piece of wing flap from 'his' Ju 188. Sadly S/Ldr Maguire was killed in a flying accident towards the end of the war.

aviation museums have some excellent items from the wreck on display as well as a fascinating story to relate. It had been a most exciting excavation with superb co-operation between museum groups and a splendid example of how working with the MoD provided satisfaction all round.

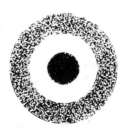

WRECKOLOGY AND
WRECKOVERY

11

In this last chapter, we embark on a travelogue of crash sites, some visited, others awaiting investigation. The East Anglian flatlands jut prominently towards Europe and, during World War 2 the area became something of a vast aircraft carrier for Allied Forces. Records kept from May 1940 list nearly 1,000 crashes in Norfolk alone and, while Suffolk's files contain more detail, they are less complete, although the total is probably similar. There is no reason to believe that bordering counties had significantly fewer crashes so, clearly, the task of detailing each incident is enormous. As these last pages are turned, we do not have a, 'closed book' at the end. Research continues: new facts emerge, eyewitnesses come forward, recollections are received from lucky survivors.

Driving through the fens and farmlands today, one sees the crumbling, overgrown airfields, empty and desolate. Their association with the war is instantly recognizable but few realize that the gap in a hedge where nothing grows any more marks where a bomber crew burned to death. Each autumn, a field of scattered fighter fragments is tractor-tumbled: the driver may or may not be aware of what happened there and with each passing season, he is less likely to have seen it. Now is the important time to record his recollections and blend them into wider history.

★ ★ ★

Mid-air collisions would become tragically commonplace over East Anglia and one of the earliest to occur cost the lives of nine Wellington aircrew before the war was eight weeks old.

Early in the war Wellington squadrons believed that their formations and firepower would protect them. In addition, various formation manoeuvres were developed to confuse attacking fighters and one of these was regarded by some as risky for bombers in close formation. Assuming a vic of bombers to be under attack by a vic of fighters, tactics called for the bombers to change from 'V' formation to a stepped-astern, vertical stack. To achieve this, the Flight Leader held formation while No 2 slid behind and below with No 3 dropping astern and lower than No 2. On command from the Flight Leader, all three aircraft would cut throttle and cause the fighters to overshoot. Abrupt throttling back was a viable tactic in the right conditions but, in close formation, at low altitude, it was dangerous. A throttled-back bomber might sag into the aircraft below or, if power on was not smoothly coordinated, one bomber might overtake the other and fly into it.

On 30 October 1939 three Wellingtons from No 9 Squadron left Honington in Suffolk for a formation practice. Flying at 800 ft, just below the cloud base, the bombers swept majestically over the aerodrome in 'V' formation. Just east of the station, Squadron Leader L.S. Lamb called the change and No 1 and 2 Wellingtons slipped in behind

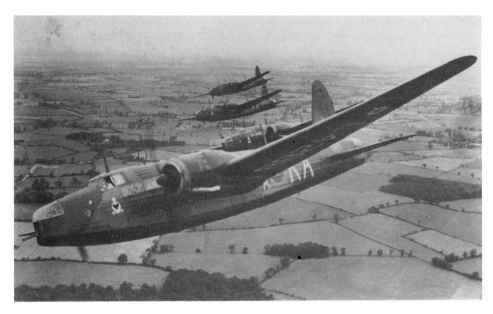

Above *'Britain Prepared' was the title of this postcard: L4288 is nearest to the camera* (Bob Collis).

Below *N & SAM member Barry Lain amid part of L4288 on display at Flixton* (Bob Collis).

him. Throttles for the Pegasus radials were cut. Seconds later, Flying Officer Chandler's bomber, *L4363*, hit Lamb's *L4288*. On the third aircraft, they were horrified to see the fin of *L4363* cut into the starboard wing of *L4288*. Swift avoiding action averted a triple tragedy as the two bombers fell, locked together and shedding pieces. Separating just before impact, both Wellingtons smashed into boggy terrain at Water Mill, Sapiston.

Crash crews found access very difficult which is probably why a lot of wreckage remained after the bodies were recovered. In 1973 a small group led by RAF Corporal Peter Agate, removed some of the wreckage and the sites were finally cleared by the N&SAM in 1982/83. *L4288* was used by the RAF in a pre-war, publicity photograph and, in a strange way, its skeletal remains continue this duty in the N&SAM collection.

Sometimes, the rewards of research are not in pieces recovered but in help given to relatives of airmen who died. In August 1987, a letter to the author from Mrs Rita Moy requested information about her brother's aircraft which crashed on 26 May 1940, 'somewhere in East Anglia'. Subsequent research revealed that No 573130 Leading Aircraftsman Ernest Peareth Armstrong was one of the brave Blenheim boys who died trying to staunch the wounds torn in Allied Lines by the Wehrmacht.

An Aircraft Apprentice Boy entrant in January, 1938, he became a Wireless Operator, Trainee Aircrew, on 5 September 1939. In October he finished training and served with 219 Sqadron until joining 235 Squadron on 19 May 1940. A week later, at 6.57 pm, 26 May, the signal to commence Operation Dynamo — the evacuation of troops from France — was issued.

Proud of his winged AG (Air Gunner) brevet, Leading Aircraftsman E.P. Armstrong in February 1940 (Mrs R. Moy).

Against momentous events unfolding, the loss that evening of Blenheim *P6956* from Bircham Newton might be considered a small matter. However, had the need not been so great, Pilot Officer C.D. Warde and his crew might not have flown in such poor weather. Climbing through overcast, Warde lost control and the twin-engined fighter entered a spin. Twirling earthwards in cloud, he struggled to recover but the Blenheim failed to respond and it was hopeless. Ordering his crew to bale out, Warde waited a little time before jumping himself. Sadly, Pilot Officer Alfred H. Murphy and Ernest Armstrong failed to escape and died when the Blenheim blew up on impact at Court Farm, Docking, in Norfolk. Ernest Armstrong was eighteen-years-old when he died and the young man's Flying Log Book is treasured by his family.

Items from crashes kept as souvenirs

may also have historical significance and one such memento is a parachute release buckle from the first German aircraft to crash in Suffolk during World War 2. Kept for many years by Police Inspector W.H. Bird, it belonged to 26-year-old *Feldwebel* Paul Randorf of *3/Küstenfliegergruppe* 906.

On 7 June, 1940, a Heinkel 115 floatplane, *8L+EL*, was flying low in the coastal mists seeking to lay its sinister cargo. As the bomber sought its target area, British searchlights illuminated it brilliantly, dazzling the pilot. Caught in the blinding glare at only 300 ft, Oblt zur See Adolf van Hüllen, lost control. At 11.31 pm, his Heinkel smacked into the grounds of The Old Rectory, Eyke, and its mine exploded. The pilot and *Feldwebel* Ludwig Fehr died instantly but Inspector Bird and others found Randorf hanging by his parachute from a tree near the Rectory entrance. Despite

serious injuries and possibly from sheer fright or shock, Randorf resisted his captors and forced them to restrain him. Wounded and afraid, he continued struggling in the ambulance travelling to the East Suffolk and Ipswich Hospital. Sadly, he died of his wounds two days later.

Pieces of *8L+EL* were scattered for some 300 yards and the Old Rectory and nearby police station suffered considerable blast damage. The aircraft itself left only a small crater but the mine detonating nearby blew a hole 20 ft across and 4 ft deep. Searching in 1982 the N&SAM found only small globules of molten aluminium so Randor's release buckle is probably the only worthwhile relic from Suffolk's first German.

For many years parts from another raider could still be found near Great Barton in Suffolk. Why it crashed remains a mystery but, in the early

Right *Official recognition chart for Heinkel 115.*

Below *Parachute release buckle from the first German aircraft to crash in Suffolk.*

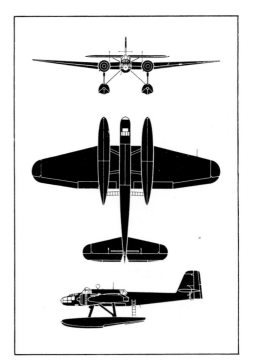

Crater caused by detonation of mine carried by He 115, 8L+EL. Remains of the float plane lie in the background (S.P. Evans).

minutes of Tuesday 30 July 1940, the populace of Bury St Edmunds heard the unmistakable sound of a low-flying, 'Jerry'. Skimming over the rooftops, it seemed to be in trouble and one onlooker claimed it burst into flames just before crashing at twelve minutes past midnight.

Daybreak saw the charred remains of Ju 88A-1, 5J+ER, smouldering across two fields. Four airmen from 7/KG4 were incinerated in the wreckage and it appears that the pilot, *Unteroffizier* Fritz Krause, attempted a forced landing but hit an oak tree and crashed, two charred parachutes hung from its branches. On 2 August the crew were buried in Great Barton village churchyard but, post-war, their remains were re-interred at Cannock Chase, the largest German war cemetery in England.

Some German airmen still rest in gentle hamlets, often alongside former adversaries. A few miles from Great Barton, at Honington, can be found the grave of *Unteroffizier* Heinrich Schaffer whose Dornier 17 of 7/KG2 crash landed at Whepstead, four miles from Bury St Edmunds, on 26 August 1940.

That afternoon, eighty bombers from KG2 and KG3 intended to attack the important RAF fighter airfields of Debden and Hornchurch. German tactics initially confused the defenders but Spitfires and Hurricanes soon engaged and took advantage of insufficient fighter protection to break up the enemy bomber formations. Pursued by Hurricanes of 111 Squadron, Dornier 17Z-3, U5+, raced for the coast. Closing in, the British fighters raked it with their machine-guns, knocking out the port engine and

Above *Charred tail unit from Ju88A-1 5J+ER at Great Barton on 30 July 1940 (G.F. Lambert FRPS via S.P. Evans).*

Below *Bullet-scarred Dornier Do 17Z-3 U5+ in an English mustard field at Whepstead, Suffolk on 26 August 1940 (G.F. Lambert FRPS via S.P. Evans).*

wounding three of the crew. At 3.40 pm, the stricken Dornier belly-landed in a mustard field and two farm workmen, harvesting wheat nearby, were first to reach it. One of them, Mr C.W. Boreham, took the proverbial pitchfork with which to apprehend the enemy. Later, he described events to a local newspaper reporter: 'I was at the top of the field loading wheat when I saw the plane coming. It was about 400 ft and only one engine running. After dropping a parachute it crashed in the field of mustard. When we got to the scene we found two of the occupants lying on the ground near the plane. They were both wounded and must have crawled out of the machine. One German, who was unhurt, was standing opposite the plane, he was a youngster about 15 or 16 years old. He said something in German which we could not understand but we could understand him when he said, 'Kamerad' and pointed to the pilot in the plane. The pilot was in the cockpit and was badly hurt. We set to work to get him out and lifted him from the machine. He made motions to us to lift his wounded leg over the wheel.'

The crew were disarmed and taken prisoner. Grievously hurt, Heinrich Schaffer succumbed to his injuries on 22 September 1940. The Dornier, *Werk Nr 1207*, was sent to the Royal Aircraft Establishment at Farnborough for examination by intelligence experts. Pictures taken by photographer G.F. Lambert illustrating the bullet-riddled bomber, provide a fascinating record of the crash and contribute to both aviation and local history.

Destroying bombers like Schaffer's Dornier, Britain won freedom for itself and, arguably, for the western world. At this crucial period, before Hitler invaded Russia and Pearl Harbor pulled America into the war, Britain, supported by her Empire, Commonwealth and people from occupied countries, was the only belligerent European nation not dominated by the Nazis. Driven from the Continent, one way she and her Allies could retaliate was through air-power but these were also days when the might of Bomber Command was more imagined than actual. Target finding apparatus and modern aircraft were coming but, for now, the RAF took the war back to Europe with what it had. 2 Group were based in East Anglia and its Blenheims forayed from the region to attack airfields, industrial targets, ports and shipping. These sorties cost them dearly but their gallantry exemplified the spirit of a nation, bloodied but unbowed, determined to hit back.

Within 2 Group was 139 (Jamaica) Squadron operating from Horsham St Faith, now Norwich Airport. On 9 December 1940, its Blenheims set off for the Ruhr in conditions described as, 'filthy' — rain and low clouds. A ceiling of 150 ft was not entirely unwelcome as it provided cover for the Blenheims who kept well below radar at only 50 ft. Shipping was a priority target so, when Flying Officer J.D. King spotted a small convoy on his port side, he turned to attack.

No sleeping gunners these — tracer whipped towards him as Jim targeted the nearest coaster. Sergeant Eric Pierce released their bombs moments before they hurtled over the vessel, barely clearing its masts. Suddenly, the Blenheim was hit. Bullets tore into the cockpit smashing the P4 compass and alcohol from it spurted into Jim's face. Startled by the stinging spray, Jim instinctively pulled up and they shot into cloud. Too late. More hits. Jim felt the ailerons go slack and the damaged Blenheim fell

Above *Jim King's bedraggled Blenheim R3698 being prepared for removal from a field near Horsham St Faith* (E. Aspinall).

Left *Twenty-year-old New Zealander Flight Lieutenant G.J. Menzies died when Blenheim T2435 was mistaken for a Ju 88* (E. Aspinall).

towards the sea. Quite how he managed it seemed a miracle but Jim pulled out just above the waves, skilfully grasping some vestige of control. Staggering just above the swell, Jim caught and prevented the port wing from slicing in then, kicking right rudder, he levelled off. Realizing his port aileron was useless and the starboard side also hit, Jim ruddered *R3698* towards home. Behind him, Sergeant Eddie Barker radioed for bearings and Eric used his compass to steer an erratic, westerly heading.

Piloting the damaged bomber demanded care. If Jim relaxed for a moment, the port wing slumped and she threatened to roll or spin: attempting to land would exacerbate the problem. Reaching Horsham, Jim felt a wheels and flaps down approach was too risky and opted to belly land. Working vigorously, he held the Blenheim level, carefully losing height and speed. Steady — steady — steady, the Blenheim eased lower. Crossing the airfield boundary, Jim kept control but then, despite his efforts, the port wing dipped too soon. If it hit, they might cartwheel into one horrific fireball. Booting hard right rudder, Jim pulled it up just in time. Scuffing the ground with its propellers, Jim knew his Blenheim had used too much space, there was nothing he could do now but brace himself and hope.

Churning turf, the bomber bellied in. Ahead lay a small bank and the aerodrome boundary. Frightened of leg injuries, Jim took his feet off the rudder pedals as the Blenheim smashed through the boundary hedge, scraped noisily across the Holt road and ripped through another hedge into the field beyond. Twisting and grinding, his bomber shed assorted pieces including the two perspex blisters on either side of the cockpit. Then, abruptly, they stopped.

Fear of fire stung Jim's response but his overhead exit failed to slide back on twisted runners. Grateful for the missing blisters, Jim squeezed free, Eddie Barker was already out but Eric had not appeared nor, thank God, had any flames, yet. Returning to the wreck, they pulled Eric to safety as help arrived. Fortunately there were no serious injuries and the dramatic spectacle of their Blenheim attracted numerous sightseers until its recovery.

Early in the new year, Jim's best friend, Flight Lieutenant Guy J. 'Lemmy' Menzies DFC, was not so lucky. Returning from operations on 22 January 1941, his Blenheim was mistaken for the similar Ju 88 by Lowestoft's AA guns who shot it down killing the crew. Fireman E.W. Lark saw the plane hit immediately and it nosedived to earth near the Somerleyton Road.

In the early 1960s, I searched for pieces of *T2435* but was too inexperienced to tell if the odd fragments found were Blenheim or not. Now the site of this sad mistake has disappeared under a housing estate and I wonder if any residents have been puzzled by scraps of aluminium in their flowerbeds.

On Lark Farm, Soham Fen, near Ely, ploughmen were at first perplexed when they hit an obstacle. Pulling the long, narrow cylinder from the soil, they discovered it was an aeroplane undercarriage leg, probably from a fighter, judging from its size. Hearing about their find, Dan Engle of the AAPS moved swiftly to research the site and arrange an excavation. His enquiries resulted in some fascinating finds from this aircraft and a so far abortive search for another.

It was 17 May 1941, when Hurricane I, *V7225*, left Mildenhall for a weather flight. Primarily a bomber base, Mildenhall was also home to 1401 Meteorological Flight whose pilots had the important but fatiguing function of data collection for the weather wizards. Flying Officer Iain Robertson MacDiarmid DFC, would need to reach high altitude, perhaps 300 millibars or approximately 30,000 ft. As the Hurricane hauled itself upstairs, he would note visibility; cloud types; air pressures; temperatures and other essential ingredients for predicting how our capricious climate might affect operations. His former fighter was an ex-87 Squadron, Battle of Britain veteran, adapted for Met Flight activities in March 1941. It could, if called upon, fulfil a fighter affiliation role and some records indicate MacDiarmid's purpose that afternoon was, in fact, to exercise with Wellingtons from 149 Squadron, also based at Mildenhall.

Whatever the Hurricane's purpose, it was seen in the Soham area apparently making a Met climb to high altitude. In ROC Post B3, Cecil Fuller was acting as plotter and observed four Wellingtons approaching from the east at 4 to 5,000 ft. Watching the Wellingtons, Cecil heard the Hurricane screaming in from above and it hurtled out of cloud towards the bombers.

MacDiarmid may have had oxygen problems and blacked out, he might have been making a pass at the bombers. Either way Cecil witnessed the last catastrophic moments of two aircraft. Plummeting into the bomber formation, MacDiarmid's Hurricane tore right through the fuselage of the leading Wellington, R1587, flown by Squadron Leader A.W.J. Clark. Cutting into the bomber, the Hurricane lost a chunk of its port wing and seemed to ricochet off the larger aircraft in its dive to oblivion. Some parachutes deployed from the bomber but all were too low and another eye witness saw one open only for it to be caught by the tumbling tail section and dragged earthwards. None of Squadron Leader Clark's crew survived when the Wellington crashed and burnt.

Forty-four years later, in January, 1985, Dan Engle organized his dig on Hurricane V7225. Appalling weather that month reminded us of the Hurricane's role but Dan faced time restraints so the 26th was fixed, whatever the conditions. Digging holes to avoid biting winds and snow squalls was almost a pleasure and the first wreckage to emerge told us that V7225 went in very steeply and upside down.

Assisted by a small machine, we pulled out pieces of lower fuselage and the smashed radiator before finding the cockpit area. Extracted from this were the control column, remains of the gunsight and both standard and meteorological instrumentation. Crushed amid the cockpit debris, we found MacDiarmid's leather flying helmet and, nearby, a George III penny. Had he carried this for luck or did it precede the Hurricane as a morsel of history dropped by a farmworker? We shall never know but the helmet underwent hours of restoration for display with the coin. To those accustomed to modern, 'bone domes', the leather helmet looks what it is, the helm of a lost warrior.

Knowing the Hurricane had reached maximum development, Hawkers had been working on a successor, the Typhoon. Carrying twelve .303 machineguns and pwered by a Napier Sabre, 24-cylinder engine, the new fighter had potential but, like all new projects hurried into combat, it had problems and one of the most serious caused the first RAF Typhoon casualty.

The book, *Fly For Your Life*, by Larry Forrester, tells the service career of the late R.R. Stanford Tuck and relates examples of what was called, 'Tuck's Luck'. Fate beamed generously towards him yet again on 1 November 1941. Now commanding 56 Squadron, Tuck planned to take one of their new Typhoon 1As, R7592, on an air test but, at the last minute, a telephone call from the station CO delayed him so he asked another pilot to check the big fighter.

Pilots of these early machines had complained of exhaust fumes making them feel ill. Tuck later recalled that R7592 was fitted with a device for measuring the mixture and strength of gases seeping into the cockpit. Carbon dioxide in a confined space could asphyxi-

Above *Buried 44 years, MacDiarmid's flying helmet was cleaned and restored for the AAPS collection.*

Above right *Whether a quirk of history or a good luck token, this George III penny was found amongst the cockpit debris of Hurricane V7225.*

ate the pilot but the smell gave warning. Far more dangerous was the odourless carbon monoxide since even small quantities are toxic. In addition, the unusual, 'car door' access to early Typhoons made it impossible to simply slow down and slide open the hood.

Being a few days off his 27th birthday, Pilot Officer James Frederick Deck was older than the average fighter pilot. His parents were English but lived in Buenos Aires, Argentina, where James grew up as one of three sons, all of whom served in the RAF.

To fire the huge, 2,200 hp engine, a Kaufman starter gun system was used to get it turning. Pressing coil booster and starter button, Tuck's ground crew had the engine running and Deck hastened out to prevent it overheating. Grumbling, Tuck returned to the dispersal hut and took his phone call as R7592, 'L' thundered away from

Duxford.

A little later and forty miles northeast, farmworker George Holmes was convalescing from a short spell in hospital and had ventured out for fresh air on this bright November day. George had no interest in aircraft and the fact that one of the RAF's latest and most secret fighters was flying over Roudham attracted little more than a glance. Then, amazingly, from about 3,000 ft, the fighter began spiralling down. Carried for miles, the screech of its revving engine grew louder and George saw the Typhoon spin viciously to destruction. Spellbound, he felt the thump as it exploded in a hedgerow along Drove Lane, not far from his cottage. Burning fiercely, it was dangerous to approach as ammunition fizzed off in all directions. One of the first to reach the scene was an ARP Warden and George remembers this man flailing his arms about like one bothered by bees, not bullets, as they zipped past.

Soon, crash trucks arrived and smothered the wreckage with foam. From deep in the ground, they pulled the burnt, shrivelled corpse of Pilot Officer Deck, 'not much longer than a spade' George recalled. A post mortem

An early Typhoon, similar to R7592 which crashed at Roudham, Norfolk, and became the first Typhoon lost in RAF service (C.H. Thomas).

established that Deck had been poisoned by carbon monoxide, high doses were detected in his liver.

Henceforth, Typhoon pilots used oxygen from engine start to shutdown. Other, structural problems with the Typhoon were eventually resolved. Disappointing at altitude and unsuitable as an interceptor, Typhoons performed well lower down and helped discourage hit-and-run attacks on coastal towns. Later, armed with cannons and rockets, Typhoons blasted across Europe in the anti-tank role.

Pilot Officer J.F. Deck is buried in Honington All Saints Churchyard. Tragically, all three Deck boys perished serving in the RAF and a stained-glass window in the Church of Saint Peter at Westleton, east Suffolk, commemorates this family's tremendous loss.

Members of the East Anglian Aircraft Recovery Group (EAARG) felt that even small pieces from the first RAF Typhoon crash would be worth finding. In March 1987 the original crater was re-opened and a huge pile of sand removed. Finds included a propeller blade, throttle controls, remains of instruments, even the intact bulb from the cockpit lamp. However, fire, foam and acidy soil had done little for aluminium items and a layer of 'daz' with burnt sand at a depth of 8 ft told us that we had reached the Typhoon's maximum penetration, below this lay solid chalk.

Promising digs can also peter out as the AAPS discovered when seeking the remains of Wellington MkIII, *Z1616*, from 75 Squadron.

It was 29 June 1942, when Pilot Officer Robert Bertram and crew departed Feltwell bound for Bremen. Shortly after take-off, the aircraft caught fire and circled over Red House Farm, Feltwell, perhaps trying to land. In the farmhouse, seven-year-old Nigel Laws was thrust beneath the table by his anxious parents as the blazing bomber headed towards their home. Years later, Nigel recalled the enormous bang and how the room lit up as incendiaries on *Z1616* ignited. None of the five crew survived.

Forty-two years later, several of those incendiaries were picked from the bottom of the saucer-shaped depression marking the site. Preliminary work by Dan Engle created an optimistic atmosphere on 27 October 1984, but, apart from some assorted fragments and a few IB's dealt with by the police, little of Z1616 remained.

A site which I am certain hides wreckage will have to remain for future archaeologists because the residents of Spashett Road, Lowestoft, are unlikely to welcome undermining of their homes.

In 1941, Lowestoft's gunners may have mistaken Menzies' Blenheim for a Ju 88 but there was no doubt about the aircraft overhead on Monday 19 October 1942. A cold, rainy morning with low clouds greeted the town's inhabitants and, as they rose for work, the Luftwaffe were already awake and bound for England. That day saw considerable German activity over the eastern counties in conditions ideal for interdiction. Defence was difficult against these tactics because day interceptors could not easily operate and the all-weather per-

Weight from the nose of an incendiary bomb found in the wreckage of Wellington Z1616 at Feltwell.

formance and radar-equipped night fighters were more effective in meeting the challenge.

From 157 Squadron, Castle Camps, Flight Sergeant N. Munro and Warrant Officer A. Eastwood were patrolling near Southwold in Mosquito *W4094* when they chased a Ju 88. Glimpsing it in cloud, they closed to 5-600 yards and caught sight of it again. At 08.40, they transmitted a 'Tally-Ho' to base and were about to fire when their Mosquito was seen. Rolling on its back, the Ju 88 evaded by going straight down into the clouds from 2,000 ft. Seconds later, they thought it had re-appeared, coming head on but this aircraft turned out to be a Beaufighter, their '88 had vanished. A few minutes later, the Mosquito crew heard that the German had crashed.

Perhaps looking back for their pursuer, the crew of Ju 88, *3E+CM, 144319*, were unaware of the trap they had entered until it was too late. Descending through the murk, they emerged near Lowestoft at only 500 ft. Despite the turbid conditions, the port's defences were alert with weapons pointing towards the approaching sound of twin Jumo engines.

Breaking cloud, the hapless Junkers was immediately attacked by shore based batteries and ships in the harbour. Bracketed in a maelstrom of light and heavy AA fire, the Ju 88 ran a gauntlet from south to north Lowestoft, frantically seeking to escape. Even a Bren gunner on the auxiliary patrol vessel, *Lovania* claimed hits, while 40 mm Bofors spat rapid rounds and heavy 3.7 in, shore batteries provided bass to this deadly orchestra. At first, the Ju 88 seemed impervious to the barrage into which it had blundered. Some accounts say the raider suddenly plunged to destruction, others thought the pilot had

The censor deleted anti-invasion scaffolding from this photograph of Ju 88 3E+CM at Lowestoft, now published with his original deletion marks which create the criss-crossed skyline. Lying in the crater is what appears to be a 1000 kg bomb.

been hit and was trying to land in a large field on College Farm, about 700 yards north-west of St Margaret's Church. Either way, the bomber struck high tension cables, flipped on its back, hit the ground inverted and exploded.

Gunners of the 478 Heavy AA Battery (Mixed) contributed to its demise and the '88 fell near their positions, gashing through some anti-invasion scaffolding. The gun-site CO, Major Frederick Cooper, was first to approach but, luckily, had not got too close when part of the bomb load detonated. Suffering from a cut forehead, Major Cooper was taken to hospital while soldiers, police and wardens cordoned off the area. When it was thought safe, firemen doused the flames and a search for

remains of the crew commenced.

All four occupants had been blown to pieces but identity discs and documents confirmed them as airmen from 4/KG6: Dr Willy Blackert, aged 30; Alfred Bohnemann, aged 23; Helmut Mollenhauer, aged 20 and Meinhard Smit, also only 20. Today, they share a common grave at Lowestoft, not far from houses hiding the crash site of their aircraft.

1942 saw US servicemen enter combat from the United Kingdom and, henceforth, American aircraft feature increasingly in this chapter, but the first to appear was RAF operated.

Prior to entering the war, America supported the Allied cause with growing frankness. In March 1941, the Lease-

Lend Bill was passed and the, 'arsenal of democracy' opened for British purchases. This procurement included aircraft and one of those acquired was the Lockheed Vega Ventura. Located in Burbank, California, Vega were a subsidary of Lockheed and developed the Ventura, to British requirements, from their famous Lodestar/Hudson series. A task envisaged for the new bomber was to replace Blenheims in the dangerous low-level role. As such, the Ventura was an inauspicious performer and was succeeded by the versatile Mosquito when enough became available. Until then, three of 2 Group's Squadrons were blessed with the bulbous bomber and, as before with Blenheims, they courageously did their best.

Last to equip was 464 Squadron consisting mainly of Australian airmen stationed at Feltwell. Receiving their first Ventura in September, they began an aggressive training programme to work out tactics with their new machines. Staying low and travelling fast were essential and frequent sorties saw spiredodging Venturas scaring parishioners throughout the fens.

For several weeks, there were no mishaps but on 4 November 1942, the inevitable happened. Bad weather that morning kept engines silent but, near noon, an improvement enabled another, low-level training exercise to be called.

For two hours, eleven of the Squadron's aircraft practised for the combat they knew was imminent. Ten aircraft had landed safely when Flight Lieutenant M.I. Dore in *AE 737* came hammering across the airfield. Climbing away, all seemed well then, inexplicably, the Ventura's nose dropped. Diving steeply, the bomber went beyond the vertical. Screaming of its plight, the agonizing howl of Double Wasp engines

This Lockheed publicity picture shows a Ventura in RAF markings. Jutting from the trailing edge of the wing can be seen exposed features of the Fowler flaps (M. Bailey).

Excavation in progress on Ventura AE737. In the foreground is a section of Fowler flap mechanism.

ceased in sudden, cruel silence. Crash crews raced into the motions of a task they knew was hopeless, *AE 737* had taken all five airmen to their deaths.

Dredging their remains from a dyke on Stallode Fen, Lakenheath, was a grim task but all were found and 464 laid to rest the victims of their first Ventura loss. Overshadowed by worthier successors, the Ventura vanished from East Anglian skies. Four decades later, AAPS members rightly felt that increased recognition of Ventura aircrews would be achieved if parts from the type went on display. Not having a fixed collection of their own, they generously invited participation by other groups and a combined effort on Stallode Fen yielded numerous finds from *AE 737*.

Working both sides of the dyke, engine parts and pieces of undercarriage appeared. Characteristic of Lockheed's medium bombers were Fowler trailing edge flaps and several portions emerged. Two, wide 'butter pat' propeller blades were hauled out while smaller items included makers' plates and remnants of radio equipment. Twin-Browning machine-guns appeared from the dorsal turret. Quantitively, these excavations were unspectacular but, as a result, the Ventura and its aircrew will be more widely honoured.

Joining the flow of materials in 1942/43 came increasing numbers of USAAF airmen, brash, but brave and eager to test themselves and their aircraft in combat. One incident involving a young fighter pilot epitomizes their hesitant start and ultimate success.

Wednesday 11 August 1943, was one of those gems in an English summer but, for 28-year-old farmer, Donald Hadingham, the rain of yesterday meant irritating delay and greater harvest effort now the sun was out. Four miles southeast of Chesnut Farm the scene was far from rural as personnel of the 56th Fighter Group tended their P-47 Thunderbolts, action must follow their enforced respite and dampness could induce minor malfunctions which they now worked to remedy.

Outside the 63rd Fighter Squadron Operations Building — an impressive title for a Nissen hut — pilots ranged chairs and relaxed until their machines were ready for air testing. Captain Walker M. Mahurin found Tuesday's inactivity caused further frustration and despondency — his performance to date was that of a tyro, not a Flight Leader with Zemke's 'Wolf Pack'. Today, however, would see him destroy his first aircraft and result in one confirmed, one damaged: both American.

It was mid-morning when crew chief, Technical Sergeant Barnes, gave 'Bud' Mahurin's P-47C clearance and he sauntered out, anticipating a routine local hop. *41-6334, UN-M*, had been his personal plane since March but Bud and Republic's portly product were about to part dramatically. 2,000 hp of Pratt and Whitney lifted his Thunderbolt sweetly away despite an ungainly 200 gallon 'bath tub' tank hugging her belly — he did not like the adverse flying effect it had but increased range was paramount for bomber escort.

Heat haze hovered over the countryside covering the agricultural activity

Captain W.M. Mahurin, 56th Fighter Group (S.P. Evans).

below. Don Hadingham, oblivious of the P-47, or other aircraft, sweated, stacking hay. Both bombers and fighters were in the area as the Eighth geared for combat, one of these, a Liberator, attracted Bud's attention: its course would take it directly over Halesworth, so he decided on a closer look. As a fighter pilot, he reasoned, it was advantageous to fraternize with bomber crews: first for the recognition problem, P-47s often returned with 'friendly' bullet holes and, second, it was advertised that a damaged fighter could move slowly into bomber formations and the bombers would protect their, 'little friend'.

Closing with the B-24, Bud dropped 15° of flap, preventing an overshoot, and slid in on its starboard side to the delight of gunners leering out. All was great fun: they waved, he waved back: they laughed, he laughed back. They motioned him in and the P-47 snuggled closer, slightly lower but level with their position — he nestled the wing of his fighter beneath the bomber's fuselage, chick to mother. His propeller arc was now no more than 3 ft away and, having passed the airfield, Bud decided enough frivolity, time for chow. Increasing speed he edged ahead of the waist, 15 ft below and clear of the two whirling Hamiltons, he was now in view of the cockpit crew peering out. Once again they waved, he responded and, as a parting gesture, decided on a demonstration of the Thunderbolt's speed — a full-power break away.

The empennage of his fighter was slightly ahead of and between the blade arcs of the Liberator's No.3 and 4 engines. He applied forward pressure to the control column and a peculiar thing began to happen, a phenomenon of aerodynamics little understood by contemporary experts let alone a comparative fledgling. Instead of diving, the tail of his P-47 raised higher, towards the bomber. Bud had neither instruction nor experience to cope with the situation — a *venturi* effect of negative air pressure created in front of each propeller was sucking his plane in. At the same time, the B-24 pilot allowed his starboard wing to drop for a better view of the Thunderbolt. In those final moments Bud did not realize that retracting his flaps would drop him out of danger, he gingerly kept forward pressure on the stick, wincing as the inevitable occurred. A loud, metallic tear needed no questions, the controls slapped uselessly and

the fighter's nose dropped to the vertical. In an instant Bud undid his harness and released the canopy. Hauling it back was easy but it took both hands on the windshield to heave his body into the airstream. Kicking and struggling he fought free, certain he was below the 500 ft required for jumping — the 'chute's response was horrifyingly slow compared to the approaching earth. The burgeoning folds arrested his descent moments before the P-47 exploded on impact, the resultant fireball roared up as he landed, stunned but unscathed.

Don stood transfixed for the brief time in which it happened. The low flying aircraft, perilously close together, interrupted his stacking and he paused, shielding his eyes from the sun with his arm, to watch them. Ducking under the bomber's wing, the fighter came up, seemed to hesitate in front and pieces flew off as the bomber chewed into it. Stone-like it fell earthwards but, just before it hit, the pilot jumped, his parachute opening as the plane blew up and he landed heavily nearby. Before Don could react, the airman was on his feet, had released his 'chute and run off towards the farmhouse. Don looked up at the limping Liberator, one wing drooped, two motors stopped, it slewed across the sky for Flixton Airfield.

Bud reached the farm and phoned Halesworth to be told a crash crew had already been despatched. From the base, the demise of Captain Mahurin was witnessed, trees obscured any sight of his escape and the smoke pall apparently indicated the need for a replacement. Returning to the smouldering crater Bud found the team probing for his body and, despite protestations, he was duly incarcerated in the 'meatwagon' and driven to hospital at Metfield for examination before a jeep took him, arms full of parachute, ignominiously back to Halesworth. Major Tukey tore off the initial strip before passing him to Colonel Zemke and, as Bud later understated, 'the conversation was more or less one-sided.' A bar on promotion for twelve months and a fine under the 104th Article of War left a chastened young airman. Luckily the Liberator crew bore no grudge, even sympathizing with the despondent fighter pilot.

Mahurin's unhappy start premised an auspicious flying career — his score of victories opened on 16 August 1943 with two confirmed, German this time, ultimately reaching 24 including one Japanese 'Dinah' and three Korean Migs. Years later I contacted Bud and tried to find some pieces of his fighter. Donald Hadingham said fragments occasionally surfaced after ploughing but my search proved fruitless and the site remains ear-marked for magnetometer survey.

On 13 August 1943, two days after Mahurin's misadventures, RAF airmen involved in another fighter and bomber collision were not as lucky.

Wellington IA, *P9228*, came from the Central Gunnery School at Sutton Bridge and was airborne for a gunnery exercise with another CGS aircraft, Spitfire *P7530*. During simulated attacks, Spitfire pilot, Flight Lieutenant H.C. Bennett, misjudged the forward momentum on a breakaway and hit the Wellington. Records relate that the bomber contributed to the accident when Flight Lieutenant E.M. Shannon, 'changed his position' after Bennett had committed his attack, this confused the fighter pilot. Both were experienced airmen but, like the sea, the sky is unforgiving and both machines crashed killing Bennett, Shannon and his crew of five.

Brushing soil off the remains of a 58-gallon fuel tank from Wellington P9228 at Stallode Fen, Lakenheath.

By grim chance, the Wellington and Spitfire straddled the Ventura site on Stallode Fen so searching for the Spitfire simply meant moving to the next field. Losing its port wing, the fighter smashed into the side of a dyke, penetrating as far as the cockpit. Bennett's burnt remains were pulled clear but his Spitfire's engine and forward fuselage were reputedly abandoned. Since 1984 several attempts to find the site have failed and P7530 joins the list of lost aircraft.

Three fields away, pieces of the Wellington were dug from the fenland's dark earth. Small items overlooked during original recovery work emerged in superb condition. Preserved in the heavy soil, we found fabric which once covered Barnes Wallis's geodetic construction and splendid examples of the structure itself. Paintwork on fabric, wood and metal delighted modellers in our midst while, shining like gold, was a brass specification plate from one of the Pegasus engines. A flying helmet and an RAF issue shoe were sombre reminders of the human toll — the loss of airmen in flying accidents seems all the more tragic.

Photographs of airmen and their aircraft add significantly to any research but pictures can also be used to trace sites and for determining the likelihood of wreckage extant. A propeller protruding from a beet field indicates the possibility that parts from B-17 Mary Ellen II may still be buried near Rickinghall, Suffolk.

During the late afternoon of 16 September 1943, American bombers attacked the airfields in France from which rose their adversaries to contest the increasingly bitter struggle for air supremacy. Returning at dusk caused navigational problems and some aircraft became lost in the gathering darkness. Six Flying Fortresses crashed or ditched as far apart as Northumberland and Wales. Nearer their base, a tragedy befell Lieutenant John D. Schley and his crew as their B-17, Mary Ellen II descended on its landing approach. Three minutes from touchdown, they bumped into a B-17 from the 95th. Hardly a collision, the Horham based aircraft continued safely, but Schley's B-17 either sustained damage to its controls or crashed taking strenuous avoiding action at too low an altitude. All ten airmen died and their loss was keenly felt at Great Ashfield where they had served since the 385th's first mission on 17 July.

As the air-war developed, airfields in occupied countries saw less attention from heavy bombers because the USAAF introduced a more suitable aircraft. This was the Martin B-26 Marauder, a sleek, speedy twin-engined, medium bomber which rose from reluctant beginnings to become superbly effective. Serving initially within the Eighth Air Force, Marauder units eventually transferred to the US Ninth Air Force whose target portfolio better suited their operations.

Flying at only 500 ft at least sixteen Marauders swept in from seaward near Reydon on 13 December 1943. One, sinking even lower than its companions, had an engine feathered and trailed an ominous stream of smoke. Seeing it settle towards the tree-line, Ron knew it was going to crash land and raced off in pursuit. An avid aviation enthusiast, young Ron Forward delighted in spotting the various types seen near his Reydon home. Marauders were especially exciting because their low altitude meant more detail and, when one belly landed nearby, Ron was enthralled to see it at close quarters.

When he found it, the authorities had already arrived but Ron got a good view of the broken bomber and heard that the crew had survived. The pilot made an excellent forced landing in the biggest field available but, even so, his Marauder still clouted an oak tree as it came to rest. Police records state that Second Lieutenant Lloyd Kisner was injured by shrapnel and taken to Southwold Hospital. A Lieutenant Oakley

Right *Wartime photograph showing wreckage of B-17F 42-30601,* Mary Ellen II *at Rickinghall, Suffolk.*

Below Mary Ellen II *photographed at Great Ashfield. The bomb and swastika symbols below the cockpit indicate the number of missions and fighter claims.*

and Flight Officer Robinson were uninjured. Their bomber had been hit by flak attacking Schipol aerodrome in Holland and was lucky to limp home.

A USAAF guard was provided for the aircraft which lay on Wood Farm for some time. It appears they were not serious about their duties and souvenir hunters had a heyday with items spirited into households around Southwold. From one of these, a gunsight and manufacturer's plate now reside in the author's collection.

Apart from locals disappearing with

Left *Lieutenant John D. Schley (left) and Staff Sergeant Clyde Gingerich both perished on board* Mary Ellen II.

Below *Low over the countryside, a B-26 Marauder of the 322nd BG (R.A. Freeman).*

N-6A gunsight and an identification plate were carefully-removed souvenirs from B-26 41-17961, ER-M of the 450th BS, 322 BG, which crashed at Reydon in Suffolk.

pieces of their aircraft whenever the opportunity arose, Americans found rural stoicism hard to comprehend. One pilot never forgot his reception when he smashed to earth at Mutford in Suffolk.

It was Thursday 3 February 1944 and Lieutenant Harold E. Comstock was struggling to get his Thunderbolt home after escorting bombers in a raid on Wilhelmshaven. The 56th had been attacked by German fighters and the battle consumed lots of fuel. Comstock and his wingman, Sam 'Stick' Stamps, fended off several attacks but their beleaguered unit was outnumbered by the tenacious enemy. Breaking combat was risky because you were vulnerable to pursuit when the Germans realized your fuel was low. The longer they kept you, the greater the chances of ditching in the icy North Sea where life

amounted to no more than minutes. Finally, the Americans disengaged and made for the coast, roughly navigating by flak concentrations bursting through dense overcast from towns below.

Sam and Hal throttled back, easing off speed to improve fuel consumption. Over Ostend, their fuel warning lights were flashing and they overheard a fellow pilot, Lloyd Langdon, radio that he was out of gas and ditching — he was never found. Urgently, the two pilots transmitted for a bearing to their base at Halesworth and coaxed their fighters across the sea. Flying wingtip to wingtip was visually comforting but little else as they hand signalled their fuel counts to each other. Just when it seemed they would make it, Hal's engine quit — he relates what happened: 'I turned the fuel selector valve to each position hoping

Fighter ace Harold E. Comstock with Thunderbolt 41-6326, UN-Y which he wrote off at Mutford (H.E. Comstock).

there might be more fuel. The clouds were at 3,000 ft above the terrain and as I broke out I could see Bungay and all of the men and equipment working on construction of the airfield. I thought I would be able to glide and was looking for a clear path where there were no people or equipment. Needless to say, I did not get that far. I was headed directly for an oak tree that looked like it had been there since Richard the Lionheart. I kicked the right rudder and hit the tree with my left wing which spun the aircraft 90° to my flight path and I went bouncing across the ground sideways. The canopy had come off and I got a lot of mud on the right side of my face and my left hip was slightly injured.

'There was a farmer ploughing the field with a one horse plough. He very kindly came over and asked me if I was, "Having a bit of trouble Yank?" It struck me very funny.'

But for the rugged construction of his Thunderbolt, Hal might not have survived. The port wing had been ripped away, the engine torn loose and the fighter's back was broken. Pieces trailed to the point of impact but Hal emerged relatively unscathed. Quite who the unruffled rustic was, Hal doesn't know but the location was Highlands Farm, Mutford and the time, 13.05 hours. PC Blyth guarded the wrecked fighter while Hal telephoned base for a jeep. 'Stick' Stamps just made it, both pilots were lucky. Several others died when their fuel ran out facing headwinds of 100 mph over the stormy North Sea.

Locals remaining unperturbed is one thing, but finding them to be clairvoyant can be even more disconcerting. Investigating a crash at Tuttington, Norfolk, uncovered an eerie tale which I relate but will not endeavour to explain.

The grey, early hours of 20 February 1944, witnessed nearly 700 heavily laden bombers opening the 'Big Week' offensive. On board a 385th B-17, bound for Tutow, a simple error had disastrous consequences. The flare pistol in a Fortress was mounted in the cabin roof, near the top-turret and handy for the engineer. Standard procedure for loading was always to remove the gun, insert the cartridge, close and lock it, put it in the holder, then fire. Attempting to load with it mounted was dangerous in case the flare slid free before the weapon was shut. Sounds simple but, fumbling with it in a cold, climbing bomber sometimes required the expedience of inserting flares with the pistol still in its mount.

High over the North Sea, the engineer on First Lieutenant Billy E. Ruby's aircraft apparently did just that. Before he could close the pistol, the cartridge slipped out, hit the floor and went off. The burning flare hit the side of the flight deck, wedging between some oxygen bottles. Instantly, a fierce, concentrated blaze erupted and Technical Sergeant Cletus D. Crouse received horrific burns struggling vainly to extinguish it. Turning towards England, Ruby ordered his crew to bale out. The tall Texan held the B-17 steady then he and co-pilot, Second Lieutenant Edward Krengulec, tried to help the injured engineer.

Eyewitnesses saw the B-17 fly over Aylsham then swing back, its cockpit a mass of flames. Seven parachutes opened safely, an eighth smouldered, then ignited. Speeding greedily upwards, flames rapidly consumed it and the airman plunged to his death. Ruby, Krengulac and Crouse were killed. Shaken but suffering only minor injuries, the seven survivors had a traumatic experience when they made their way to a nearby farmhouse. Greeting them, the woman who answered the door said they were expected. She had dreamed of their crash the night before and, inside, the fliers stared in disbelief at a breakfast table laid for exactly their number.

Some weeks after Billy Ruby's B-17 blew up, a ring belonging to him was found and sent back to Great Ashfield. Who the clairvoyant woman was is a

First Lieutenant Billy E. Ruby, a brave Texan who died in his blazing bomber at Tuttington, Norfolk.

Stewart Evans (left) and Paul Crickmore struggle to remove a section of Liberator armour plating from a pond at Benacre, Suffolk.

mystery but fragments from the lost bomber are still scattered across the farmland — did she foresee people searching over four decades later?

Whether they believed in predicting the future or not, many airmen were superstitious but orders were orders whatever the date. On 13 March 1944, the diary of the 93rd BG, 409th Squadron, Hardwick: 'Back to France again — this time to La Pol. Our luck holds no longer; on the way to the target, a dozen miles or so from the airdrome, one of our ships, piloted by First Lieutenant Alfred C. Chamberlain, of Ellsworth, Maine, crashed. The pilot was using instruments and it is believed the ship stalled and went into a spin from which it never recovered. Miraculously, four of the enlisted men on the crew escaped alive. The wreckage was found south of Lowestoft.'

In fact, the bomber seems to have broken up as it fell and pieces were strewn over a wide area around Benacre. During 1971/72, several searches occurred and, pumping water from a pond, we removed a well-preserved section of armour plating, printed on which were cruise control instructions and other technical details for B-24J, *42-100363*. This came from the flight deck but the pond also yielded a waist gun, propeller blade, bomb fin and belts of ammunition. From another pond, two fields away, Pete Snowling hauled out one of the Twin Wasp engines. This had originally fallen in the field and lay for some time until farmworkers rolled it out of their way and dumped it in the pond.

In case this book gives the wrong impression, most aircraft were salvaged at the time. Taken near Bury St Edmunds, on 27 March 1944, pictures show a thorough dismantling job underway on Halifax *LW671*. Based at Snaith, Yorkshire, this 51 Squadron aircraft attempted to land at Rougham but overshot and crashed, happily without serious crew injuries. No aviation archaeologist need waste time on that

A recovery team dismantle Halifax LW671 after it crashed at Rougham near Bury St Edmunds.

site but the pictures have historical merit of their own.

Travelling east, a photograph taken at Flixton on 27 April 1944, is supported by a sprinkling of B-24 parts found on Abbey Farm, near the old airbase. These evidence the loss of First Lieutenant Wayne I. Case and crew when a sudden change of wind direction caught the fully loaded Liberator as it took off for Blainville Sur L'Eau railyards. In addition to the ten Americans, two RAF air-

Above *NFS firemen douse the remains of a 446th BG Liberator at Abbey Farm, Flixton.*

Below *The de Havilland Canada Mosquito KB161 was named* VANCOUVER *British Columbia Canada and ended its days at Chittering in Cambridgeshire. Seen here on an air test with its port Merlin feathered.*

men working in the radar shack also died when part of the bomb load exploded.

Firemen from Bungay were wisely held back until the risk had receded, it was already too late to think of rescue. Over forty years later, bomb fragments and scattered parts of B-24H *42-50306* were gathered from farm and woodland by the N & SAM.

Not only did American airmen and aircraft contribute to the crescendo of air activity over Britain during the war years, the resources of her northern neighbour, Canada, were also utilized. In material terms, Canada lacked the same scale of indigenous industry, her manufacturers became primarily responsible for sub-contracted construction of existing types. This avoided enormous design and development costs and reduced lead times, but was still a complicated business requiring local tooling, sourcing and modifications to suit North American standards.

Prior to hostilities, fear of attacks on its vital British factories had already prompted the de Havilland Company to consider assembly in its Canadian subsidiary, de Havilland Canada. Their plant at Downsview, near Toronto, initially made Tiger Moths and Ansons but a pressing need for more Mosquitoes resulted in the factory gearing to produce Canadian variants, the first of which was the B.MkXX, a Canadian version of the British B.MkV.

Supply problems, specification changes and other delays prevented achievement of output plans but in August 1943 the first Canadian-built Mosquitoes arrived in England. Virtually all factory-fresh combat aircraft needed additional, minor modifications to meet operational needs and the Mosquito was no exception. At RAF Henlow, 13 MU adapted the Canadian aircraft before their release into squadron service.

The very first Canadian Mosquito operation occurred with 139 Squadron on 2 December 1943, when Flight Lieutenant G. Salter and Warrant Officer A.C. Pearson DFM, participated in a raid on Berlin. Their aircraft, *KB161, XD-H*, proudly carried the name, *VANCOUVER British Columbia Canada* and had reached the Squadron in November. This debut was slightly marred by frozen controls and engine problems but *VANCOUVER* would more than make up for it during the six months of operational existence.

During this period, *VANCOUVER* and increasing numbers of her sisters flew with 139 Squadron as part of the Light Night Striking Force (LNSF). Flying nuisance raids and spoofs, the LNSF would harass and confuse German defences. For this, the speedy Mosquito was ideal. Using electronics and window, a small force might look like a main attack. Sometimes, similar tactics *did* conceal the Main Force. This was one role. Equipped with G-H and, later, the target-imaging, radar, H2S, Mosquitoes also marked for the Main Force and made raids of their own.

To fly a Mosquito at high altitude and use its electronics required physical stamina, experience and skill. Sometimes, Mosquito aircrew had completed operational tours on heavy bombers before transferring to the LNSF. Flying Officer Alan J.A. Woollard DFM, flew 27 trips on Lancasters with 106 Squadron before being posted to 29 OTU, North Luffenham, to teach navigation and the use of 'Gee'. Eager to fly Mosquitoes, Alan successfully passed decompression chamber tests in late 1943 and went to 1655 CU, Marham, for Mosquito training. At Marham, Alan met and teamed up with Flying Officer Geoffrey W. Lewis and the pair were posted to 139 Squadron early in 1944. From 24 February to 14 March, Geoff and Alan flew eight Gee raids then Alan departed for training on H2S. When he returned in April, they commenced the first of thirteen H2S operations, the last four being flown in Mosquito *KB161*, VANCOUVER, *British Columbia Canada*.

On Thursday 11 May 1944, twelve aircraft of 139 Squadron departed Upwood to attack Mannheim and Ludwigshafen. Geoff powered *VANCOUVER* away at 22.05 hours with a cargo of TI flares to mark the I.G. Farben Chemical works in Ludwigshafen. Poor visibility handicapped their attack but Alan found the objective and released the major part of their flare pattern. Then, at two, four-second intervals his bombing button was pressed to unload the last of their flares in the planned pattern.

Barometric fuzing triggered ignition at 2,000 ft. Alan had no way of knowing if all flares had released so he jabbed the button several times and set the fuze switch to 'safe'. Safety drill also required bomb doors to be opened on descent over the sea in case of a hang up.

Complying with this, Alan opened the doors but he and Geoff were unaware of the rogue flare still tucked, like a time-bomb, in the belly of the *VANCOUVER*. Crossing the English coast, they descended towards Upwood, now only a few minutes ahead.

At 2,000 ft the hang-up exploded, suddenly filling the cockpit with dense, white smoke. Unable to see, Geoff opened his small window and the smoke partly cleared. Both airmen knew the Mosquito must have a major fire in its belly and the only chance they had was to jump. Alan released the floor hatch,

clipped on his parachute and attempted to leave. Diving at over 300 mph, the slipstream pinned him against the back of the hatch, unable to budge. Realizing Alan's predicament, Geoff came swiftly to his aid. Putting his right foot unceremoniously on Alan's head, Geoff shoved hard and Alan shot clear. No one could do the same for Geoff.

A flash of flames hurtled blindingly by as Alan fell into darkness. His parachute opened and the silence was uncanny after two hours between the Mosquito's Merlins. Now, the navigator felt afraid of what lay below and suffered horrible images of his body, impaled on one of East Anglia's many spires. Just then, he saw tree tops against the night sky but he swished past, thumping heavily into an open field. Knocked breathless, the grateful navigator lay there a few moments as his senses advised a lack of bones broken. Releasing his parachute, it was nearly half-past one in the morning and pitch dark as Alan fumbled along the hedgerow, trying to find a gate. At last, he found himself in a narrow lane and came to a house with a large, unwelcoming guard dog. Walking on, he reached a more welcoming homestead and was pleased to see a telephone line emerging. Understandably startled, the family took him in. Contacting Upwood was difficult for the lines were busy. When he got through, an exasperated operator told him they were busy, there had been a plane crash — as if *he* did not know!

Explaining how he was fully aware of that produced rapid results and transport was despatched immediately. Alan thanked his helpers: the family's small daughter, now awake, was firmly convinced Father Christmas had called again. At Upwood, Alan heard that Geoff was dead. Unable to escape, he died when *VANCOUVER* exploded on farmland at Chittering, Cambridgeshire. Four weeks earlier, Alan attended Geoff's wedding, now he faced his friend's funeral. Flying Officer Geoffrey William Lewis, aged 23, was laid to rest at Overseal, Derbyshire, in the church of St Matthew. Alan Woollard flew eight more sorties before his Mosquito was shot up over Berlin, to crash in Sweden. Pieces lay scattered across three fields but its crew survived.

In 1976 I heard from a local resident that parts of a Mosquito were buried on Field View Farm, Chittering. A full day's search found no confirmation but, the following week, a sliver of propeller was picked up with a handful of other fragments. Unable to obtain strong read- ings from what was, after all, an aircraft made mainly of wood, we resorted to trenching by machine on 15 February 1976. Three were cut in parallel, each 40 ft long and 4 ft deep. Finally, we detected a cluster of brass woodscrews and followed them down to a mass of mangled electronics and woodwork. As excavations of the warplane progressed, a more peaceful user of the air drifted gently overhead in the shape of hot air balloon, *G-BANT, Shades*. Waves were exchanged but we had no time to stop, I wonder if they guessed our purpose. A satisfying day's work on an historic aircraft removed a lot of electronics, sadly, rather mangled; the pilot's armoured seat; dinghy equipment and one engine.

Now silent forever, a Merlin engine from Mosquito KB161.

SEPARATE HINGED SECTIONS FOR BOTH PILOTS

THIS TRIANGULAR GLASS SECTION PROTRUDED INTO AIRSTREAM TO PROVIDE SOME FORWARD VIEW FOR PILOT IN REAR SEAT. HE PERHAPS HAD TO LEAN FROM SIDE TO SIDE...

22

I'M NOT SURE, AFTER 39 YEARS, BUT I FEEL THE WHITE 22 WAS PAINTED OVER THE FIRST TWO LETTERS-DG, WHICH WERE BLACK OR DARK GREEN. SEE OTHER DRAWING...

22 DG + NR

I WAS VERY IMPRESSED BY THE INSTRUMENTATION IN THIS AIRPLANE

I DON'T REMEMBER SEEING A BELLY TANK... MAYBE DROPPED EARLIER OR KNOCKED OFF IN TREES...

AMBULANCE

HEAVY LAMINATED GLASS WINDSHIELD

TREE TOPS SHATTERED

WRECKAGE IN THREE DISTINCT SECTIONS: ENGINE NACELLE, WING AND FUSELAGE... DESCENDING Bf 109 G-12 HAD APPARENTLY MUSHED THROUGH TREE TOPS AND BOUNCED UPHILL, BREAKING INTO THREE LARGE PIECES. VERY HEAVY BULLET-PROOF WINDSHIELD HAD BOUNCED NEARLY TO THE TOP OF THE HILL. MEDICS CARRIED INJURED PILOT TO AMBULANCE AT TOP.

Less than a week after the loss of KB161, another contribution to East Anglian aviation history happened in Suffolk. Highly unusual, some of the following facts are revealed for the first time.

It was a fine, spring evening and Harold Gayfer was strolling with his mother in a lane near Lound Hall. Hearing a low-flying aircraft, the youngster looked towards the coast and saw a single-engined, low-wing monoplane flying towards them. Harold spent most of his pocket money on aircraft-spotting books and, at first glance, a Hurricane came to mind but, somehow, it did not look right. Closer now, its identity clicked — a Messerschmitt 109! Too suprised even to duck, Harold gaped as it passed by, so low he saw the pilot. No alert had sounded, not a shot was fired. As it disappeared over the tree-tops, Harold heard the Daimler-Benz falter into silence.

Rushing for his bicycle, he chased off to see where it had crashed and soon found himself in Herringfleet. There, just beyond the bottom of Mrs Girling's cottage garden, lay his Messerschmitt. American soldiers were guarding the wreck but showed him how it had gone under roadside telephone wires and cut through some tree tops before crashing. A police car had taken the pilot to hospital with a broken left leg and light injuries to his right wrist but Harold heard that he seemed glad to be in England and kept repeating, 'England good' to his rescuers. It was true. Carl Wimberger had defected, he was pleased to reach England.

An Austrian, Carl Wimberger joined his country's Air Force in 1937 and was being trained at the time of the Anschluss in 1938. Discharged by the Germans, he was recalled when war broke out and became a pilot. For some time, he performed target-towing duties then went to 3/Erg. Zerstorer Gruppe. Following this, he was posted to a fighter training school but failed the requirements for 'Wild Sau' nightfighters. In January 1944, Wimberger was injured flying a Bf 109 at night. Recovering from this, he went to 1/JG102, dayfighter school, near Zerbst.

Unhappy with his situation, and, perhaps, his country's predicament, the 25-year-old Oberfeldwebel decided on defection. During the afternoon of 15 May 1944, the opportunity came when he took off from Zerbst in a twin-seat Me 109G-12, 22DG+NR, fitted with a long-range drop tank. Taking advantage of 10/10 cloud to hide his flight, he flew a compass bearing for England and kept in cloud at 7,000 ft. Hanover was glimpsed, then the Zuider Zee.

Nearing Britain, his cloud cover disappeared and Wimberger worried about the island's defences. Losing height, he lowered his undercarriage to signal surrender as he approached the coast. Off Lowestoft, at only 40 ft, he passed some ship-board balloons and climbed for safety. Having flown over 400 miles, his fuel warning lamp flickered then came full on. As power faded, he raised his undercarriage and tried to glide for open land but fell short into a disused gravel pit. Whether or not his exact words were, 'England Good', he was lucky to be alive and undoubtedly pleased to be here.

These sketches of the ME 109 at Herringfleet were made by Bob Harper, Assistant Intelligence Officer of the 448th BG (R.L. Harper).

Searching the overgrown gulley years later, I found nothing of Wimberger's unusual Messerschmitt. Some sites are that frustrating but others yield more than expected: on display at Parham is a beautifully restored Wright-Cyclone, arguably the most complete radial recovered from an East Anglian site.

At 06.50 hours on 23 May 1944 Flying Fortresses from the 351st BG, Polebrook, were forming for a preinvasion raid on the Epinal marshalling yards in France. Intending to attack the airfield at Bourges, Liberators from the 458th BG also assembled nearby. Maybe it was a mistake in planning, timing or orders but something went seriously wrong. In bright sunshine, the two formations converged. Majestically, inexhorably, disastrously, the two formations enmeshed.

In a few, terrifying seconds, their organized patterns fell apart as aircraft, wheeling and banking, climbing and diving, desperately tried to evade the inevitable. From another formation overhead, crews watched with fascinated horror. Trying to avoid one B-24, they saw a B-17 turn on its side and slice through another Liberator. Flopping earthwards, the pieces of B-24 carried First Lieutenant K.C. Barton and his crew to their deaths. Flown by First Lieutenant Peter E. Crowe, the wretched B-17, its nose and two engines gone, fell into a slow, remorseless spin. Miraculously, three gunners parachuted to safety before the Fortress embedded itself on marshland near the River Dove at Hoxne. At Waterloo Plantation, Eye, the Liberator burnt fiercely, convulsing in a series of blasts as part of its bomb load detonated. Later, Bomb Disposal dealt with sixteen 250 lb bombs in and around the wreckage.

Crowe's B-17 jettisoned five of its six 1,000 lb bombs and they exploded on open land without causing injury. One of the survivors reportedly told Mrs A.K.G. Flowerdew, Gardiners Farm, that a 1,000 lb bomb remained on board when it crashed. The wartime Aircraft Crash and Accident Form confirms five explosions, one bomb unaccounted for.

In 1967, three local men, George Vyse, Peter Adcock and David Grimmer, uncovered wreckage of the lost bomber and removed an engine, machine-guns, and ammunition. The story of their activities appeared in the press and the USAF spent some time searching for the missing bomb. Eventually, an American spokesman expressed satisfaction that the area was safe, the missing bomb might have exploded at the time. He admitted, however, that there *was* a possibility it had sunk too deep for detection.

Convinced the bomber's No 4 engine lay in a dyke, near the surface, but away from the bulk of the wreckage, Ron Buxton hired a machine and organized a dig for 20 August 1972. Carefully digging around it exposed the whole nacelle in superb condition. Scooping mud from the dyke revealed a 6 ft length of tree trunk wedged between the engine and propeller. The broken stump stood nearby and led to the theory that this engine had been torn off in the bomber's final moments. Lacking power for a direct lift, the digger driver resorted to sloping an access route into the crater and dragged the engine free.

By comparison, the mangled wreckage revealed at Metfield offered few opportunities for restoration but such sad pieces serve to tell the tale of *Lucky Penny* and her crew on D-Day plus two, 8 June 1944. The 491st Group diarist noted what happened.

'This mission was one best forgotten.

Right *At Hoxne, Ron Buxton supervises removal of an engine and propeller from B-17G-45-BO, 42-97325, of the 508th Squadron, 351st BG. Now restored by him, the engine is displayed in the 390th BG MAM, Parham (S.P. Evans).*

Below *Wreckage of B-24, Lucky Penny at Metfield on 8 June 1944.*

Bottom *Wreckage of B-24, Lucky Penny at Metfield on 3 May 1973.*

Most everything that could possibly go wrong went wrong. Starting out early in the morning an excited gunner lost his life when he ran into a rotating prop. A short time later Lieutenant Sharp, flying *42-110169*, crashed within the confines of the field killing the entire crew... At 08.25 aircraft crashed and burned...the plane had circled three times with No 1 feathered...the tower tried to contact on both command frequency and on UHF with no acknowledgement. The aircraft made a normal approach. 300 yards out the aircraft pulled up to go around and began to retract gear, pulling up sharp and to the left. At 200 ft it stalled and spun in. Two explosions at five minute intervals completely destroyed the aircraft.'

Lucky Penny and her crew were blown to pieces. Nearly thirty years later, debris emerged during ditch clearance and farmer, Terry Godbold, gave permission for us to enlarge his ditch and clear what we found. In wreckovery terms, the parts were mediocre but we felt that even a small display would help lift the unfortunate crew of *Lucky Penny* from the obscurity of casualty statistics.

June 1944, saw the Allied beach-head established and ferocious fighting took place as the armies battled it out. Hard-earned air superiority was a clear benefit for the invading forces. Both in quantity and, generally, in quality, the American and British pilots were proving superior. Not that one man is better than another, more simply, he was given better training but, as we have seen many times, this had its own cost. On the last day of that momentous month, another young American made his own, supreme sacrifice, not roaring in, low over the beach-head, guns blazing, but in a flat-spinning fighter from which he struggled to escape as it fell to earth at Heywood, near Diss.

In 1986, Jeff Carless and Nigel Beckett organized a search for this aircraft and invited a small number of devotees to help. The site lay in a 26 acre field, amalgamated from three small fields, at the top of Boot Lane. As is often the case, this made precise location difficult but Nigel eventually came across an area of concentrated surface fragments.

Working nearby, a farmhand came to watch activities. Jake Calver was a youngster at the time but remembered how slowly the fighter, a Thunderbolt, seemed to fall. He waited for the pilot to appear as, almost lazily, the aircraft spiralled lower. Still no parachute. Moments before impact, a figure detached itself, a candle of silk streamed, then pilot and plane hit the earth simultaneously. Rescuers rushed across as two more P-47's circled, trying to indicate where, in the barley crop, lay the prone figure and half-opened parachute. Flames and smoke pillared from the burning wreckage as farmworkers found the pilot about 100 yards away. Nothing could be done, the young airman was dead.

Nigel had a hunch that the fighter's engine was still buried and, once cleaned, would be the first, major find by the newly formed EAARG. Within minutes of scraping off topsoil, Nigel's hunch proved itself as a row of cylinder heads appeared. Several, back-aching hours of hand digging avoided damaging the R2800 and moved enough earth for the small Massey-Ferguson tractor to try lifting the engine. Shackling chains about its bulk saw the big broken power-plant move for the first time in 42 years. Brushing earth from remains of the cowling, Jeff noted a yellow and black diamond pattern which confirmed his research.

On 30 June 1944 three Thunderbolts from 353rd FG, Raydon, were airborne on an evening navigational training exercise. That day, the unit had been busy strafing in France so it was good to get height in untroubled skies and enjoy the thrill of flight. Second Lieutenant William K. Lahke had taken off at 18.50 and made for the coast. Twenty minutes later, Second Lieutenant Robert W. Larson and Lieutenant Craft were aloft and heading for a rendezvous with Lahke. By now, Lahke's P-47 was near Tibenham, just below the overcast cloud, at 3,000 ft. Larson and Craft closed to within 400 yards of Lahke's fighter, steadied, then slid nearer for a formation join up. It went wrong: Larson and Lahke scraped together, almost gently but disastrously for one of them. As they hit, the left wing tip and aileron broke off Larson's P-47 and it pitched upwards before falling away. Lahke had serious damage to his right wing, engine and propeller but, luckily, was able to keep control. Larson's Thunderbolt dropped into the flat spin from which it never recovered.

Items recovered from an aircraft can pay tribute to its crew and excavations are happier in the knowledge that they survived. When we heard of plans to extend the port at Parkeston Quay, we realized that a promising B-24 site was in jeopardy so launched our own form of rescue archaeology. Passengers to Harwich on the nearby railway could hardly be expected to realize that the 'island' in a scruffy looking lagoon near the station was actually a large section of Liberator wing. For us to reach it, we needed permission from British Rail which entailed a legal agreement, insurance and, if necessary, reimbursement of wages for *their* staff to supervise *us*. All this for the pleasure of paddling in some

Watched by Nigel Beckett, Jeff Carless (left) shackles a chain to the digger bucket during recovery of an engine from 353rd FG Thunderbolt, 42-8511, at Heywood in 1986.

very smelly water seemed stupid but we felt that the story of the Liberator, *Lucy Quipment* was worth it.

17 July 1944 saw the 493rd BG attacking targets to support the Invasion. Over Coulanges railway bridge, flak crippled two of *Lucy Quipment*'s engines and shrapnel peppered her fuel tanks. She really had some loose equipment and pilot, Lieutenant Robert L. Millhollin

realized that their chances of reaching Debach were slim but none of the crew were hurt and fuel, vapouring from holed tanks, had not ignited: *Lucy* had served them well, they wanted to take her home.

Nearing England, it was obvious the risks of taking their invalid down through 10/10 cloud were too great. Millhollin and his co-pilot, Lieutenant Henry E. Davis edged into the overcast sky but were unable to break clear without getting dangerously low. Nursing power from their two good engines, *Lucy* climbed into sunlight near what they hoped would be the English coast. Millhollin ordered his crew to prepare to bale out then turned *Lucy* seawards and rang the alarm.

Ball-turret gunner, Sergeant Raymond J. Romac recalled, 'The navigator (Lieutenant John S. Balliet) dropped from the bomb bay and I waited in the camera hatch until I saw him sail away beneath. Then I went. I remember while I was standing there looking down at the edge of the hatch, I changed my mind about going out feet first and dived instead. The slipstream must have flipped me around so I was feet down in the air. The only trouble was that the chute didn't open when I yanked the rip-cord, I had pulled the ring completely out and the silk was still in the pack. It strikes me funny now that I wasn't excited at the time, I simply flipped open the flap on the pack and I tossed the silk up into the air. I guess I'm a lucky guy. . .I'm here to tell the tale. I was calm at first but I guess I let my feelings get away with me as I watched old *Lucy* fly away into the cloud. I remember how I painted up all the turrets with names for the crew, my Rosemary was painted there too. I think I started to cry, I'd lived a long time with *Lucy* and hated to see her go.

The next thing I knew, I was singing, trying to calm myself down, I guess.

'As soon as I dropped through the overcast, the ground seemed to rush up to meet me, it came up too fast, the wind had kicked me into an awkward position and I hit hard on my left foot, spraining my ankle. Luckily, no bones were broken but my ankle hurt like the devil. I limped to a nearby road where I was picked up by two RAF men in a jeep. They brought me to a police station and I got some hot coffee. A Constable then took me to the RAF fighter base and later I joined the rest of the crew. I sure was glad to see the boys.'

Waist gunner, Sergeant William R. Lockridge, had a happier parachuting experience and picked flowers for the packers after floating gently into a meadow, something he had promised them if he ever had to use his parachute! Sergeant William C. Bass, tail gunner, had a far more uncomfortable time. 'I had wondered, many times, how I would take it if we ever had to bale out. As we circled several times through the pea-soup, I still figured we might ditch in the Channel or crash land. Then, 'Pop' our pilot, started up to altitude and I knew we were going to have to hit the silk. We immediately checked each other's 'chute harness and put on life preservers in case we landed in the water. When the order came through to parachute out, I was the third to go. We rolled through the camera hatch, one after another as fast as possible in hopes we'd land close together. I remember I kissed my chute just before I jumped and the gesture brought me luck. As I fell, I saw the little 'chute pull out, and the big canopy, and that white silk blossomed out was the most beautiful sight I'd ever seen.

'It was sad to watch old *Lucy*, our Lib,

fade away into the clouds, particularly when I saw, for the last time, my wife's nickname, "Ruskin" painted on my tail turret.

'I guess I had an even more exciting time getting down than the rest of the boys. When I saw I was over land instead of water, I was happy, but I didn't actually hit the ground. I came sweeping over the house tops, picking up my feet to keep from kicking off the chimneys and finally ended up in the top of a high tree. It was on the edge of a cabbage patch behind a house. Getting out of that tree was the hardest part of the whole jump. In the first place, I probably scared the wits out of one English lady, she was the only one around — she stood there, screaming and throwing up her hands and then ran off to get a Bobby.

'I remember sitting there saying to myself, "What a hell of a place to be". I suppose I could have slipped out of my harness and gotten down to the ground without much trouble but I kept thinking, "I've gotten down this far okay, I'll probably break my leg if I try to climb down this tree. Finally, the local citizens got me down by ladders, ropes and what not. From thereon, people just waited on me and the other boys on my crew who had been rounded up. The policeman gave us tea and cookies. Men and officers from a nearby RAF station warmed us up with brandy. Finally, our own officers got there and saw to it that we got plenty to eat but, after it was all over, it was sure nice getting home.'

Staff Sergeant Herbert C. Goldman, radio operator, had a soggy landing in the Stour. Disentangling himself, he began wading ashore then noticed a man on the bank signalling with scooping movements of his hands. Unable to figure it out, Goldman continued but was intercepted by a rescue craft to learn the man had been trying to warn him away from a minefield!

Nineteen-year-old Staff Sergeant Thelbert W. Niehoff was further out and floundering in his heavy flying clothing when a launch sped to his rescue. As he struggled, his rescuers caught the top-turret gunner by the seat of his flying pants and pulled him on board. Waist-gunner, Sergeant John W. Thompson, had no further adventures beyond landing in a turnip patch. Flight Officer Stanley P. Friedman navigated *Lucy* home and baled out only to be taken as a German by suspicious farmworkers. Fortunately, he was rescued by an RAF officer.

Lucy Quipment had limped home, her crew were safe. Wearily, the old bomber settled seawards but did not quite make it. Had she crashed in Harwich or Parkeston, the results would have been devastating but fate guided her final flight towards a piece of wasteland separated from the Stour by the railway embankment. Slithering into a large shallow pool, *Lucy* left her tail near the point of impact, bounced, then disintegrated in a 500 yard trail of fragments. Total destruction was assisted by anti-tank blocks, *Lucy* shattered one of them, spreading her remains for some distance beyond. Countless pieces of Liberator lay everywhere.

In later years, Carless Chemicals built a refinery on part of the site, reclaimed from the marshland. No doubt, remnants of Lucy lie beneath their storage tanks. Plans for further building prompted action and a small team gathered on site in August 1976. Short on sanity but saturated with enthusiasm, our first task was to winch ashore the abandoned wing section. Ian Hawkins bravely waded through the

Above *A picture taken by USAAF photographer Russell Zorn shows scattered fragments of* Lucy Quipment *near Parkeston Quay in July 1944 (R. Zorn).*

Below *August 1976. A similar view to that taken 32 years earlier shows the digger-dogsled team in action.*

foul-smelling water to attach the winch cable. Gradually, the 'island' of wreckage eased landwards including a complete main undercarriage leg and tyre, still retracted in its housing.

While others dismantled this, I paddled about searching for smaller items. Wearing waders, I found most of the pool accessible and soon grew accustomed to the stench. Clinging mud hindered movement but I found a partially burnt fuel tank which I emptied and adapted to float pieces ashore. Others concocted their own methods and soon we had a worthwhile selection of artefacts to tell the tale of *Lucy Quipment*. A major problem was getting larger pieces across the lagoon but we discovered a crude causeway just below the surface. Using a piece of wing as a sledge, we became our own dog team. The secret lay in gaining momentum on firm footing before you hit the sludge.

Miss the causeway and you received a very unhealthy baptism and the smell lingered for days, as two of the team discovered.

Airmen from another Liberator are commemorated by a plaque in Kirby Bedon church. Hit by flak over France on 18 August 1944, *Broad and High* from the 467th BG struggled to reach Rackheath. That evening, eleven-year-old Tristan Everett was helping with the harvest when the big silver bomber was seen dragging itself homewards. Tristan sensed it was going down and saw it crunch into a beet field. Grating noisily for some distance, the B-24 smacked into an embankment, breaking its back and crushing the nose. Four of the crew perished and Tristan heard later that the pilot, Lieutenant Roger L. Leister, was lost on another mission.

Month by month, crashes continued. Little wonder that wreckage still exists,

B-24 42-50439 which crashed at Kirby Bedon, Norfolk on 19 August 1944.

Above *Wreckage of a 491st BG Liberator, 44-10489, near Stanford Water, Norfolk, on 9 September 1944.*

Above right *A P-51 Mustang fighter still resides in this pool near Ranworth.*

Right *479th FG Mustang which crash landed at Kirton on 27 September 1944 (S.P. Evans).*

there were just too many to clear at the time. Some sites, difficult to access, remain unexplored even though there is a likelihood that parts may be found.

Climbing out of North Pickenham on 9 September 1944, Lieutenant Warczak had problems when his No1 and No4 engines caught fire. From 900 ft, the incendiary-laden B-24 flopped to earth in the Stanford Battle Area. Warczak and two gunners escaped through a slit in the fuselage as flames consumed their comrades. Access to the Battle Area is difficult but Mother Nature herself beat us on another site. Hacking through undergrowth, it was hard to believe this was Ranworth, Norfolk and not the Burmese jungle. Without Mr Grapes, the marshman, we would never have found the site and, as it was, three pumps failed to make much headway lowering the water.

Fragments confirmed the wreck as a Mustang and, waist deep, I could stand on large pieces of the sunken fighter. Identifying this P-51 has baffled aviation historians. Tiny pieces of red and yellow nose art were found, even two, rusting machine-guns, lying in nearby reeds, but no evidence to tell us the all-important serial number. Arthur Foster, a Ranworth resident during the war, told us the pilot parachuted clear when a wing came off but who he was is

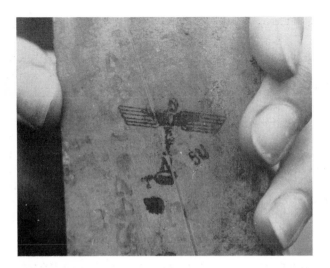

Excavations of the site of B-17 43-388431 at Knodishall were disappointing although this fragment has at least got the manufacturer's logo.

unresolved and his fighter still rests in the marsh.

Recovery crews had no problem when Captain C.A.P. Duffie slithered his Mustang to earth on Saturday 27 September 1944. An ace of the 479th Group, he belly landed on Corporation Farm, Kirton, skidded through some hedgerows into a stubble field and emerged, unharmed, in the next parish, on Hall Farm, Falkenham. A picture tells us there is no prospect of finding anything on either farm.

Disappointment was the only reward at Knodishall, Suffolk, where a Kimbolton based B-17 cremated itself after the crew baled out. Corroded beyond recognition, our bucket of bits contained few finds. One piece, stamped, 'Boeing' was at least a tangible link with events on 31 October 1944, when British guns destroyed the luckless B-17. What pilot, Lieutenant Charles W. Goodier, said on the subject is not recorded.

Few crashes contain anything approaching humour, most, like two Lancasters at Hockwold, were ghastly events. It was just before Christmas, on 18 December 1944. No. 63 Course, 3 Lancaster Finishing School, was near-

ing completion and, that night, the sound of Merlins shook surrounding hamlets as bombers thundered away on a training exercise. After air-to-air firing, circuits and practice landings at Waterbeach, Methwold and Tempsford, the bombers returned to Feltwell. Several were on circuit, preparing to land when, at 21.51 hours, two collided in the dark winter sky. Lancasters R5674, 'K', and R5846, A5-H, both crashed, killing their crews.

In 1984, the AAPS found all four Rolls-Royce Merlins from R5846 along with machine-guns and other equipment. Compressed in sandy soil, where the fuselage had burnt forty years earlier, Andy Brown discovered a scorched, money-packed leather wallet. Stuck to the outside were the remains of a letter addressed to 'WOP/AG, John W. Hutton, Sergeants Mess, RAF Feltwell.'

'My Dear Son,
I hope your cold is better. . . I was disappointed to hear you will not be home for New Year. . .'

Like so many sons, John never got home.

Returning the wallet to his sister revealed why he had so much cash, he was saving for a spree on his 21st birthday.

January 1945: Hitler's final, western offensive was being turned. Initially, bad weather protected the Wehrmacht but, as it cleared, bombers pulverized tactical targets and avenging fighters fell on troops and transport. For months, Mustangs harassed German communications and, training in England, P-51's hedge-hopped across the countryside. As always, such realism was bought at a price.

On 4 January 1945, Second Lieutenant Thurmann E. Sands was in a flight of 479th FG Mustangs which flew from Wattisham on a navigation exercise involving low level flying. Prior to take-off, pilots were warned to keep widely spaced, look well ahead and keep 50 ft higher than their leader. For the first hour, all went well. At 11.15 am, the Mustangs dropped from 2,500 ft for a low-level run towards the coast. Sands was piloting an old P-51B, serial 43-6393, retired from combat and used mostly by pilots newly arrived from America.

Two minutes after descending, the leader of the Flight flashed low over Haughley Station, Suffolk. The 10.25 from Ipswich to Bury St Edmunds had just pulled out, trundling slowly along the tracks. Lou Massari, an NCO with the 385th BG, was a passenger on the train and saw the first Mustang streak overhead then swing up in a right turn after simulating an attack on the locomotive. A second P-51 roared over, climbing out in the same manner. Lou heard another coming in and pressed his face to the window, looking for it. Beyond the station was a hummock. To Lou, the Mustang simply failed to pull up and hit the hillock in a disintegrat-

Photographed during excavations at Hockwold, this wallet and contents were returned to the family of Sergeant John W. Hutton, RAF.

The burning remains of Sands' P-51 are smeared across the Suffolk countryside.

ing fireball. Lou was completely unaware that the Mustang had also hit the engine of his train.

Driver, George Baker, had drawn LNER locomotive 7764 slowly away from Haughley. He and fireman Cyril Broad were startled when a plane tore low overhead, swiftly followed by another. The third aircraft was even lower, Thurmann Sands' flying career and life ended in a terrible misjudgement. His P-51 came *under* the telegraph wires, ripped through a fence bordering the permanent way and clipped the locomotive. The boiler cladding and steel sheets between the funnel and cabin were pulled open as the force of impact slammed the Mustang to earth. Sands' mutilated body was found near the end of a fire-scar spread across three fields.

George Baker had head wounds and flying glass cut Cyril Broad but their injuries were not serious. None of the passengers were hurt but their train was delayed for an hour while USAAF personnel from Great Ashfield removed the body of Lieutenant Sands. Coincidentally, a B-17 from Great Ashfield was over Haughley, going in to land, when the crash occurred. As the Flying Fortress descended, its crew saw Mustangs buzzing a train and radioed base to report that one of the P-51s went too low, hit the engine and shredded itself to pieces in fields beyond the railway line. Calling for an ambulance the B-17 pilot, Frank Walls photographed the trail of burning wreckage.

Forty-two years later, this trail was followed by Jeff Carless, picking up small pieces from Sands' Mustang. Near the back-plate of a machine-gun, Jeff found a florin and threepenny-piece both dated, 1944. The unfortunate Sands barely had time to understand this strange coinage and the money is now displayed, with pieces of his fighter, in the East Essex Aviation Museum, one of whose members is in touch with the Sands family.

Items found on crash sites need not be large to represent the story but Jeff Carless is hoping for more than mere fragments from, *Floogie II*. Normally flown by 357th FG ace, Otto Jenkins,

Right *Coins and a piece of P-51 picked up at the site where Second Lieutenant Thurmann E. Sands crashed* (East Essex Aviation Museum).

Below *The site where this 357th FG Mustang* Floogie II *fell still awaits investigation* (M. Olmsted via S.P. Evans).

Above *Wreckage of a 453rd BG B-24J, 44-10515, at Crown Farm, Deopham on 6 February 1945.*

Below *17 January 1988. Work in progress at Crown Farm.*

this Mustang was lost on 13 January 1945, when Lieutenant Schleiker became disorientated in bad weather and spun in near Woodbridge. Sadly, Schleiker died and *Floogie II* was burnt out. Indications are that wreckage of the fighter still lies buried.

'Spun in'. Time after time in the annals of aviation history, those two chilling words appear. Even to read, in terse, official files, of airmen trapped, spinning earthwards, touches a sense of fear. Repeatedly, fliers endured that risk, some even survived the experience, but many did not. Meeting in the mist on Crown Farm, Deopham, Norfolk, during January 1988, we reflected sombrely on a similar winter's morning, 43 years earlier. Spinning from cloud, a Liberator and its crew were blown to pieces only yards from the farm. Pictures showed a hideous heap of debris, only

a mainwheel and one engine were recognizable.

On 6 February 1945, the planned target for the 453rd BG, Old Buckenham, was a synthetic oil plant at Rothensee. In the event, clouds obscured it so they bombed marshalling yards in Magdeburg. Second Lieutenant Roy F. Flatt and his crew were lost during assembly when they spun in following a near miss with another B-24. Local people told us that the bomber broke up as it fell and that wreckage was scattered over several parishes. Carrying a full load, the fuselage impacted behind Crown Farm at 9.30 am and several bombs detonated, seriously damaging the farmhouse and putting farmer's wife, Mrs Law, into a state of shock. Fortunately, six of the 500 lb bombs did not explode, otherwise she might not have survived.

Every autumn, reminders of this inci-

A crushed flak helmet with chaff wedged inside.

Top *Sunglasses were worn by USAAF gunners to help reduce glare from sun and cloud surfaces.*

Above *Battery and fragments of torch found at Deopham. Many pieces of wreckage still litter this site.*

dent surfaced during ploughing and our search obtained readings over a wide area. Below the surface, we found some sad relics. A crumpled flak helmet, strangely, stuffed with strips of chaff; fragments of a torch and a battery made

specifically for the Signal Corps US Army. Perhaps the most poignant article was a spectacle case containing the remains of some sunglasses. Other pieces still await excavation: this site may take years.

Death, so near war's end, seems even more bitter. Some fliers appeared to tempt it. Captain Robert Fifield of the 357th FG extended his combat tour three times. On 3 May 1945, just five days before VE Day, he died when his Mustang crashed at Westleton, Suffolk. Three days later, another P-51 pilot taunted the Grim Reaper and, fittingly, his story closes this chronological and personal selection of crashes.

Sunday 6 May 1945 was a beautifully clear day with a few scattered clouds enhancing the tranquillity of anticipated peace. For the 20th Fighter Group, combat pressures had disappeared. Their last mission had been over a week ago and, having survived so far, you would have to be damned unlucky not to get home. Lieutenant Vincent J. Rudnick had been assigned to the 79th Squadron on 28 October 1944 and had amassed 254 combat hours pursuing the remnants of an exhausted Luftwaffe from skies over the Reich. Opportunities for kills were rare and Rudnick's hours reflected hard work but only a ½ Heinkel III, with another damaged, during a strafing attack on Weiden airfield on 20 February 1945. His aircraft that day had been *Mine 3 Express*, now his regular ship. This, weathered P-51 had seen more action than her pilot. Records show she went to Russia on the shuttle mission during September 1944 and she is believed to have been called, *My Lucky Blonde*. Maybe Rudnick's girl was a brunette and did not like him spending time with a blonde so he changed the name of the aircraft. In any event, he

Above *Captain Robert Fifield, 357th Fighter Group, Leiston* (M. Olmsted via S.P. Evans).

Below *Wreckage of Fifield's Mustang, 44-63710, at Westleton. Note victory tally on right* (M. Olmsted via S.P. Evans).

Captain R.H. Pollock (left) and Lieutenant Vincent J. Rudnick pose by Mine 3 Express (J. Hoffman via D. Morris).

probably never realized that this would be their last date as he fired up the powerful Packard Merlin.

Lifting away from King's Cliffe, Rudnick sought a safe section of sky in which to carry out the purpose of his flight, filed simply as, 'local training, acrobatics flight'. At 14.45 hours he was 12,000 ft over the village of Stoke Ferry, searching the sky to ensure all was clear before he commenced a loop. Satisfied there were no aircraft in the vicinity, Rudnick put the Mustang's nose down, building up speed before pulling back on the stick. The fighter responded smoothly and he felt himself compressed in the seat as she pulled 'G'. The horizon dropped away and *Express* pointed heavenwards before coming over on her back, speed falling away — this may have been the problem. Like most thoroughbreds, the Mustang could be temperamental and directional instability was a known feature of the type. At the top of the loop, the Mustang threw her pilot and snapped into an inverted spin, ruining Rudnick's day. His Mustang had bolted and no amount of coercion on the controls could rein her in. Down, down, down she spun, the altimeter swiftly in reverse, a gyrating kaleidoscope of fields whirling before the pilot's eyes. Rudnick wrestled the controls for 8,500 ft before abandoning, *Mine 3 Express* to her fate.

Just outside Stoke Ferry, Tim Chaplin was supervising land reclamation work, oblivious of the Mustang's presence until a change in engine tone indicated trouble. Jim heard it begin its terminal scream then saw the silver fighter, on its back, spinning viciously earthwards. A parachute appeared then the engine's agony terminated abruptly to restore the tranquillity of a Sunday in summer. Rudnick landed unscathed near the Oxborough Road and was picked up by a Mr Vine who drove him to view the remains of his aircraft. The P-51 had impacted near an empty cottage called, *Springside*, damaging some outhouses and, locals allege, later causing the gable end to fall out. Amongst others at the scene was a young lad named Harry Hall who grew up to run his own building firm and operate a JCB.

Just over forty years later, on Saturday 15 June 1985, Harry was revisiting the site armed with his digger and determined to recover what remained of, *Mine 3 Express*. Photographs provided by Dave Knight and Ray Corby of the 20th Fighter Historical Group looked promising and had puzzled the two specialists for months. Sent to them by a veteran, the pictures illustrated the site where P-51D-5-NA, *44-13720*, MC-X, had crashed, 'in the vicinity of King's Cliffe'. The site lay near a stream with an oak tree and cottage nearby but hours spent scouring the countryside, failed to match the pictures.

On the other hand, I had found a site but could not identify it. Working through an organization called, 'Friends of the Eighth', which links people interested in Eighth Air Force history, I eventually contacted Dave Knight and described the crash site of a Mustang, identity unknown. We were both delighted, he had his site, I had my Mustang and a dig was arranged.

Wreckage of Mine 3 Express *at Stoke Ferry. Skeletal tail section protrudes from crater. The angle of the main plane, top right, gave rise to the mistaken conclusion that a lot of the fighter was buried* (20th FHG).

Judging by the photographs, the site looked good. It consisted of a crater, less than 20 ft wide, protruding from which was the fighter's skeletal rudder and a rear section of main plane, indicating a steep angle of impact. Our assumption was that the engine and forward section were buried so Harry began by removing a section of topsoil.

Fire-fighting foam had been sprayed on the wreck and this badly corrodes aluminium. A layer of white, powdered crystals, nicknamed 'Daz', appeared and, with corroded fragments, clearly indicated the original extent of the crater. Some oddments were found by sifting this layer, amongst which were the oil cap and fragments of engine casing. Below this layer, we came across sand, both yellow and, strangely, purple, which caused discussion about it being natural or a consequence of the crash. Laboratory tests later proved that the discoloration was a result of the crash.

Disappointment edged in as those with building experience related the resistance sand could offer and, at six ft, we had clearly gone below the level of wreckage, this being confirmed by the magnetometer. A few fragments emerged from the edges including a section of black and white striped cowling and a piece of tyre but that was clearly it. One slight consolation was an unintentional salute from the Red Arrows whose two sections passed overhead using the traditional fighter formation, Finger Four. For those involved, the dig disappointed, but the research answered questions and completed another historical footnote.

Fragments of shattered warplane are clues to unearth not only wreckage but, more importantly, the drama behind each incident and often even small pieces will reveal a fascinating story. A fate shared by airmen in this book was to fall from East Anglian skies. The fortunate returned home, some to regale grandchildren with their experiences, others to quietly contemplate lost friends or shiver in relived nightmares. This book is intended to inform and to offer a tribute to the survivors and the fallen. It is intended as a tribute from the writer's generation whose children have grown up under peaceful skies, to the airmen who helped to win that peace. I hope that I may have succeeded.

APPENDIX

For researchers and historians the following appendix provides additional information on aircraft and incidents related in Chapter 11.

Page 195
30 October 1939 10.50 hours.
Wellington *L4288, KA-A*, 9 Squadron. 5 killed.
Squadron Leader L.S. Lamb: pilot (Captain).
Flying Officer P.E. Torkington-Leech: pilot.
Sergeant C.A. Bryant: Pilot.
Leading Aircraftsman S. Hawkins.
Aircraftsman 1 E. Grant.

Page 197
26 May 1940 17.45 hours.
Blenheim IV *P6956*, 235 Squadron
Pilot Officer C.D. Warde: Pilot.
Pilot Officer Alfred H. Murphy: Navigator, KIA.
Leading Aircraftsman Ernest Peareth Armstrong: wireless operator, KIA.

Page 198
7 June 1940 23.31 hours.
He 115 *8L+EL* 3/*Küstenfliegergruppe* 906.
Oberleutnant zur See Adolf van Hüllen: pilot, KIA.
Feldwebel Ludwig Fehr, KIA.
Feldwebel Paul Randorf, died of injuries 9 June 1940.

Page 199
30 July 1940 00.12 hours.
Ju88A-1 *5J+ER, W.Nr4102*, 7/KG4. 4 killed.
Unteroffizier Fritz Krause: Pilot. DoB 10.4.16.
Obergefreiter Johannes Berlage, DoB 18.6.13.
Gerfr Bruno Glaser, DoB 12.4.17.
Uffz Willi Böhlke, DoB 21.9.13.

Page 200
26 August 1940 15.40 hours.
Do 17Z-3 *U5+, W.Nr 1207*, 7/KG2.
Uffz F. Knorky, PoW/wounded.
Uffz W. Simon, PoW/wounded.
Uffz W. Simon, PoW/wounded.
Uffz Heinrich Schaffer, PoW/wounded.
Died 22.9.40.
Gefr L. Schadt, PoW.

Page 203
22 January 1941 12.27 hours.
Blenheim IV *T2435*, 139 Squadron. 3 killed.
Flight Lieutenant Guy Jerrold Menzies DFC: Pilot, aged 20, born Christchurch, New Zealand. Buried at Catton, Norfolk.
Sergeant Roy Tribick: wireless operator/air gunner, aged 21.
Sergeant Edwin Jones Bonney: Observer, aged 27.

Page 203/204
17 May 1941 14.25 hours.
Hurricane 1 *V7225* 1401 Met. Flight
Flying Officer Iain Robertson MacDiarmid: aged 24.
Buried in Barbour Cemetery, Rossneath, Dumbartonshire.
Wellington *RI587*. 6 killed.
Squadron Leader A.W.J. Clarke: pilot.
Pilot Officer G.H. Cotton: pilot.
Sergeant C.E. Bushford: observer.
Sergeant G.D. Gray: rear gunner.
Sergeant R.A. Petter: wireless operator/air gunner.
Sergeant A. Pepper: wireless operator/air gunner.

Pages 206
29 June 1941. 23.28 hours.
Wellington *Z1616*, 75 Squadron. 5 killed.
Pilot Officer Robert Bertram: pilot, aged 26.
Sergeant Joseph Guy Quin: observer, aged 25.
Sergeant George Walter Mathew Archer: air gunner.
Sergeant (RNZAF) Richard John Grenfell: Wireless operator/air gunner, aged 22.
Sergeant (RNZAF) Norman Mitchell: wireless operator/air gunner, aged 25.

Page 207
19 October 1942 08.50 hours.
Ju88A-4 *3E+CM 144319*, 4/KG6. 4 killed.
Leutnant Dr Wilhelm Blackert: pilot, aged 30.
Uffz Alfred Bohnemann: radio operator, aged 23.
Uffz Helmut Mollenhauer: air gunner, aged 20.
Uffz Meinhard Smit: observer, aged 20.

Pages 209
4 November 1942 15.45 hours.
Ventura Mk1 *AE737*, 464 Squadron. 5 killed.
Flight Lieutenant M.I. Dore: pilot.
Flight Sergeant T.H. Martin: navigator.
Flight Sergeant J.F. Palmer: wireless operator/air gunner.
Sergeant H.P. Painting: air gunner.
Sergeant C.S. Thomson: air gunner.

Page 213/214
15 August 1943 12.00 hours
Spitfire II *P7530* Central Gunnery School.
Flight Lieutenant H.C. Bennett. Killed.
Wellington 1a *P9228* Central Gunnery School.
6 killed.
Flight Lieutenant E.M. Shannon: pilot.
Flying Officer M. Smith: second pilot.
Pilot Officer R.P.T. Akeroyd: wireless operator/air gunner.
Flying Officer G.F. Wood DFC: wireless operator/air gunner.
Pilot Officer B.C. Dreaver DFC: air gunner.
Flight Sergeant H. Nutteridge: air gunner.

Page 216
16 September 1943 22.00 hours.
B-17F *42-30601*, *Mary Ellen II*
550 Squadron 385 Bombardment Group. 10 killed.
Lieutenant John D. Schley: pilot.
Lieutenant John T. Baum: co-pilot.
Lieutenant John F. Ellingsen. navigator.
Lieutenant Earl. R. Bates: bombardier.
Tech. Sergeant Walter J. Roth: top turret gunner.
Tech. Sergeant John R. Egbert: radio operator gunner.
Staff Sergeant Willard G. White: ball turret gunner.
Staff Sergeant Chester E. Truex: tail gunner.
Staff Sergeant Harold A. Waldner: left waist gunner.
Staff Sergeant Clyde G. Gingerich: right waist gunner.

Pages 216
13 December 1943 15.40 hours
B-26 Marauder *41-17961*, *ER-M*
450 Squadron. 322 Bombardment Group.
Andrews Field.
Crew as text — full crew unknown.

Page 217
3 February 1944 13.05 hours.
P-47C *41-6326*, *UN-Y* 63 Squadron 56 Fighter Group.
Lieutenant Harold Elwood Comstock.

Pages 219
20 February 1944 09.40 hours.
B-17G *42-40004*, 548 Squadron 385 Bombardment Group.
3 killed.
Lieutenant Billy E. Ruby: pilot, KIA.
Lieutenant Edward Krengulec: co-pilot, KIA.
Tech. Sergeant Cletus D. Crouse: top turret gunner, KIA.
Staff Sergeant Howard E. Anderson: gunner.
Lieutenant Tony Thorncock: bombardier.
Sergeant Edward J. Roddy: gunner.
Staff Sergeant A.J. Guinta: gunner.
Tech. Sergeant Henry B. Parker: radio operator.
— two crew members unknown.

Page 220
13 March 1944 09.15 hours.
B-24J *42-100363* 409 Squadron 93 Bombardment group.
6 killed.
Lieutenant Alfred C. Chaimberlain: pilot, KIA.
Lieutenant Beaufort A. McKethen co-pilot: KIA.
Lieutenant Raymond H. Piotrowski: navigator, KIA.
Lieutenant Eugene Z. Talley: bombardier, KIA.
Technical Sergeant Frederick H. Brewer: top turret gunner, KIA.
Staff Sergeant Charles N. O'Brien: tail gunner, KIA.
Technical Sergeant Anthony Cassey.
Technical Sergeant Kendale.
+ two unknown survivors.

Page 221
27 April 1944 16.00 hours.
B-24H *42-50306*, 704 Squadron, 446 Bombardment Group.
10 killed.
Lieutenant Wayne I. Case: pilot.
Flight Officer Roswell S. Mayer: co-pilot.
Lieutenant Joseph S. Boulos: navigator.
Lieutenant Amuel B. Canant: bombardier.
Technical Sergeant Emmett D. Bogwell: Engineer top turret gunner.
Technical Sergeant Lewis W. Phillip: radio operator.
Staff Sergeant August R. Kendall: gunner.
Staff Sergeant James L. Rachal: gunner.
Staff Sergeant Morgan H. Whitton: gunner.
Staff Sergeant Charles M. Douglas: gunner.

Page 228
23 May 1944 06.50 hours.
B-17G *42-97325* 508 Squadron 351 Bombardment Group.

6 killed.
Lieutenant Peter E. Crowe: pilot, KIA.
Lieutenant Norris H. Nelson: co-pilot, KIA.
Lieutenant Robert A. Russeth: navigator, KIA
Lieutenant Frank Rubin: Bombardier, KIA.
Technical Sergeant Gerald W. Fiebelkorn: top turret gunner, KIA.
Technical Sergeant Theodore W. Popp: radio operator, injured.
Staff Sergeant Frank T. Lopez: tail gunner, KIA.
Staff Sergeant Joseph T. Duggan: Left waist gunner, injured.
Staff Sergeant Edwin G. Harden: ball turret gunner, injured.
B-24J *42-110172* 754 Squadron 458 Bombardment Group.
10 killed — (collided with B-17G *42-97325*).
Lieutenant Kenneth C. Barton.
Lieutenant William J. Fuqua Jr.
Lieutenant Charles G. Hobblitt.
Lieutenant Preston W. Campbell Jr.
Staff Sergeant Roy A. Torkelson.
Staff Sergeant Charles A. Leonard Jr.
Staff Sergeant Harold R. McGlynn.
Staff Sergeant Carroll J. Labbee.
Staff Sergeant Maynard T. Halsted.
Staff Sergeant Richard E. Arnold.

Page 228
8 June 1944 08.15 hours
B-24J *42-110169*, *Lucky Penny*, 853 Squadron, 491 Bombardment Group.
9 killed.
Lieutenant Fletcher E. Sharp.
Lieutenant Sammy T. Rowan.
Lieutenant Edwin W. Foster.
Staff Sergeant Rudolph C. Schopa.
Staff Sergeant Grover L. Buchanan.
Sergeant Warren H. Rudolph.
Sergeant Clyde V. Jones.
Sergeant Carl W. Frack.
Sergeant Lester J. Datthyn.

Page 230
30 June 1944, 19.45 hours.
P-47D *42-8511* 351 Squadron 353 Fighter Group.
Lieutenant Robert L. Larson, KIA.
P-47D *42-8628*, 351 Squadron 353 Fighter Group.
Lieutenant William K. Lahke — landed safely after collision with *42-8511*.

Pages 231
17 July 1944 13.20 hours.
B-24H *41-29545*, *Lucy Quipment*.

Page 235
18 August 1944 18.55 hours.
B-24H *42-50439*, *Broad and High*, 788 Squadron, 467 Bombardment Group.
Lieutenant Roger L. Leister: pilot, uninjured.
Lieutenant Frank Bales: co-pilot, serious head injuries.
Lieutenant William M. Sherrill: navigator, KIA.
Technical Sergeant Darlton W. Pontius: engineer, KIA.
Technical Sergeant George Lifschitz: radio operator, KIA.
Staff Sergeant Neil Matzek: nose turret gunner, minor injuries.
Staff Sergeant Philip A. Snyder: waist gunner, KIA.
Technical Sergeant Jessie Duff: tail gunner, minor injuries.
Staff Sergeant Ernest Schreiner: waist gunner, minor injuries.

Page 236
9 September 1944 07.50 hours.
B-24J *44-10489*, 491 Bombardment Group.
Lieutenant John S. Warczak Jr: pilot.
Lieutenant Jerry R. Miller: co-pilot, KIA.
Lieutenant Nicholas Molnihoff: Bombardier, KIA.
Technical Sergeant Walter S. Peterson: ball turret gunner, KIA.
Technical Sergeant Mason C. Carr: rear gunner, KIA.
Staff Sergeant Henry Chavez: waist gunner.
Staff Sergeant William R. Boling: top turret gunner.
Staff Sergeant Robert L. Watkins: nose turret gunner, KIA.

Page 238
31 October 1944 08.55 hours.
B-17G *43-388431*, 379 Bombardment Group.
Aircraft is believed to have been hit by British AA guns while they were in action against a V1.
Full crew unknown.

Page 238
18 December 1944 21.51 hours.
Lancaster *R5674*, 3LFS 7 killed.
Pilot Officer (RAAF) Horace William Harler: pilot, aged 20.
Flying Officer Douglas Edwin Parsons: air bomber, aged 22.
Flight sergeant (RAAF), Percy Alfred Ewins, aged 23.
Sergeant Cyril Frank Farley: Air gunner, aged 19.

Sergeant James Foster: air gunner, aged 23.
Flight Sergeant Dennis William Harris: navigator, aged 23.
Flight Sergeant Peter Aspinall Gledhill: flight engineer, aged 21.
Lancaster R5846, A5-H 3 LFS. 7 killed.
Flight Sergeant (RNZAF) Thomas George Jacobs: pilot, aged 22.
Flight Sergeant George Ridley Telford: navigator, aged 36.
Sergeant John Watson Hutton: wireless operator/air gunner, aged 20.
Sergeant James Duffin: air bomber.
Sergeant Leslie Arthur Raymond Potter: flight engineer, aged 19.
Sergeant Frank Albert Oxlade: air gunner, aged 19.

Sergeant Cyril Symonds: air gunner, aged 19.

Page 243
6 February 1945 09.30 hours.
B-24J 44-10515, 734 Squadron, 453 Bombardment Group.
10 killed.
Lieutenant Roy F. Flatt: pilot.
Lieutenant Robert W. Mccormick: co-pilot.
Lieutenant Henry D. Daniel: navigator.
Lieutenant Ralph W. Andrew: bombardier.
Sergeant James E. Tryce: engineer.
Sergeant Fred H. Dieckhoff: radio operator.
Sergeant Joseph K. Rilett: tail turret gunner.
Sergeant Carl W. Toll: nose turret gunner.
Sergeant Hubert W. Williams: top turret gunner.
Sergeant Antonio Portella: waist gunner.

INDEX

American Air Force units, numerical order

Royal Air Force units, numerical order

German Units, alpha-numerical order

Miscellaneous units/organizations

255